USING
MICROSOFT
WORKS

Using Microsoft®
Works 3 for the Mac®

Greg Schultz

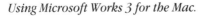

Using Microsoft Works 3 for the Mac.

Library of Congress Catalog No.: 91-68387

ISBN: 0-88022-833-4

95 94 93 92   4 3 2 1

Interpretation of the printing code: the rightmost double-digit number is the year of the book's printing; the rightmost single-digit number is the number of the book's printing. For example, a printing code of 92-1 shows that the first printing of the book occurred in 1992.

Screen reproductions in this book were created using Exposure Pro from Baseline Publishing, Memphis, TN.

Using Microsoft Works 3 for the Mac is based on Version 3.0 of Microsoft Works for the Macintosh.

Publisher: Lloyd J. Short

Associate Publisher: Rick Ranucci

Product Development Manager: Thomas H. Bennett

Book Designer: Scott Cook

Production Team: Claudia Bell, Jodie Cantwell, Paula Carroll, Michelle Cleary, Brook Farling, Jay Lesandrini, Cindy L. Phipps, Caroline Roop, Linda Seifert, Jeff Strum, Johnna VanHoose, Lisa Wilson, Phil Worthington

Dedication

For Amanda and Brittany

May they be the power users of the next generation.

Acquisitions Editor
Tim Ryan

Product Director
Kathie-Jo Arnoff

Production Editor
Pamela Wampler

Editors
Elsa M. Bell
Barbara K. Koenig
J. Christopher Nelson
Heather Northrup

Technical Editors
John S. Dranchak, Logic Control
Rita Lewis, Lewis Technical Writing Services

Composed in *ITC Garamond* and *MCPdigital*
by Que Corporation

About the Author

Greg Schultz has written and edited instructional texts on a variety of microcomputer topics. He is author of Que's *Using GeoWorks Pro*, coauthor of the second edition of Que's *Using Quicken 3 for the Mac*, and has served as technical editor for Que's *Using DacEasy*, 2nd Edition, and *Using MS-DOS 5*. He has taught more than a thousand hours of classroom microcomputer training and has managed training for the northwest branch of a national computer training organization.

In addition to a masters degree in adult education, Mr. Schultz brings to his work a 20-year background in publications and retail management, during which time he has been active in applying computer technology to business problems.

Trademark Acknowledgments

Que Corporation has made every effort to supply trademark information about company names, products, and services mentioned in this book. Trademarks indicated below were derived from various sources. Que Corporation cannot attest to the accuracy of this information.

1-2-3 is a registered trademark of Lotus Development Corporation.

Apple, AppleWorks, LaserWriter Mac, and Macintosh are registered trademarks of Apple Computer, Inc.

CompuServe is a registered trademark of CompuServe, Inc., and H&R Block, Inc.

GEnie is a trademark of General Electric Company.

IBM is a registered trademark of International Business Machines Corporation.

MacWrite is a registered trademark of Claris Corporation.

Microsoft Excel, Microsoft Word, Microsoft Word for Windows, and Microsoft Works are registered trademarks of Microsoft Corporation.

Rolodex is a registered trademark of Rolodex Corporation.

WordPerfect is a registered trademark of WordPerfect Corporation.

Trademarks of other products in this book are held by the companies producing them.

Acknowledgments

This book reflects the contributions of a number of skilled, creative individuals. The author would particularly like to thank Kathie-Jo Arnoff for gathering and weaving together the many threads of the project. Rita Lewis furnished screen shots and rewrites. Pamela Wampler provided a strong hand at the editorial helm. Elsa Bell, Barbara Koenig, Chris Nelson, and Heather Northrup contributed thoughtful editing of various chapters. Warm thanks to John Dranchak for his strong technical editing. And finally thanks to Tim Ryan who provided good counsel and an island of calm in what was a sometimes stormy process.

Contents at a Glance

Table of Contents

2   Understanding Works Basics 29

VI Using Advanced Features

14 Using Macros 377

xxvii

Introduction

icrosoft Works 3.0 is an outstanding example of integrated software. A single program encompasses five major purposes for which Macintosh computers are used: word processing, spreadsheet analysis, database management, drawing, and communication. Using an integrated menu system and screen interface, you can create powerful documents that share information from different modules. For example, you can combine names and addresses from a database with a form letter or perform spreadsheet calculations with database information.

Works modules work in similar ways, so your understanding of one module transfers to another module. In addition to the core modules, Works comes with a selection of document templates, called *stationery*, a complete communications tool kit, and a well-developed tutorial and on-line Help system.

This book helps you master the rich collection of features Works provides. This single program contains all the resources many Macintosh users will ever need. You can run a small business, create a newsletter, manage home finances, write school papers, and accomplish many more computing activities without ever starting up another program.

USING
MICROSOFT
WORKS

The Works Modules

With the Works modules—the word processor, the spreadsheet, the database, the drawing program, and the communications program—you can create impressive documents quickly and easily. This section describes each module.

The Word Processor

The Works word processor can create professional documents, complete with headers, footers, and footnotes. An improved spelling checker and a new 190,000-word thesaurus help ensure accuracy. Works' integrated features enable you to move text easily and to add text and illustrations from other modules or outside sources. Powerful formatting features enable you to enhance the appearance of your document by changing fonts and type sizes. You can use the Draw module to add graphic enhancements.

The Spreadsheet

Using the Works spreadsheet, you can analyze personal or business finances and analyze the what-if questions that affect financial success. You can use 64 built-in functions to automatically perform complex mathematical operations such as mortgage interest calculation or investment analysis. A charting feature is part of the spreadsheet. The newly included quick charting feature lets Works do the work of developing a chart. You also can use features from the Draw module to enhance and clarify spreadsheets and charts.

The Database

You can put any type of information you want to organize and analyze into a Works database. Using flexible design tools, you can create gridlike arrangements of records or use on-screen forms that resemble printed forms. After you collect your data, you can use calculated fields to manipulate and analyze information. Multiple filters enable you to specify precisely the records you want to retrieve. A built-in report writer enables you to print a retrieved record with totals and subtotals included.

The Draw Module

In Works Version 3.0, the drawing module has been separated and enhanced to work as a stand-alone feature. The word *draw* has a special meaning in computer graphics. Draw designates object-oriented graphics, drawings defined by mathematical formulas rather than by a fixed-dot pattern. Such graphics can be scaled to any size without developing "jaggies." They can be used to produce smooth, professional-looking illustrations. The word processor, database, and spreadsheet all have a draw layer that provides a way to easily place graphics and other visual enhancements into other modules.

The Communication Module

The Works communication module has kept up with the increasing popularity and sophistication of on-line technology. Through links with an improved Apple Communications Toolbox, several new or enhanced features, such as enhanced terminal emulation, have been added. Works also provides stationery that contains prepared sign-on scripts for major commercial information services.

Who Should Use This Book?

Using Microsoft Works 3 for the Mac is useful to a wide range of users. The book makes no assumptions about your Macintosh experience. All features are fully explained. Numerous screen shots help you check your progress. If you are new to Works, this book can help you get started through its sections on basic techniques.

If you are an experienced user of Works, you will find coverage of all the new and enhanced features in Version 3.0. Tips and cautions throughout the book increase your skills and help you avoid pitfalls. As an experienced user, you may be particularly interested in new features such as the enhanced Draw module covered in Chapters 5 and 6, or the ability to use up to 16 named filters for a database, explained in Chapter 10. Appendix B contains a detailed listing of features new to Version 3.0.

What This Book Contains

This book is divided into six major parts. The following sections briefly outline chapter contents.

Part I: Getting Started with Works

Chapter 1, "Macintosh Basics for New Users," provides the fundamental information needed to navigate the Macintosh interface. This chapter explains how to work with both System 7 and System 6, and explains basic skills, such as those needed to manage menus and dialog boxes. This chapter also introduces folders and file management techniques.

Chapter 2, "Understanding Works Basics," explains techniques common to all Works modules. This chapter discusses program installation and start-up, as well as the use and creation of stationery templates. In addition to explaining Help features, much of this chapter covers standard procedures for opening and saving documents.

Part II: Using the Word Processor

Chapter 3, "Creating Documents," examines the basics of word processing. This chapter explains text entry, editing, and page layout features, and introduces printing procedures.

Chapter 4, "Enhancing Documents," shows you how to apply character and paragraph formatting and change character styles, as well as how to use the spelling checker and thesaurus. This chapter also demonstrates tabs, headers, footers, and footnotes.

Part III: Using Draw

Chapter 5, "Creating Drawings," is the first of two chapters devoted to the greatly enhanced Draw module. This chapter introduces drawing tools and describes techniques for managing graphic objects.

Chapter 6, "Enhancing Documents with Draw," builds on the previous chapter to show the ways you can use Draw to enhance documents. This chapter includes instructions for creating multicolumn documents. Other sections show how to import drawings and how to use Draw with other Works modules.

Part IV: Using Spreadsheets

Chapter 7, "Creating Spreadsheets," presents the basic steps in building a spreadsheet in Works. This chapter explains screen navigation and spreadsheet terminology. This chapter also introduces the use of ranges and demonstrates display options. The chapter concludes with an explanation of how to preview and print your spreadsheet.

Chapter 8, "Applying Spreadsheet Functions," is entirely devoted to a description of the purpose and use of the 64 spreadsheet functions built into Works. This chapter describes the syntax of each function and provides examples of how to use the function.

Chapter 9, "Working with Charts," concentrates on the tools available for the graphic interpretation of spreadsheets. This chapter describes the Works chart types and demonstrates the charting tools. This chapter also presents the quick charting feature. The chapter concludes with a discussion of how to enhance charts by formatting both chart and text elements.

Part V: Using the Database

Chapter 10, "Creating Databases," teaches database terminology and concepts. Sections deal with creating a database, editing and formatting fields, and calculating within the database. This chapter demonstrates data entry views and explains ways of sorting and filtering data.

Chapter 11, "Preparing Database Reports," shows how to extract useful information from your database by creating reports. This chapter explains the design of a report and describes formatting. This chapter also shows automatic creation of totals and subtotals. A section of the chapter shows how to extract information from your database to create labels and form letters.

Part VI: Using Advanced Features

Chapter 12, "Using Works Communications," provides an introduction to the Works communication module. This chapter introduces communications concepts and terminology and explains how to use communications stationery. Much of the chapter is devoted to an explanation of the settings available to synchronize communications with a remote computer.

Chapter 13, "Integrating Works Applications," focuses on how Works modules work together. This chapter describes methods of moving data and explores issues of file compatibility. An example based on a mail-merge document demonstrates the ease of module integration. The chapter concludes with a discussion of importing and exporting Works files to other computer programs.

Chapter 14, "Using Macros," explains how to record keystrokes to be replayed automatically. This chapter explains techniques for creating, saving, and running macro files. This chapter also includes macro concepts and troubleshooting tips.

The Appendixes

Appendix A, "Works Command Reference," covers the menus common to all Works modules, and then describes the unique menus found in the individual modules. The commands are listed in alphabetical order under the module names. Commands are listed with their keyboard shortcuts.

Appendix B, "New Features of Version 3.0," describes the enhancements found in Version 3.0. The Appendix lists the new features and enhancements in each module.

Appendix C, "Works with System 6 and 7," lists the differences in the way Works appears and behaves under the two systems.

Conventions Used In This Book

The conventions used in this book have been established to help you learn to use the program quickly and easily. Here are some of the conventions:

- Material you type appears in **bold** type.

- Screen messages appear in a `special typeface`.

- Key combinations use a - to separate the keys (⌘-S, for example). Press the first key and, while holding it down, press the next key. Release both keys at once.

- Tips, notes, and cautions give additional information to help you get the most out of Works 3.

Introduction

Getting Started with Works

Includes

USING
MICROSOFT
WORKS

Macintosh Basics for New Users

I f you are a new Macintosh user, your enthusiasm may have dropped when you picked up the 426-page reference manual that accompanies System 7 software or the equally hefty volumes found with earlier systems. Take heart. The basics of using the Macintosh are not complex. Much of Apple's high esteem among users rests on the brilliant design of the Macintosh operating system. Its intuitive quality and ease of use have made the Macintosh a model of how a computer and a computer user should interact.

This chapter condenses, into relatively few pages, the core of what you need to know to run your Macintosh. With this information, you can do enough to use the system-based features of Works. When you want to learn more about the operating system that manages your Macintosh, you can dig through the wealth of important and well-written information that Apple provides. At present, you presumably have a copy of Works at your fingertips and are ready to get it running. Read on to get started.

The screen illustrations in this book are taken from a machine using System 7, but the descriptions generally apply to any Macintosh. When exceptions arise, they are mentioned in the text. If you are an experienced Macintosh user, you may want to begin with Chapter 2, "Understanding Works Basics," which describes features specific to Works.

USING
MICROSOFT
WORKS

Macintosh System Choices

Every Macintosh, whatever its type, requires *system software* to run. The system program manages the demands of application programs and hardware, provides the on-screen interface with which you interact, and controls storage and retrieval of programs and data.

NOTE

The Macintosh operating system and Works both have a wealth of screen and keyboard shortcuts that can speed frequently repeated activities. Throughout this book, commands and techniques have been chosen for their clarity for beginning users rather than their speed. When you are familiar with the basics, consult the command reference in Appendix A for useful shortcuts.

Through the years, Macintosh system software has been upgraded in a way that allows older machines to benefit from new features. Some features have only been available on newer machines, but the software can run on every type of Macintosh. In 1991, Apple introduced System 7, perhaps the most significant system upgrade since the Macintosh was introduced. New features such as file sharing, TrueType, and virtual memory propelled the Macintosh to new levels of performance and convenience.

The disadvantage of System 7 is that it needs a great deal of disk space and memory. To use System 7, you need a hard disk and at least 2 megabytes of RAM (random-access memory). The good news is that, if you don't have a Macintosh that can support System 7, you can still use System version 6.0.4 or later. System 6 is less demanding of disk and memory space.

With Works, you can use either System 6 or System 7. Works can use System 7 features such as Balloon Help and TrueType, but most of the features of the integrated Works environment do not require the support of System 7. You can comfortably choose either system, confident that Works will perform well in either case.

Supplementing Memory

Whichever system you choose, you can improve Works' performance by providing adequate memory. When running, Works consumes about a megabyte (one million bytes) of memory. If, for example, you also use System 7, which consumes a megabyte of memory, you have used 2 "megs" of memory before opening any document in Works.

One of the great advantages of an integrated program such as Works is its capability to run several modules in memory and switch between them. For example, you can open a database, copy a chart, click a button to switch modules, and paste the chart into a word processing document. Running several modules at once requires enough memory to hold the system, Works, and all your documents.

The more memory you have, the more documents and larger documents you can have open at the same time. The minimum memory recommendation for using Works with System 6 is 1 megabyte. If using System 7 and Works, the recommended minimum amount is 2 megabytes. If you plan to make full use of the possibilities of multiple active modules or complex documents, consider doubling the minimum recommendation.

Macintosh memory has recently been available in the range of about 50 dollars per megabyte. If you are even moderately mechanical, you can install memory by yourself. Some vendors provide instructional videos and inexpensive tool kits to help you with the process. Consult Macintosh magazines and newsletters for prices and sources.

Mastering the Mouse

The basics of using the Macintosh mouse boil down to three words: *point*, *click*, and *drag*. This section discusses the three techniques in order.

Pointing moves the mouse to the screen area where you want to work. Roll the mouse on your work surface to move the mouse in the direction you want the pointer to travel. If you run out of work space, lift the mouse back to a convenient position and resume rolling. When the mouse isn't touching anything, the pointer won't move.

Many mouse users buy a mouse pad. Usually a square of foam-backed fabric, the pad provides a clean, slightly resilient area to move the mouse where the ball won't slip as it might on a polished surface. A mouse pad is a convenience, not a necessity.

After pointing to the place you want to work, you press (click) the mouse button to signal the Macintosh to take an action. The mouse button doesn't take much force to activate. A light press or tap is sufficient. What happens on-screen when you click depends on what aspect of Works you are using. The most common outcomes are the selection of a command or the activation of some Works feature. If you want to select more than one object at a time, hold down the Shift key while clicking the mouse. Each time you Shift-click, another object is selected.

In addition to clicking, you also can double-click. Frequently, something you do by clicking once, moving the mouse, and clicking again or pressing Return, you can do with a quick double tap of the mouse button. This technique is one of the major shortcuts available with the mouse. After you master this technique, you will use it frequently. The computer monitors the time between clicks. If you are too slow (tap..........tap), the Macintosh interprets your action as two separate single mouse clicks. At the right speed (tap..tap), the computer correctly interprets the double-click and performs the appropriate action, usually saving you a step or two.

The third technique, dragging, means moving the mouse while you hold down the mouse button. This technique often is used to move objects across the screen. Dragging also is used to highlight something you want to change. This process, called *selecting*, is vital when you want to point out an object or area to which you want a program command to apply.

In figure 1.1, the dark area on the screen has been highlighted (selected) by dragging the mouse pointer across the area. The selected area could now be deleted, copied, or otherwise modified. The program looks for the selected area when a command is chosen and applies the effect of the command to that area. Note that you can select some objects (icons, for example) simply by pointing to them and clicking.

Fig. 1.1
Text selected by dragging.

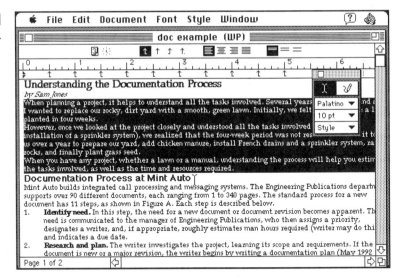

Understanding the Desktop

The Macintosh uses the concept of a *desktop* to present its documents and tools. The desktop program called the *Finder* opens automatically when you start your Macintosh.

Part I

Getting Started with Works

The desktop contains *icons*, small images that graphically represent items such as documents, disks, file folders, and other elements of your system. Most icons open into windows when double-clicked. Icons of particular importance include the icon for your start-up disk in the upper right corner of the screen and the Trash icon used to discard files. A menu bar across the top of the screen enables your mouse to open menus containing commands used for file and disk management. Desktop features are identified in figure 1.2.

Fig. 1.2
The desktop is where you manage your Macintosh.

Menu bar

Hard disk

Active window

Trash icon

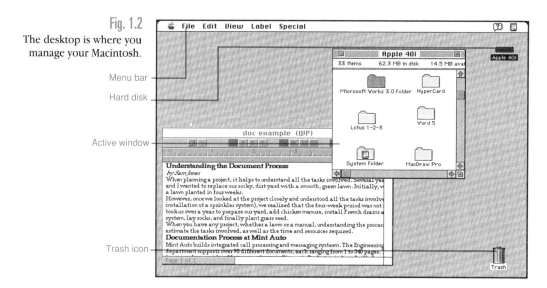

Managing Windows

Figure 1.2 also contains two windows. You can have several windows open at a time, but only one can be active. The active window responds to your mouse and menu commands. You can identify the active window by its position on top of other windows. In addition, the title bar of the active window shows striped lines across it. To make an inactive window active, click the mouse anywhere within its boundary. The window moves in front of any other windows on the screen, and commands or mouse actions now affect it.

Moving Windows

In Works, you often want to have several windows open at the same time. If you are switching from one document to another, moving windows so that you can see the contents of several at one time (see fig. 1.3) is often helpful. Moving a window is a simple process:

1. Point to the title bar at the top of the window.

2. Hold down the mouse button and drag the window to a new location.

Fig. 1.3
Moving windows enables you to see several windows at once.

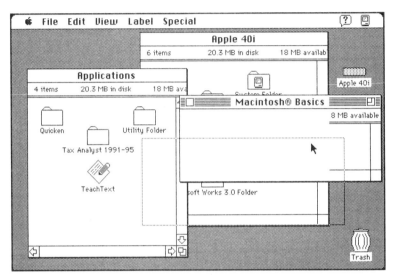

Resizing Windows

Windows can be resized to create useful working arrangements (see fig. 1.4). You may find, for example, that a tall, narrow window of figures next to a word processing document can save you the time involved in switching windows to look for data. However, as a window is reduced in size, you see less of its contents. The next section explains how to use scroll bars to overcome this problem.

Fig 1.4
Resized windows can aid
your work.

Close box

Zoom box

Size box

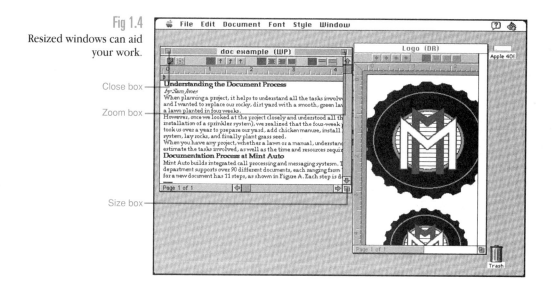

To resize a window, use the following steps :

1. Using the mouse, point to the size box in the lower right corner of the window.

2. Hold down the mouse button and drag to the new size.

If you want to make a window as large as possible, click the zoom box in the upper right corner of the window. Clicking again causes the window to zoom back to its original size.

To close a window, click the close box in the upper left corner of the window. If the window is represented by an icon, it will close back to that icon.

Using Scroll Bars

When a window is small, or when what it contains is large, some information in the window is hidden. Scroll bars at the bottom or right edge of the window enable you to move the window contents so that you can see everything, even in a small window.

A scroll bar consists of three parts: the bar itself, running vertically or horizontally at the right or bottom of a window; the scroll box, which moves in the bar; and the scroll arrows at either end of the bar. Figure 1.5 shows a window with scroll bars. Note that one scroll bar is gray, and the other is white. A gray bar indicates more content beyond the window border. A white bar indicates that all content in the direction controlled by that bar is visible.

Fig. 1.5
A window with scroll bars.

Scroll box —
Scroll bar —
Scroll arrow —

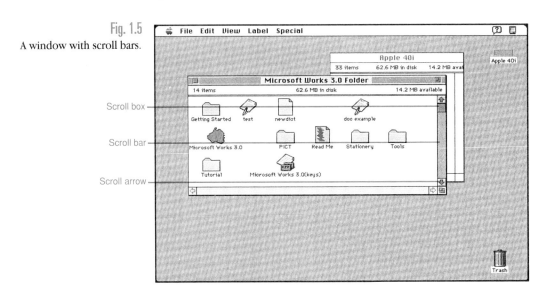

To use a scroll bar, follow these methods:

- To move quickly through the entire contents of a window, drag the scroll box from the top to the bottom of the scroll bar with the mouse pointer. The position of the scroll box is proportional to your position in the window. In other words, if the box is half-way down the scroll bar, you are halfway through the window contents.

- To move one full window at a time, click the areas on either side of the scroll box.

- To move a little bit at a time, click the scroll arrows at the top or bottom of the scroll bar.

- To scroll the contents of the window continuously in the direction the arrow points, point to one of the small scroll arrows and hold down the mouse button.

Using Menus and Dialog Boxes

Across the top of the screen in any program, you find a menu bar. The words on the bar are menu titles. Each menu contains logical groupings of commands. To open a menu, position the mouse pointer on the menu title and hold down the mouse button. To select a command, drag the mouse in an open menu until the desired command is highlighted. Release the mouse button to activate the command (see fig. 1.6).

Fig. 1.6
Commands are selected by dragging the mouse to highlight them.

Menu bar
Menu titles
Keyboard shortcut
Grayed out command

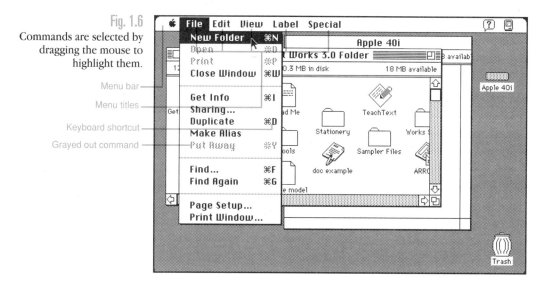

Often, commands have *keyboard shortcuts* that enable you to activate the commands without using the mouse. The shortcuts generally involve the ⌘ key and one or more other keys. Keyboard shortcuts are listed to the right of a command on the menu. As you become more familiar with a program, you will probably memorize shortcuts for frequently used commands. Appendix A contains a full listing of keyboard shortcuts. In some situations, menu choices are not available. In such cases, the command is grayed out, and you cannot select it.

Menu Variations

Some programs (including Works) use submenus and pop-up menus. A submenu, sometimes called a *cascading menu*, is indicated by a small triangle (▶) to the right of the command name. To open the submenu,

Chapter 1
Macintosh Basics for New Users

drag the mouse pointer to the command containing the submenu. The submenu opens. To use it, drag the mouse sideways into the submenu, and then highlight the command you want (see fig. 1.7).

Fig. 1.7

A submenu is indicated by a black triangle pointing right.

Submenu marker

Submenu

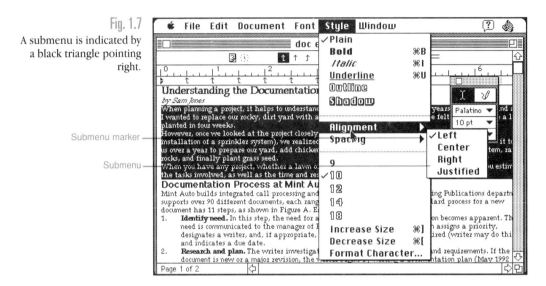

Dialog Boxes

When the Macintosh needs to display a message or when additional information is needed to carry out a command, a *dialog box* appears on your screen. Menu commands followed by three dots also open a dialog box when chosen. Dialog boxes (see fig. 1.8) contain a variety of components that you can use to make choices. The most frequently encountered components are listed in table 1.1.

Fig. 1.8

A typical dialog box.

Text box

Check box

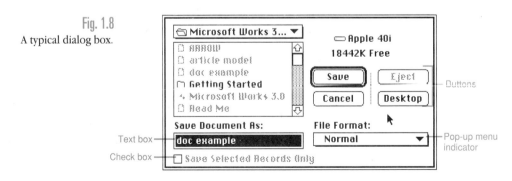

Part I

Getting Started with Works

	Component	Purpose
	Button	Activates a command.
	Radio Button	Selects/deselects a single item from a group (not illustrated) in fig. 1.8.
	Check Boxes	Selects/deselects multiple items.
	Text Box	Enables you to enter or modify information from keyboard.

Table 1.1
Dialog Box Components

Pop-up menus often appear in dialog boxes. A pop-up menu is indicated by a black triangle pointing downward. Pointing to the triangle and holding down the mouse button opens the pop-up menu (see fig. 1.9).

Fig. 1.9
A pop-up menu.

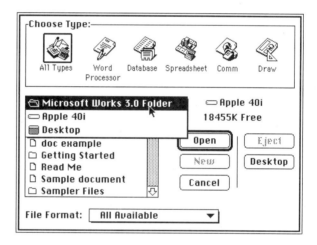

The Apple Menu

At the far left of every menu bar is an apple image that can be opened to show a specialized menu. The Apple menu, shown in figure 1.10, includes *desk accessories*, small programs that often provide utility features, and *control panels*, which control many of the standard settings for your Macintosh. A complete discussion of desk accessories and control panels is beyond the scope of this chapter, but you must know about a few items to use Works successfully.

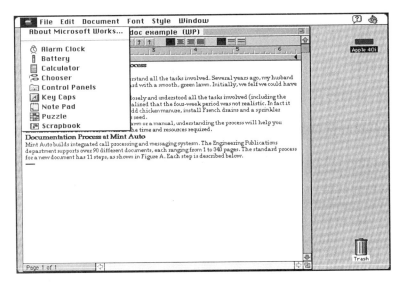

Fig. 1.10
The Apple menu.

Chooser

When you open the Apple menu, one of the items you see is the Chooser (see fig. 1.11). This desk accessory controls the selection of printers. The selection of printer icons matches those you chose when you installed your system software. To specify the printer your Macintosh will use, click the appropriate printer icon.

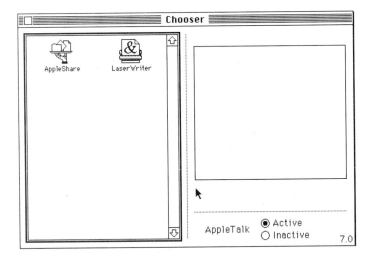

Fig. 1.11
The Chooser desk accessory controls printer selection.

Part I

Getting Started with Works

If you have multiple printers or want to install a different printer, consult your system documentation.

Control Panels

Control panels are presented differently in System 6 and System 7, but the underlying concepts are the same. A control panel lets you adjust settings for items such as the mouse, keyboard, sound, and other system features. Although you can use the default settings with Works, you should become familiar with control panel options so that you can fine-tune features such as date and time settings, the keyboard repeat rate, and mouse behavior.

To adjust a control panel, open the Apple menu, choose the Control Panels command, and double-click the control panel you want to adjust (see fig. 1.12). With System 6, choose the Control Panel command from the Apple menu, and then scroll the list of control panel devices that appears at the left of the Control Panel window. Click the icon for the device you want to change.

Fig. 1.12
Control panels enable you
to control system settings.

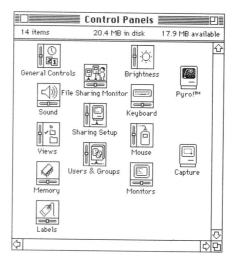

Managing Folders

A Macintosh equipped with a hard disk may contain more than a thousand files. Whether you have hundreds of files or thousands, you must be able to manage them effectively. Just as a file drawer crammed with a thousand unsorted documents is unmanageable, a hard disk with all its files in a single location is difficult to manage. Your Macintosh uses *folders* to solve the problem of file storage.

You can keep your correspondence in one folder, your novel in another folder, and your budget in a third. You can create hundreds of folders on your hard disk. The Macintosh uses an icon of a file folder to represent its electronic folders.

Electronic folders possess a feature their cardboard cousins do not: you can store computer folders within other computer folders. You can create a folder for your correspondence, for example. Within this correspondence folder, you can create more folders, one for business and one for personal correspondence.

To navigate the system of folders, the Macintosh uses a dialog box that shows the files and folders available in the current location (see fig. 1.13). A scrolling list enables you to view the documents and folders you can open, and buttons enable you to move to other locations or open files. This kind of dialog box appears when you choose commands for managing files, such as Open or Save As.

Fig. 1.13
A folder dialog box.

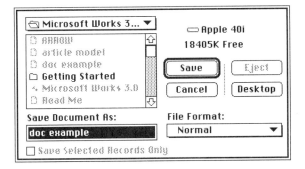

Navigating the Desktop Structure

The Desktop button (called *Drive* in System 6) is the key to changing folders. Clicking it displays a scrolling list of the folders and disks present on the Macintosh desktop. If a disk is in the external drive, it is listed also (see fig. 1.14). To see the contents of a folder or disk displayed on the desktop, double-click its icon; or, in the Open dialog box, select the folder or disk and click the Open button. The scrolling list title and display changes to show the contents of the new location (see fig. 1.15).

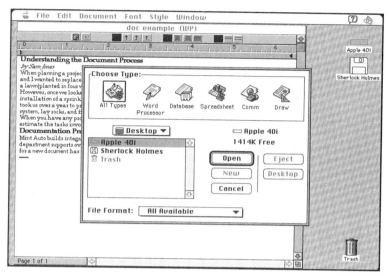

Fig. 1.14
The Desktop display
includes a disk in the
external drive.

Fig. 1.14
The Desktop display
includes a disk in the
external drive.

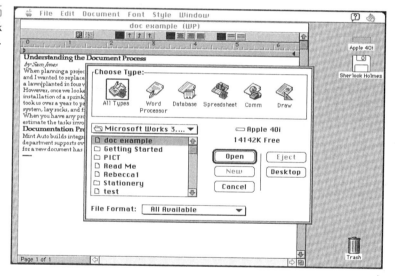

Fig. 1.15
Clicking a folder or disk
icon displays its contents.

In addition to icons for folders and disks, you will see icons that look
like small sheets of paper with the upper right corners folded down.
These icons represent documents. Double-clicking one of these icons
opens the document and its associated application. Document management in Works is discussed in Chapter 2, "Understanding Works Basics."

Creating Folders

The operating system and applications programs create new folders when they are installed, but you can create new folders and modify the desktop structure to suit your working style. To create a new folder, open the File menu and choose the command New Folder. A new empty folder, named *untitled folder*, appears in your present location.

If you want the folder located at a specific level of your hierarchy of folders, you can either move to the proper level of folders before creating the folder or later drag it into or out of the folder where it was created. Notice that your new folder is selected (highlighted). If you type a name, it will replace *untitled folder*. To change the name of other folders, hold down the mouse button and drag the mouse pointer across the folder name to select it, and then type a new name.

Do not rename or alter the folders named *System Tools* or *System Folder*. Programs look for folders with these exact names to locate resources the programs need. Changing their name or location can cause your programs to behave unpredictably.

Using the Clipboard and Scrapbook

The Clipboard and the Scrapbook are two Macintosh features that you will find helpful when using Works. The Clipboard provides a way to move text and images from document to document; the Scrapbook furnishes a handy storage place for reusable selections.

Using the Clipboard

The Clipboard is an area of memory where material cut or copied from a document is temporarily stored. In Works, items such as illustrations or blocks of text are often moved from one document to another by use of the Clipboard.

In Works, you can see the current contents of the Clipboard by opening the Window menu and choosing the command Show Clipboard (see fig. 1.16). When operating outside Works, the Show Clipboard command is usually found on the Edit menu.

Fig. 1.16
You can view the Clipboard
from within Works.

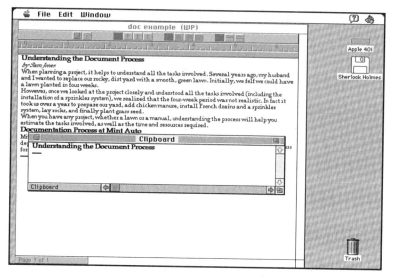

The Clipboard can hold only one item at a time, regardless of the size of the item. If you copied a large document to the Clipboard and then deleted or copied a single period from your screen, the period would displace the entire document. If you need to get rid of something without replacing the contents of the Clipboard, use the Clear (rather than Copy) command from the Edit menu. This command bypasses the Clipboard.

If something is on the Clipboard, you can use the Paste command to place it in a document. In fact, you can paste it repeatedly in different locations. Pasting puts a copy of the Clipboard contents into the document, leaving the original material untouched. You also can use the Clipboard, a Macintosh system feature, to move information between application programs.

Storing Selections in the Scrapbook

When you frequently use an item like a company logo or name and address, the Scrapbook provides a storage location that resembles its namesake. The Scrapbook is a desk accessory, provided by the Macintosh system, that enables you to store text and images you use frequently. Because the Scrapbook is on the Apple menu, the Scrapbook is available in nearly all applications.

Use these steps to place an item in the Scrapbook:

1. Select the material you want to copy from your original document.

2. Open the Edit menu and choose Copy. The selected material is copied to the Clipboard.

3. Open the Apple menu and choose Scrapbook. The Scrapbook window opens (see fig. 1.17).

4. Open the Edit menu and choose Paste. The copied item is pasted into the Scrapbook.

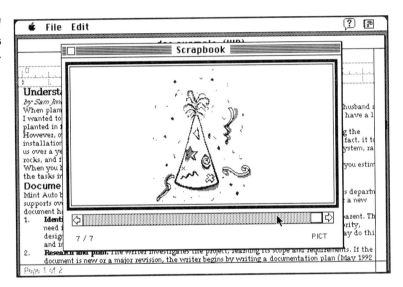

Fig. 1.17

The Scrapbook stores frequently used items.

A scroll bar along the bottom of the Scrapbook window enables you to move through the stored items. To move an item from the Scrapbook into a document, reverse the process above—copying from the Scrapbook, switching to your document, and then pasting the Scrapbook image in place.

Chapter Summary

ou could learn hundreds of facts about your Macintosh operating system. This chapter narrowed down the information to the least you need to know to get up and running with Works. You learned the relative merits of System 7 and System 6, ways of using the mouse, and how to manage windows. Other basic skills included in this chapter were the use of menus and dialog boxes and the management of folders. The chapter concluded with an introduction to the Clipboard and the Scrapbook.

Understanding Works Basics

T his chapter looks at fundamental features common to all the activities within Works. Like most Macintosh applications, Works is an integrated program with many consistent features throughout its modules. Works is based on the premise that business users want a program that incorporates the tools to perform their routine tasks. Therefore, Works includes a word processing module, a database module, a spreadsheet module, a drawing module, and a communications module. In addition, Works is constructed so that you easily can use data from one module in another. Works also takes into account the fact that most business users are not computer experts and do not want to spend precious time learning new programs. Commands and their keyboard equivalents in one module usually match those in all others, so you have to learn only one type of action for each task you want to accomplish with the program.

As stated in Chapter 1, the File and Edit menus, as well as portions of the Window menu, are carried over into each module. These menus provide standardized commands for basic actions such as opening and closing files, printing documents, cutting and pasting data, undoing errors,

USING
MICROSOFT
WORKS

getting help, and moving between documents within a module. In addition, Works provides on-line help ensuring that you do not get lost in the program. These features enable you to get up and running quickly.

Works 3.0 has added enhancements that make the program run more smoothly on the Macintosh. These enhancements include an easier installation program, updates to each module to make them more user-friendly and interdependent, as well as a library of templates, called *Stationery*, to help you become more productive.

Installing Works

Works' installation utility offers you two installation options: standard and custom. If you choose the standard installation, all you have to do is click a few buttons and feed disks to your Macintosh during the process. A custom installation takes a little more attention because you select which modules are loaded. In both cases, you may want a book and a cup of coffee or tea handy because, depending on the speed of your machine, the process of decompressing the Works files can take a while.

Standard Installation

NOTE

Before beginning your installation, make a backup copy of your master disks. If your original disks are later damaged or lost, you will have a way to modify or restore the copy of Works you are about to place on your hard disk.

Standard installation loads every feature of Works onto your hard disk. The complete installation requires about 3 megabytes of disk space. Note that Works itself takes up approximately 1 megabyte of disk space, Tools takes up 1.7 megabytes, and various supporting modules take up 500 kilobytes. If there are features of Works you may not need, use the custom installation described in the next section. You can install additional features later by running the installation program again in custom mode and selecting the features you want to add.

Although the installation utility guides you with on-screen prompts, the following steps give you an idea of what to anticipate during the standard installation.

1. Before beginning the installation process, turn off any virus-checking software running on your Macintosh.

2. Insert Works Disk 1. The Install window, which includes the Installer icon (see fig. 2.1), opens.

3. Double-click the Installer icon to start installation.

4. Click OK to move past the initial Welcome window.

5. In the Easy Install window, click Install to put all program features on your disk (see fig. 2.2).

Fig. 2.1
Double-click the Installer icon to begin installation.

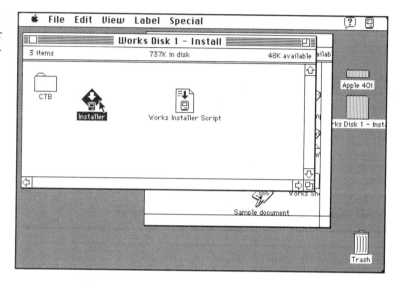

Fig. 2.2
Click the Install button to put all program features on your disk.

Chapter 2
Understanding Works Basics

The installation continues, prompting you to change disks as needed. As the installation nears completion, you are prompted to enter your name and company name. When the installation is complete, a dialog box presents a button that, when pressed, restarts your computer with Works installed.

Custom Installation

Custom installation enables you to select the exact modules you want to install. Clicking the Customize button in the Easy Install window (see fig. 2.2) opens a screen that contains a scrolling list of items you can choose to include in the installation. Click once to select the Works 3.0 program, and then scroll through the list. Hold down Shift while clicking additional features you want to add. To help with your planning, table 2.1 contains the list of program elements you can include (or exclude).

Table 2.1
Program Elements for Custom Installation

Program feature	Description
Works 3.0 Program (required)	The core program
Spelling Checking	A spelling checker
Thesaurus	A thesaurus
File Conversions	File formats for importing and exporting files
Communications Tools	Communications scripts/settings/protocols
CTB Resouces for System 6	Communications Tool Box used with System 6
Learning Microsoft Works	On-line tutorial stacks used with HyperCard
Getting Started	Examples for use with written tutorial
Microsoft Works Help	Context-driven, on-line help system
Stationery	Template library
Run Works from Server	Script for running a network version of Works
Install Works from Server	Script for installing Works onto network nodes from a server

Your decisions on what to include can have a substantial effect on the amount of hard disk space required by Works. For example, the HyperCard-driven tutorial requires more than 700 kilobytes of disk space. You may want to install the tutorial initially, and then, after you have finished using it, remove it to regain the disk space.

If you are not using a network, you do not need the elements that install and run Works from a server. If you are using System 7, you can leave out the CTB (Communications Tool Box) for System 6. When you have selected the features you want, click the Install button and follow the prompts.

NOTE

To run the tutorial, you must have HyperCard 2.1 installed on your Macintosh. If you don't, check the Macintosh systems manual for instructions on how to install HyperCard.

Starting Works

The Installation program puts Works in a folder named, logically, *Microsoft Works 3.0 Folder*. Opening that folder reveals the program icon as well as folders containing major elements such as Stationery and the Tutorial (see fig. 2.3).

Fig. 2.3
The program and its associated folders.

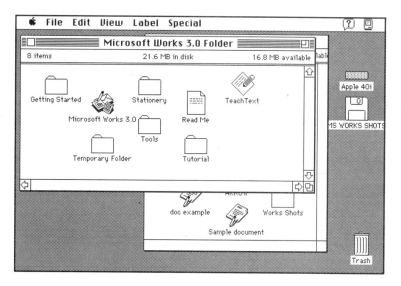

To start Works, double-click its program icon. After a copyright and registration screen, the Choose Type dialog box opens. In this chapter, the section "Standard Works Procedures" discusses the use of this important feature.

Chapter 2
Understanding Works Basics

Using System 7's Application Menu with Works

Chapter 1 introduced the Macintosh operating system, including the concepts of the Finder, desktop, and how windows, folders, and icons work. The Macintosh provides an outstanding environment for integrated software through *multitasking*. Multitasking is the ability to perform more than one operation at a time.

System 6 introduced an adjunct to the Finder, called *MultiFinder*, that enables you to open more than one application at a time (although you can run only one at a time). MultiFinder enables you to switch between dormant applications to activate a new program by clicking a small icon that appears on the far right corner of the menu bar. With each click, the icon changes to indicate which program is active.

In System 7, Apple completely rewrote the operating system and merged MultiFinder's functions with those of the Finder, along with additional enhancements, to provide true multitasking. Certain functions—such as printing, copying, and deleting documents—now can operate in the background while you work within an application. Works, like all Macintosh programs that are compatible with System 7, supports these multitasking features. This section describes how the new Finder in System 7 operates with Works.

To open applications, all you have to do is double-click a document's or application's icon in the Finder window, or drag a document on top of its application. You can use the Finder to open as many applications as the memory allows. When you open another application or document, its window appears on top of older windows in either a *tiled* (diagonally layered) or *stacked* (piled layers) arrangement on top of the Finder window. Each window is accessible by clicking its title bar with your mouse, but clicking the title bar can be difficult if you have too many windows open on your screen. Instead, you can use the Application menu for moving between applications.

The Application menu in System 7 replaces the MultiFinder icon used in System 6 on the far right corner of the menu bar. With the Application menu, you can switch between applications by pulling down a menu and selecting a command. To use the Application menu, pull down the menu and select the application's icon from the list. Note that the Finder also has an icon on the list, enabling you to return to the desktop whenever you want. As displayed in figure 2.4, the active application is indicated with a check mark to the left of its icon.

Fig. 2.4
The Application menu with
the Works icon selected.

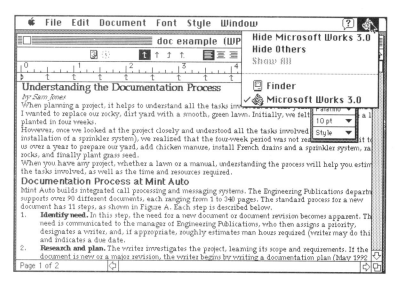

The Application menu also provides a means to hide the clutter on your screen (and also increases your available memory). Use one of the two commands to hide your currently active window (Hide Application) or the Finder window and any other application's window (Hide Other). Use either the Show All command or reselect the dimmed icon of an application to display the windows. This versatile system enables you to have all the functions of the Finder, opening and closing applications, deleting items, copying items, and loading disks, available at all times no matter where you are in Works. In addition, you have the power of other Macintosh applications at your fingertips to enhance your work in Works.

Standard Works Procedures

The procedures involved in opening, saving, printing, closing, and quitting are used repeatedly in Works and are identical in each Works module. These key activities and other procedures common to every Works module are explained in this section.

Starting a New Document

When Works starts, it automatically presents the Choose Type dialog box (see fig. 2.5). From this dialog box, you can open existing files or create a new file. At the top of the Choose Type dialog box are icons representing the five Works modules. If you want to open an existing document, see the section called "Opening Existing Files." To create a new document file, you need to specify the module you want to use.

Fig. 2.5
Create a new file using the
Choose Type dialog box.

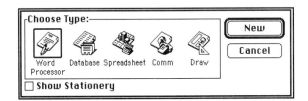

When you click the icon of the Works module you want to use, the New button, previously grayed out and inactive, becomes available. Clicking New opens a new blank document and launches the Works module you have selected. As a shortcut, you can simply double-click the module icon to launch the module and open a new blank document.

Until you name and save your new document, it exists only in the computer's memory. If the power fails or you shut down without saving, the contents of your new file are gone. Consequently, one of the first steps to take after creating a new file is to name it and save it. For information about saving, see this chapter's section called "Saving Your Work."

Opening a New File

When working in a module, you can create a new file by opening the File menu and choosing New. A scaled-down version of the Choose Type dialog box appears with the active Works module selected. Click the New button to create a new file. You can have several files open at the same time, limited only by the amount of free memory available.

You are not limited to opening another file in your current module. By selecting another module's icon and clicking New, you can open multiple modules at the same time. To switch from one open document to another, select the document you want from the list presented when you open the Window menu (see fig. 2.6). Again, remember to name and save your new file so that it is recorded on the hard disk.

Fig. 2.6
Switch between open
documents using the
Window menu.

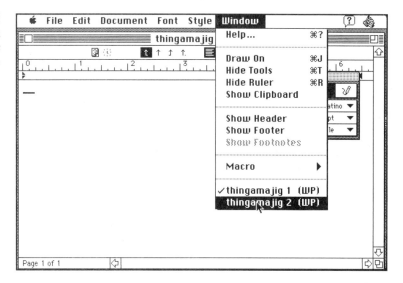

Managing Files

The concept of *filtering* is key to understanding how Works manages its
modules and their files. In Works, filtering is the act of organizing
documents by their module type. In addition to the name you give a file,
Works attaches a designator that tells Works which module created the
file. Although you don't see the designator when you view a list of file
names, it is reflected in the code that follows the name of an open file on
the title bar. (WP) stands for Word Processing, (DR) for Draw, (SS) for
Spreadsheet, and(DB) for Database.

Works uses the designator to filter file names when you open a list of
documents. If you are using the spreadsheet and you choose the
command to open files and select the spreadsheet icon, Works presents
a list that is limited to spreadsheet files, together with any other folders
in the current folder. If you switch to the database, select the database
icon, and open a list of files, the list of files is filtered to show only
database files.

You can use the All Types icon to remove type filtering (see fig. 2.7).
When this icon is chosen, the lists of files that Works presents show
every file type. You may want to see every file to verify the presence of a
certain file or to launch another module by double-clicking a file name
associated with that module.

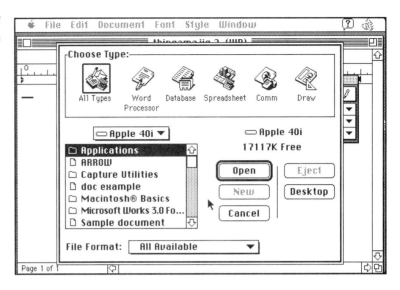

Fig. 2.7
The All Types icon removes
file type filtering.

At the bottom of the Choose Type dialog box is an additional filtering
feature called *File Format*. File Format is a pop-up menu containing a
list of all the possible formats you can open using Works. Usually the box
says `All Available`.

Opening the menu and scrolling presents a list of file formats for Works
and for a number of other computer applications, both Macintosh and
PC (see fig. 2.8). The File Format menu enables you to filter by file
format rather than file type.

The default selection, All Available, shows every type of file the selected
Works module can read. In other words, if you had the word processor
type selected and the All Available *format* chosen, a scrolling list of files
in the Document list box would show all word processing documents
that Works could read. If you changed the format type to Normal, the
basic Works format, only word processing documents created by Works
would appear in your file list.

To review, the default procedure, which is suitable for most situations,
shows files of all *formats* the active module can read. If you want to view
files that are of a different *type* than those of the active module, choose
the All Types icon. If you want to exclude all file formats except one,
choose the desired *format* in the File Format pop-up menu.

Fig. 2.8
The File Format pop-up
menu.

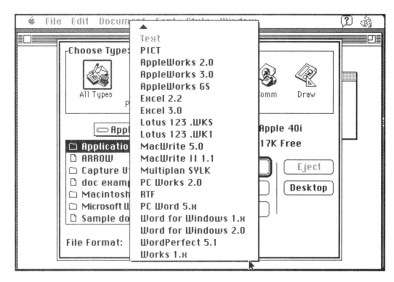

Opening Existing Files

When you understand how Works filters the list of files available to open, the process of opening is simple. Use the following steps:

1. Open the File menu and choose the Open command. The Choose Type dialog box appears.

2. Click the icon that represents the module in which you want to open a file.

3. Use the scrolling list to locate the file.

   You can change the folder where you are searching by clicking the Desktop button and selecting another folder from the list by double-clicking its name.

4. Highlight the document you want and click Open.

   You also can double-click the file name.

The current folder is named in the box at the top of the scrolling list of files. The list shows any files and folders stored in the current folder. To move to another folder or disk, point to the black triangle following the folder name and hold down the mouse button; a pop-up menu opens to show other disks and folders. Drag the highlight to the one you want and release the mouse button.

If a folder is shown in the scrolling list, you can move to it and see its contents by double-clicking the folder name. To return to the folder from which you started, open the pop-up menu at the top of the list and choose the desired folder.

Saving Your Work

One of the first computing lessons you should learn requires only two words to convey: Save Frequently! Few computing experiences are more frustrating than the loss of hours of work through equipment failure or accident. Saving is fast and simple, so there is no reason not to save often.

The process of saving a file is the same in all modules. You use the Save and Save As commands on the File menu. The first time a file is saved, you can use either command with the same result. Because the file is unnamed, the Save As dialog box opens to give you an opportunity to enter a file name and the location where you want the file to be saved. After that initial save, you can save later versions of the document under the same name using the Save command, without accessing the dialog box.

Saving a New Document

To name and save a new file, follow these steps:

1. Open the File menu and choose the command Save As. The Save As dialog box opens (see fig. 2.9).

2. In the text box titled Save Document As, type a name for the file. The name can be up to 31 characters in length. Do not use a colon (:) in the name; you can use all other punctuation.

3. Click the Save button to store the file in the current folder.

The Save As dialog box opens with the Save Document As text box, containing the generic file name Untitled, selected. Typing a new file name in the text box replaces the generic one. By default, the file is saved in the current folder. Use the Document list box and current Folder pull-down menu to move to the folder where you want to save your document. For instance, if you created a folder labeled Drawing to hold your images, you can direct the saved document there by locating the Drawing folder and double-clicking to open it.

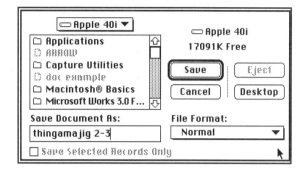

Fig. 2.9
The Save As dialog box.

To the right of the Save Document As text box is a list box labeled `File Format`. Usually, you save your file in the standard Works format, Normal. Clicking in the File Format box opens a pop-up menu showing other formats. Saving to these formats produces files that can be read by other programs. Saving with the Stationery format turns your document into a template that can be reused as a basis for other documents. Using templates is explained later in this chapter, in the section "Using Works Stationery." After you have specified the name location and format for your file, click Save to store your file with its new name and location.

Saving an Existing File with a New Name or Location

You also can use Save As to change the name or location of an existing file. To change the file name, type in a new name in the Save Document As text box and click Save. Works saves the current version of the file under the new name. You now have two versions of your data. To change the file location, use the file list box and current file pop-up menu to scroll to a new folder location, or click the Desktop button to move to a new folder and navigate from there. When you click Save, the file is saved in a new location.

When you save an existing document in another folder, you can create different versions of the document with identical names. Suppose you created a document called *Art*, and then saved it in your Drawing folder. A day later you revised Art and, to transfer it to another machine, saved it to a disk. You would now have two different versions of Art, an old one in your Drawing folder and a revised one on a disk. Nothing is wrong with this procedure, but you need to be aware of the possibility of confusion. For instance, just before saving the new version of Art to a disk, you could have saved the new version in the Drawing folder so that you would have identical versions on the disk and the computer.

Saving with Speed

The first time you save a document, the Save command opens the Save As dialog box so that you can choose a name and storage location. After that, choosing Save from the File menu quickly saves your file with its designated name and location. No dialog box appears. The Save command is the command to use for routine and frequent saving as you work on a document.

The keyboard shortcut for the Save command, which saves the current file, is ⌘-S.

Saving a Workspace

A workspace is a particular collection of documents you may want to open at the same time. For instance, you might have a word processing document and two Draw documents open in Works so that you can switch between them to move information. Grouping documents is an effective way to organize your work. Works treats such groupings as documents that can be manipulated together or individually. When you choose the command Save Workspace from the File menu, Works asks you to give the arrangement a name, and then saves a record of which documents were open. If you save a workspace containing a document that has not been saved, that document is not saved in the workspace. As a reminder, Works presents a dialog box with the message, Untitled documents will not be saved in the workspace file.

You open a workspace just like a document. Workspace documents appear in the Choose Type dialog box's file list box along with the names of their contents. When you double-click the workspace name, all the documents it contains are reopened in the same arrangement when you saved the workspace.

Deleting Files

The Trash Can on the desktop is used for removing files. The process is easiest when Works is not running, enabling you to open folders and locate the files you want to remove. Drag the files to the Trash to remove them. The Trash Can icon bulges to show it has contents. When you have collected all of your trash files, open the Special menu on the menu bar, and choose the command Empty Trash. If you are using System 7, you receive one final caution before your files are gone forever. System 6 users don't get a warning.

If you haven't selected the Empty Trash command, you can remove a file from the Trash. Double-click the Trash icon to open it; then drag the file out of the trash. If you use System 7, you can remove a file from the Trash when you get the warning after invoking the Empty Trash command.

Setting Works Preferences

Works provides a way to set a series of basic options both for all modules and for individual modules. To change settings, choose the Preferences command, which appears on the Edit menu of all modules (see fig. 2.10). The options shown vary with the module, but by clicking different icons in the dialog box, you can see and set options for any module. Preference settings for individual modules are discussed in the chapters devoted to the module. This section describes the settings that affect all modules.

Fig. 2.10
The Preferences
dialog box.

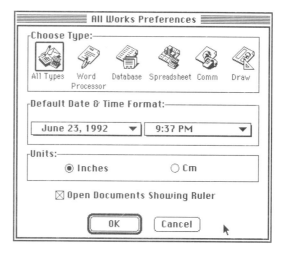

To set preferences that affect all modules, click the icon labeled All Types. The dialog box offers pop-up menus to set date and time formats, a selection of inches or centimeters (cm) as the default unit of measurement, and a check box that specifies that documents in modules in which a ruler is used open with the ruler showing. Click Cancel to leave the options unchanged. If you want to change an option, make the appropriate selection; then click OK to record the new settings.

Printing

Three commands on the File menu control printing choices: Print Preview, Print, and Print One. Using these options, you can preview a document before printing to see how it will look on paper; when you print, you can select print quality and the pages you want to print, or you can choose the Print One command to bypass the dialog box and print one copy quickly with the current settings.

Some printing choices depend on the capabilities of the printer you use. Use the Chooser desk accessory, found under the Apple menu, to specify your printer. If your printer does not appear in Chooser, you need to install a *printer driver* in your Macintosh system folder.

A printer driver is a small software utility that tells your computer how to communicate with your model of printer. Drivers for most popular Apple printers are included with system software, but if the driver for your printer is not, it is probably packed with the printer. For additional information on this topic, consult your system software manual or your printer documentation.

Previewing a Document

You can save substantial amounts of time and paper by using the Print Preview command. Choosing this command from the File menu opens a display similar to the one shown in figure 2.11. In the thumbnail view, you cannot distinguish individual words (unless you use large type), but you can get a sense of the document layout and page breaks. When you select Print Preview from the File menu, the screen displays the first page of your document, and the cursor changes to a magnifying glass.

If you click the page with the magnifier, the page zooms out to reveal its full size. Drag the hand cursor to move the page on the screen or to view other areas. Click the close box to return to the first screen. If you have more than one page, use the Previous and Next buttons to flip through the document. If you are satisfied with the document, click the Print button and the Print dialog box opens. To make revisions, choose Cancel or click the close box, and Works returns you to the document.

Controlling the Print Settings

The Print dialog box is part of the Macintosh system software, which controls printing for all Macintosh applications. The exact appearance of the dialog box depends on the printer you are using. Figure 2.12 shows a print dialog box for an ImageWriter, and figure 2.13 shows one for a LaserWriter.

Fig. 2.11
The Print Preview window
shows layout.

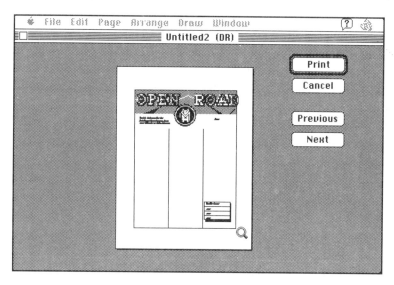

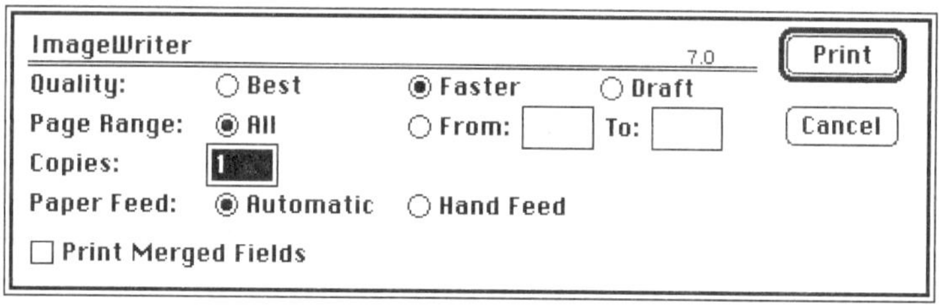

Fig. 2.12
Print dialog box for an
ImageWriter.

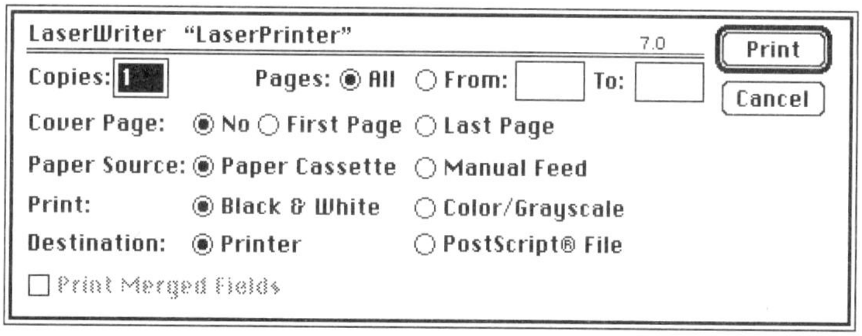

Fig. 2.13
Print dialog box for a
LaserWriter

With an ImageWriter, you can choose paper size, orientation, and a limited number of image sizes. The LaserWriter has settings for number of copies, page range, paper feed, color, and output destination. If you use a different printer, a different selection of choices is offered in the dialog box.

Chapter 2

Understanding Works Basics

Sending a Document Directly to the Printer

The handy Print One command sends the current document directly to the printer, using the settings presently in the Print dialog box. Use this command if you don't need to make any adjustments in printer settings.

Closing and Quitting

When you are finished with a document, you may want to close it and start another, or you may want to quit Works. You also can close all documents if you have several open at the same time.

Closing Documents

To close the active document, open the File menu and choose Close, or click the close box in the window's upper left corner.

If you have unsaved changes in the document, a dialog box opens asking whether you want to save the changes. Click Yes to save, No to discard the changes or Cancel to quit the process. To close a document that is open but not currently active, use the Window menu to make the document the active window; then choose Close.

Close All methodically closes all open files. When you choose the Close All command from the File menu, the dialog box shown in figure 2.14 opens. Clicking the box to save all changed files without further prompting is a good idea. Otherwise, you have to respond to a dialog box for each file you close. When you choose OK, the process proceeds automatically.

Fig. 2.14
The Close All dialog box.

```
┌────────────────────────────────────────────────┐
│  Are you sure you want to close     ┌────────┐  │
│  all open Works documents?          │   OK   │  │
│                                     └────────┘  │
│  ☐ Save all changed files without   ┌────────┐  │
│     further prompting               │ Cancel │  │
│                                     └────────┘  │
└────────────────────────────────────────────────┘
```

Quitting Works

If you go directly to Quit, you are given a chance to save your files. Works asks whether you want to save changes and, after you have responded, proceeds to close down the program. You do not have to use Save or Save As before using Quit.

Using Works Stationery

Stationery is a name used by Works (and Macintosh System 7) to designate documents saved as templates—sample documents you can use as the foundation for activities in all modules of Works. When you open a stationery file, Works creates a new unnamed document that contains the contents and formatting of the stationery template from which the document originated.

You can add to or modify any aspect of the new document, and the original stationery document remains unchanged and ready to produce another sheet of stationery the next time you need one. Although the word *stationery* implies word processing documents, stationery templates exist for all Works modules.

To increase your productivity and give you a head start with Works, the program comes packaged with stationery. As you will learn in a following section, you also can create your own reusable stationery for repetitive or complex jobs.

Opening Prepared Stationery

When you open a stationery document, you open an untitled copy of the original. The original remains unchanged, ready to provide another copy whenever needed. You can edit stationery documents to update them, but their principal purpose is to provide reusable templates.

You can reach stationery from the File menu using either the New or Open command. To use a prepared stationery template to create a new document, follow these steps:

1. Open the File menu and choose New.

   Click the module icon you want, if it does not have a box around it.

2. Click the Show Stationery check box.

   Choosing the check box expands the dialog box to present a scrolling list where you can choose stationery documents and a Preview window where you can get a miniature preview of the selected document (see fig. 2.15).

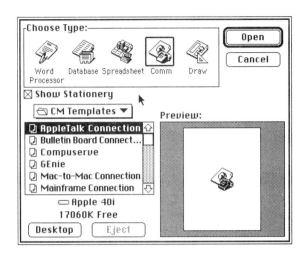

Fig. 2.15
Choosing Show Stationery
expands the Choose Type
dialog box.

3. Click once on a stationery document name from the scrolling list. A preview of the stationery document's contents appears at the right.

4. Click Open to create a new document based on the selected stationery or double-click the name of the stationery document in the file list box. Works displays an unnamed copy of the file for you to work with. Be sure to name and save your new file promptly so you don't risk losing your work.

Creating Stationery

Any Works document you have created is a potential piece of stationery. For example, you can start with a blank spreadsheet or start from an existing stationery spreadsheet if you like. In both cases, make the changes you want, remembering that everything in the spreadsheet is duplicated each time you use the stationery. Don't leave in items that you won't want in each copy. When your spreadsheet or document is ready, follow these steps to change a normal spreadsheet document into stationery:

1. Create the document you want as stationery.

2. Open the File menu and choose Save As.

NOTE

When you save a file as stationery, its stationery file name won't be reflected in the title bar of the on-screen document. Works creates a separate new stationery file that you will see when you next look at a list of stationery in the New or Open file lists.

3. Name the document.

  Switch to a new folder if desired.

4. Open the File Format pop-up menu and drag to select
  Stationery (see figure 2.16).

5. Click the Save button.

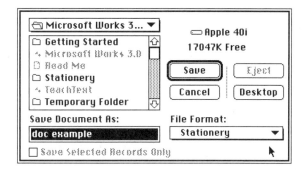

A duplicate of your file has been saved in stationery format. Your original
file remains open and can be used or discarded as desired. The new
stationery appears as a template option for use in generating a new file.

Getting Help

Works has an outstanding on-line, context-based help system. If you use
System 7, you get the added feature of Balloon Help, which provides
interactive help when you point to an object on the screen.

Help In Works

If you are using System 6, you can find the Help command on the
Window menu. With System 7, you can use either the Window menu or
the Help Menu icon on the menu bar. Either way, choosing Help opens
a window that contains icons representing each Works module (see
fig. 2.17).

Fig. 2.17
Choose Help from the
Window menu.

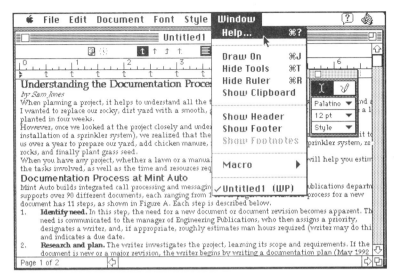

Figure 2.18 displays the initial Help dialog box. When you click the icon for a module, an index of help topics opens. Clicking on a topic about which you want to get additional information displays an additional outline of topics. Click a subtopic within this outline to display the help data. The Help window contains several buttons to help you navigate through topics. Table 2.2 describes the purpose of each of these buttons. The Quick Help button opens a window that presents "help on Help," a digest of techniques for navigating the Help menu.

Table 2.2
Help Window Buttons

Button	Purpose
Contents	Returns you to the Help Contents window.
Search	Opens a search dialog box to locate topics.
Back	Reverses your steps through Help windows.
History	Lists your previous steps. Click one to go to that location.
Arrows	Pages through Help.

Balloon Help

Balloon Help is a feature available only to users of System 7. A small icon, shaped as the balloon used for text in comic books, activates a menu (see fig. 2.19). Choosing the command Show Balloons, activates a feature that displays explanatory balloons of text when you point to objects on the screen. The command changes to Hide Balloons, which you can choose to turn off the feature. Although you can use Balloon Help with Works, not all objects on the screen have balloon explanations.

Fig. 2.18
The Help dialog box.

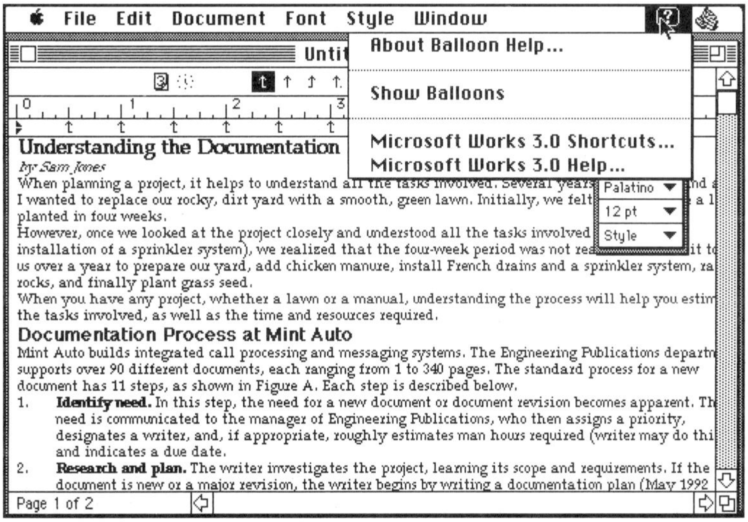

Fig. 2.19
The Balloon Help menu.

Works adds two menu items to the Balloon Help menu. The Microsoft Works 3.0 Shortcuts command opens an electronic booklet jammed with tips and shortcuts (see fig. 2.20). Because the Balloon Help menu is present at all times, you can use it to open this handy guide in any situation. The Microsoft Works 3.0 Help command on the Balloon Help menu enables you to conveniently access the Works help program.

Fig. 2.20
The Works 3.0 Shortcuts
dialog box.

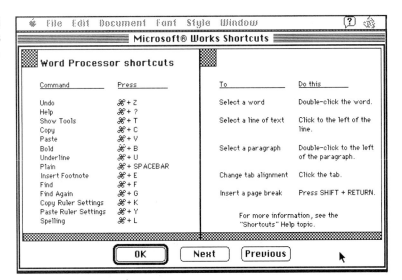

Chapter Summary

In this chapter, you learned techniques common to all Works modules. Program installation and start-up were discussed as well as standard procedures for opening, saving, printing, and closing documents. How to set Works preferences was explained, and the use and creation of stationery documents was demonstrated. The chapter concluded with an explanation of the help features available in Works and System 7.

Part I

Getting Started with Works

PART II

Using the
Word Processor

Includes

USING
MICROSOFT
WORKS

Creating Documents

Word processing is the most popular application of computers. In your use of Microsoft Works, a majority of your projects probably will include word processor documents of some type. Additionally, the word processor is the common denominator of integrated documents in Works. You can import spreadsheets, charts, and database information into a word processor document, and you can export word-processed text to the other modules of Works.

The Works word processor is powerful and capable, and is well qualified for the central role it plays in the program. In addition to a complete set of standard features, the word processor includes some attractive bonuses:

- Icons to automate common formatting tasks

- Customizable templates called *stationery*

- Headers, footers, and footnotes

- Links to Draw for graphic enhancement

Works' close integration of its modules enables you to move text around and into other types of documents. You also can save your documents in various formats that enable you to move the documents into other Macintosh and PC-based applications.

USING
MICROSOFT
WORKS

This chapter discusses the major features of the word processor and explains the basics of creating a document. In subsequent sections, you learn to edit a document and manage layout elements such as margins and indents. The chapter concludes with sections on saving and printing your work.

Starting the Word Processor

When you start Works by double-clicking its icon, the Open dialog box, shown in figure 3.1, appears. To switch to the word processing module, double-click the Word Processor icon. The word processing menu appears at the top of the screen and, unless you choose a specific document in the scrolling list, a new, untitled document is opened.

Fig. 3.1
The Open dialog box.

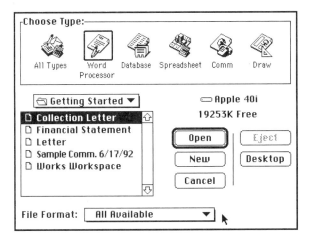

Touring the Word Processor Screen

Because this chapter is the first in the book to describe the screen layout of a Works module, this chapter introduces some features common to all module windows. Figure 3.2, for example, shows some features that are common to all Works module screens. Later chapters describe only the unique features of a specific module.

Part II

Using the Word Processor

Features Common to All Works Module Screens

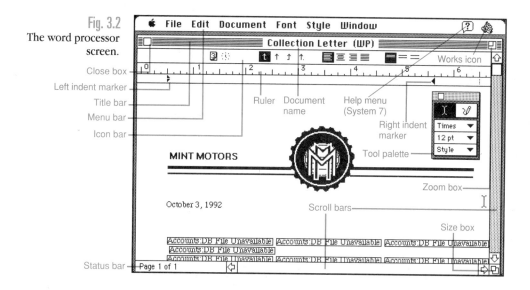

Fig. 3.2
The word processor screen.

Close box
Left indent marker
Title bar
Menu bar
Icon bar

Ruler   Document name   Help menu (System 7)   Works icon
Right indent marker   Tool palette
Zoom box
Scroll bars
Size box

MINT MOTORS

October 3, 1992

Accounts:DB File Unavailable Accounts:DB File Unavailable Accounts:DB File Unavailable
Accounts:DB File Unavailable
Accounts:DB File Unavailable Accounts:DB File Unavailable Accounts:DB File Unavailable

Status bar — Page 1 of 1

The *title bar*, at the top of the window, includes the document name. When you first open a new document, Works gives it the generic name *Untitled1*. When you first save a document, you give it a name, and that name then appears in the title bar.

Next to the file name (in parentheses) is an indication of the Works module that created the document. In this case (WP) tells you that this document is a word processor document. This information may seem self-evident right now, but you can have several windows of different types open at once. In a multiple-window situation, identifying a window type from its title bar is quite handy.

At the left end of the title bar is the *close box*. Clicking this box closes the window. If you have unsaved material on the screen and you click the close box, a dialog box appears asking whether you want to save your changes to the document. Clicking Yes opens the File Save dialog box.

At the right end of the title bar is the *zoom box*. Clicking the zoom box shrinks or enlarges the window. Scroll bars appear at the right and the bottom of the window. Their use is described in Chapter 1, "Macintosh Basics for New Users."

Chapter 3
Creating Documents

To the left of the bottom scroll bar is an area called the *status bar*. Varied messages and information appear here, depending on your current activity. Typically, this area shows the current page number and total pages in your document.

Features of the Word Processing Screen

In addition to the features shared by all Works screens, the word processor screen contains a powerful tool: the *ruler* (see fig. 3.3). The top part of the ruler contains a row of icons called *ruler buttons*. The buttons serve as shortcuts for a variety of commands. Below the buttons is a scale, measured in inches, used to align margins, indents, and tabs. The triangular markers at the bottom right and left of the ruler can be dragged to new positions to change document margins and indents.

On the document screen, a flashing vertical line called the *insertion point* indicates where the text you type will appear. A short horizontal line, the *end mark*, shows the end of the current document.

Fig. 3.3
The ruler appears at the top of the document window.

Insertion point ——
End mark ——

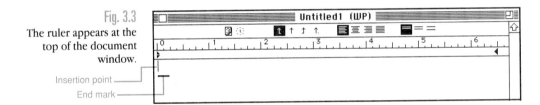

Understanding the Word Processing Menus

Above the document window, menu names appear on the *menu bar*. The File, Edit, and Window menus appear in all Works modules. Other menu names change depending on the module you are using.

The following paragraphs give a general description of the six word processing menus. A detailed command reference of all word processor commands appears in Appendix A.

The File menu contains the commands used to open, close, and save document files and the commands for page setup and printing. You also quit Works from this menu. If you are on a network using Microsoft Mail, the Open Mail and Send Mail commands at the bottom of the menu are active. If you don't use Microsoft Mail, the mail commands will be grayed out and not available for use.

The Edit menu includes the commands that cut, copy, and move material within and between documents. The Find, Replace, and Undo commands are all useful for correcting problems. The GoTo Page command helps you move to a specific location. The Preferences command enables you to customize fonts and footnotes.

An improved spelling checker and the new 190,000-word thesaurus are the highlights of the Document menu. Other tools in the Document menu add professional touches to your documents by inserting footnotes, page breaks, and time/date stamps.

The fonts installed in your Macintosh System folder are applied to your documents through the Font menu. The adjacent Style menu is used to change font sizes, styles (bold, italic, and so on), and spacing.

The Window menu controls the display of open documents. Depending on the amount of memory in your Macintosh, you can have as many as 32 windows open at once. The Window menu also controls the display of the ruler, the tool palette, and drawing tools. The Works macro utility is entered here, and the Help, Clipboard, and Header/Footer commands are on this menu.

Creating New Documents

When you start the word processor, it opens a blank untitled document like the one shown in figure 3.4. The flashing insertion point in the upper left corner indicates where characters will appear when you begin typing. If, after starting one document, you choose to start a second one, open the File menu, choose New, and then double-click the Word Processor icon in the Choose Type dialog box. A new blank word processing document opens on top of the original one.

If you drag the new document down a bit, using the title bar, you can see the original document behind the new one (see fig. 3.5). To bring the first document forward, click any visible part of its window. You also can bring a window forward, even if it is not visible, by opening the

Window menu and choosing the window you want from the list of open windows at the bottom of the menu (see fig. 3.6).

Fig. 3.4

A new blank document in the word processor.

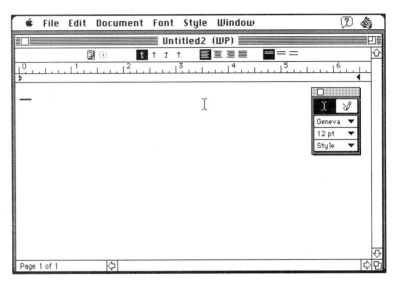

Fig. 3.4

A new blank document in the word processor.

Fig. 3.5

Document pulled down to reveal document behind.

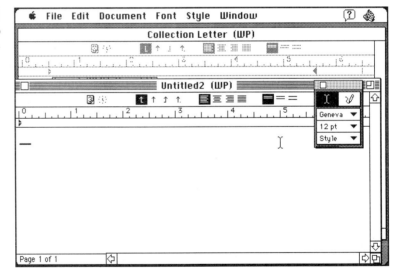

Part II

Using the Word Processor

Fig. 3.6
Window menu showing
two windows.

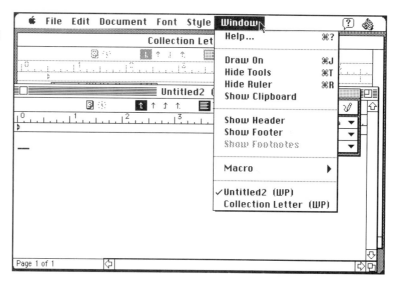

Fig. 3.6
Window menu showing
two windows.

Creating Your Document

Although you have a powerful, complex program at your service, typing a basic document is easy. Follow these steps:

1. Open the File menu and choose the New command. A new, untitled document opens.

2. Begin typing your text. When you reach the end of a line, do not press Return. Works automatically moves you to a new line—a feature called *word wrap*.

3. When you want to end a paragraph, press Return.

4. To create a blank line, press Return without typing any text.

5. To make simple corrections, press Delete. The character to the left of the insertion point is removed.

Moving through Your Document

After you fill your screen with text, you may want to move through your document. You can move left or right one character, or up or down one line by using the keyboard arrow keys. To make larger moves, place the mouse pointer where you want the insertion point to appear, and then

NOTE

If you were trained on a typewriter, you may feel that you need to press Return at the end of each line. Pressing Return at the end of every line is not only unnecessary—it can cause problems. Each time you press Return, you create a new paragraph. If each line in your document becomes a paragraph, strange things happen when you use para-graph-oriented commands for spacing and formatting. When you see how easily Works manages line breaks, you will soon break the habit.

click the mouse. You also can use the scroll bars to move the document in the window. If you have an extended keyboard, you can use the keys listed in table 3.1 to speed up moves.

Table 3.1
Movement Keyboard
Shortcuts

Key	Result
Home	To beginning of document
End	To end of document
Page Up	Up one document window
Page Down	Down one document window

Correcting Mistakes

Small revisions are simple. To delete an error, position the insertion point to the right of the error by using the mouse or keyboard arrow keys. Then press Delete. Press Delete as many times as necessary to erase the error.

Using Basic Editing Techniques

To many users, the most appealing feature of computerized word processing is the capability to edit freely without having to retype the entire document. Creating and experimenting with documents is less tedious because you easily can revise or enhance your work. Works contains excellent editing tools. In this section, you are introduced to the principal ones.

Selecting Text

Using Delete works well to correct small problems, but suppose that you want to remove an entire sentence or paragraph. The answer lies in *selecting*, which is a way of highlighting text you want to change. To select text, hold down the mouse button while dragging across the text you want to highlight. As you move the mouse, a reverse (black) highlight appears across the selected text (see fig. 3.7). When you release the mouse button, the highlight remains until you click the mouse button again. Now when you choose a command, it applies to the selected text.

Fig. 3.7
Document with text
selected.

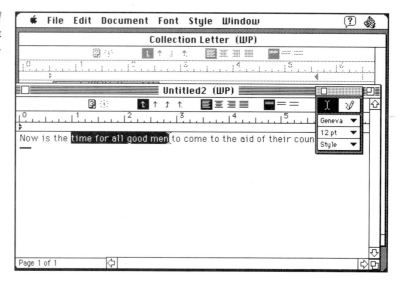

In addition to selecting text for correction, you also select it when you want to change its appearance or when you want to copy or move the text. When you are new to Works, you may forget to select text before choosing a command. If nothing is selected, your command has no effect. Remember the little phrase *select-do*. This phrase can help you remember to select something for a command to act on before choosing the command.

Using Selection Shortcuts

Because you select text frequently while editing a document, Works contains selection shortcuts. Several shortcuts involve using an area of the document screen called the *selection bar*. This bar is a narrow border running down the left edge of your document. You can tell when your mouse pointer moves into the selection bar because the pointer turns into a bold arrow pointing right (see fig. 3.8). If you are a new mouse user, you may have to practice a bit to put the pointer exactly in the selection bar. On a smaller screen, the area is quite narrow. Now that you know how to use the selection bar, try the shortcuts in table 3.2.

Fig. 3.8
The mouse pointer turns
into an arrow.

Mouse pointer —

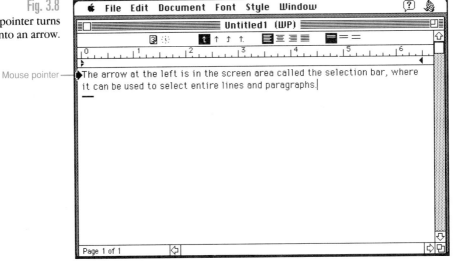

Table 3.2
Selection Shortcuts

Selection	Action
A word	Double-click the word
A line	Click in the selection bar, next to the line
A paragraph	Double-click in the selection bar, next to the paragraph
Any amount of text	Drag the mouse pointer across the text
The entire document	Open the Edit menu and choose Select All, or press the ⌘ key and click in the selection bar

An alternate way to select text requires more explanation. Click the mouse at the beginning of any area you want to select. Move the mouse pointer to the end of the selection, hold down the Shift key, and click at the end of your selection. The area between the first and last mouse click is highlighted.

You can modify a selection by holding down Shift while dragging the mouse to increase or decrease the selected area. In all cases, you remove a selection by clicking the mouse anywhere on the document screen.

Inserting and Deleting Text

To insert text, click the mouse where you want the text to appear and begin typing. The new text pushes existing text to the right while Works word wrap automatically adjusts line length. Another feature that new Works users find convenient is described by the phrase "typing replaces selection." When any block of text is selected, the first character you type replaces the whole block. For example, if you want to replace a sentence, select it and start typing. You don't have to delete the original sentence before you begin typing the replacement.

To delete text, select it and press the Delete key. The selected material is removed from the screen and placed in a temporary storage area in memory. The only way to retrieve deleted text is to immediately select Undo from the Edit menu. You must select Undo before performing any other command.

Material removed using the Cut command is handled differently from material removed with Delete. When you cut something, it disappears from the screen, but Works temporarily places the cut material in a storage area in computer memory called the *Clipboard*. Only one item can be stored on the Clipboard, regardless of size. If you cut another item, the second item bumps the first one out of storage and out of existence. A cut item stays on the Clipboard until replaced by another one or until you leave the program.

To restore cut material to your screen, open the Edit menu and choose the Paste command. The contents of the Clipboard (the last item cut) return to the screen at the location of the insertion point.

The Edit menu also contains a Clear command. When you select something and choose Clear, the selection is removed from the screen and is *not* stored on the Clipboard. After you Clear an item, it is gone for good. This command is useful when you have put a selection on the Clipboard with the intention of using the selection elsewhere and yet you need to remove something else from the screen. Using Clear bypasses the Clipboard, leaving its contents intact.

Moving and Copying Text

You can move any block of text to a new location by using the Cut and Paste commands (see fig. 3.9). Use these steps:

1. Select the text you want to move.

2. Open the Edit menu and choose Cut. The selected material is placed on the Clipboard.

3. Position the insertion point where you want to paste your text.

4. Open the Edit menu and choose Paste.

If you cut something by mistake, immediately open the Edit menu and choose Undo. Your deletion is restored in its original location.

Fig. 3.9
The Edit menu, showing commands and keyboard shortcuts.

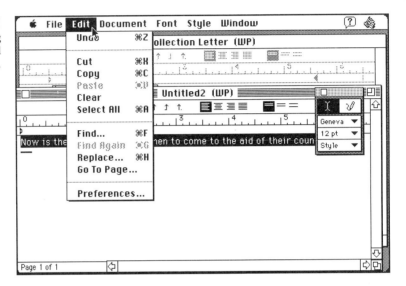

The Copy command, also on the Edit menu, leaves the selected text on the screen, while duplicating the text on the Clipboard. To place a copy in a new location, follow these steps:

1. Select the text you want to copy.

2. Open the Edit menu and choose Copy. The selected material is copied to the Clipboard.

3. Position the insertion point where you want to paste your text.

4. Open the Edit menu and choose Paste.

Table 3.3 shows the keyboard shortcuts to the frequently used Cut, Copy, Paste, and Undo commands. These shortcut keys are used universally in Macintosh applications. The Command key is the large key with an apple or "propeller" icon (or both) on it. Notice that the shortcut keys are next to one another on your keyboard.

TIP

In the Clipboard, the original contents remain until displaced by another cut or copied item. As a consequence, you can paste the same item repeatedly in various locations. Just move the insertion point and choose Paste again. This technique is useful for creating repetitive documents such as forms or lists.

Part II

Using the Word Processor

	Command	Keyboard shortcut
Table 3.3 Shortcut Keys	Cut	⌘-X
	Copy	⌘-C
	Paste	⌘-V
	Undo	⌘-Z

Finding and Replacing Text

Imagine that you have just created a multipage article about a famous person named McDonald. Imagine further that you mistakenly spelled the name *Mac*Donald in at least one location. How can you discover whether you made the error again?

Without a Find or Replace command, you would have to scroll through every line of your document, looking for other instances of the error. In Works, you open the Edit menu and click Find or Replace. In this section, you learn how to use these quick and accurate tools to correct or revise repetitive errors.

To search for text, follow these steps:

1. Open the Edit menu and choose the Find command. The Find dialog box opens (see fig. 3.10).

2. Type the word or phrase you want to find in the Find What text box, and then click the Find Next button. Works scrolls to and highlights the first occurrence of the word.

3. To continue the search, click the Find Next button. The message `All occurrences of [word] have been found` appears when the search is complete.

4. When you are finished, click Cancel to end the search.

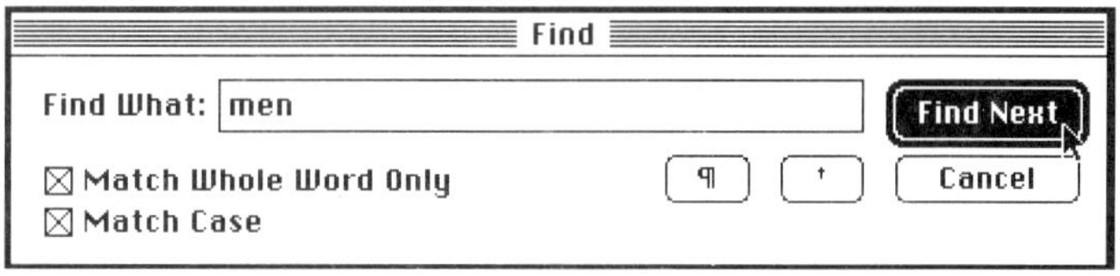

Fig. 3.10
The Find dialog box.

Find

Find What: men   [Find Next]

☒ Match Whole Word Only   [¶] [']   [Cancel]
☒ Match Case

Chapter 3
Creating Documents

Controlling Searches

Two check boxes in the Find dialog box change the way the search works. Normally, the search finds all instances of the word you type, even if the word is embedded in another word. For instance, if you search for *cat*, you also may find *cat*alog and and s*cat*. If you click an X in the Match Whole Word Only box, the search finds only complete words that match your entry. In the previous example, only *cat* would be found.

The second check box controls matching case (capitalization). If you enter the command to search for *CAT* (in capitals), and then click an X in the Match Case box, your search will not find *cat*. If you typed *cat* (small letters), your search would not find *CAT*. You can combine the use of both check boxes. With both boxes checked, you find only the exact word matching the capitalization of the word you typed in the text box.

The two buttons in the Find dialog box, containing a paragraph mark and an arrow respectively, are discussed in the section of this chapter called "Searching for Special Characters."

Replacing Words

Using the Replace command is very similar to using Find. The Replace dialog box appears in figure 3.11. Features not present in the Find dialog box are the Replace With text box and the Replace and Replace All buttons. The other elements of the box work as just described for the Find command.

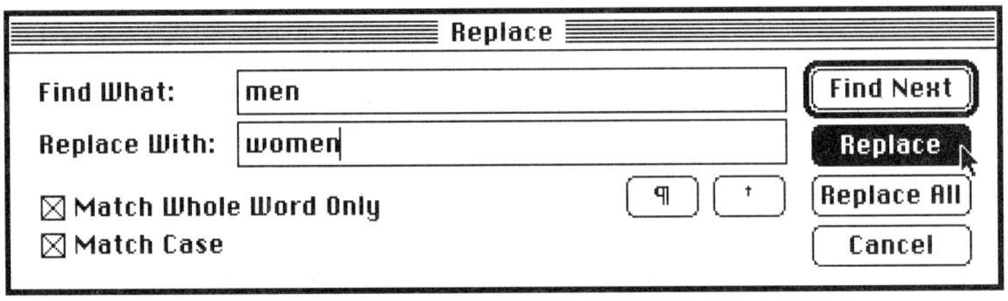

Fig. 3.11
The Replace dialog box.

Replace		
Find What: men		**Find Next**
Replace With: women		**Replace**
☒ Match Whole Word Only ¶ ↑		**Replace All**
☒ Match Case		**Cancel**

To replace one word with another, use these steps:

1. Enter the word you want to find and its replacement in the appropriate text boxes.

2. Click Find Next. The first instance of the word to be replaced is highlighted.

Part II

Using the Word Processor

3. Click the Replace button to replace the highlighted word.

4. Click Find Next to skip the replacement and find the word again.

Once you are sure your replacements are going correctly, you can click the Replace All button and the remaining changes are made rapidly without your intervention.

Don't be too quick to click Replace All. Unless you have set up the options carefully, you can get strange results. One common problem comes from not clicking the Match Whole Word Only box. If you replaced all instances of *cat* with *dog* without specifying whole words, you could come up with words like *dogalog.*

The Find and Replace commands have limitations. When the Find dialog box is open, you have to close it to edit. And when you use Replace, you can specify only a single word or phrase as a replacement. The command Find Again on the Edit menu enables you to make varied replacements of a single word or phrase. Find Again finds the word currently in the Find What text box even though the dialog box is closed. When you choose Find Again, the next instance of the word is highlighted and you can edit it directly.

Searching for Special Characters

In Works, *special characters* are the paragraph mark and the tab symbol. Both symbols are invisible in Works documents. Why would you need to find and change invisible items? Because these two items have a profound effect on the structure of your documents. If you want to rearrange your text in certain ways, fusing two paragraphs into one, for instance, you must change a special character.

Think of the paragraph mark and the tab symbol as invisible instructions that tell the word processor to do something. Each time you press the Return key, you put an invisible paragraph mark in your document. The paragraph mark is equivalent to an instruction that says, "End this sentence and move down to the next line." Each press of the Tab key puts in an invisible tab symbol. The tab symbol says, "Jump from here to the next tab stop." If you want to add or remove these instructions, you have to locate the special characters. After you grasp the concept of how the special characters work, you will know where to find them, but when you are new to word processing, the Find and Replace commands are helpful.

To find special characters, use the buttons that represent the characters in both the Find and Replace dialog boxes. The paragraph mark is represented by a traditional symbol (¶), the tab by a small arrow (↑). Clicking a symbol enters it into the Find What text box. You can then proceed to find or replace the symbol by using the procedures you use with words or phrases. Works highlights the apparently empty spaces that contain the characters. One useful tactic to delete either symbol is to use the Replace command and leave the Replace With box empty.

Managing Document Layout

After your text is in place, you may want to change the layout of your document. Perhaps you have a printed letterhead that requires you to start the letter an inch or two down the sheet. You may want to center your address between the margins, or the margins themselves may be too wide or narrow. This section addresses these issues and others related to document layout.

Setting Page Size and Orientation

Because specifying the correct document size and orientation is critical to printing, the Page Setup command, found on the File menu, links printer and page information. When you choose Page Setup, a dialog box related to the printer you have selected appears. For information about selecting a printer, read the section called "Printing Your Work." Figure 3.12 shows the dialog box for a LaserWriter printer. The dialog box contains radio buttons used to select paper size, and check boxes used to choose printer-specific effects such as image reduction. The two buttons under the Orientation heading choose vertical (often called *portrait*) or horizontal (*landscape*) printing.

Fig. 3.12
The Page Setup dialog box.

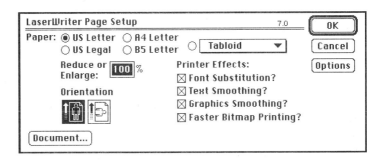

Setting Margins

The Document button at the bottom of the Page Setup dialog box opens the secondary dialog box, shown in figure 3.13. This box contains Margins and Numbering sections used by the word processor as well as grayed out sections used by other Works modules. To change document margins, type new measurements in inches. You also enter starting numbers for pages and footnotes in this dialog box. This feature enables you to start at a page other than 1 if, for example, you need consecutive page numbering for multiple documents. If the Title Page check box is selected, a page number is not printed on the first page. Numbering begins with 2 printed on the second page.

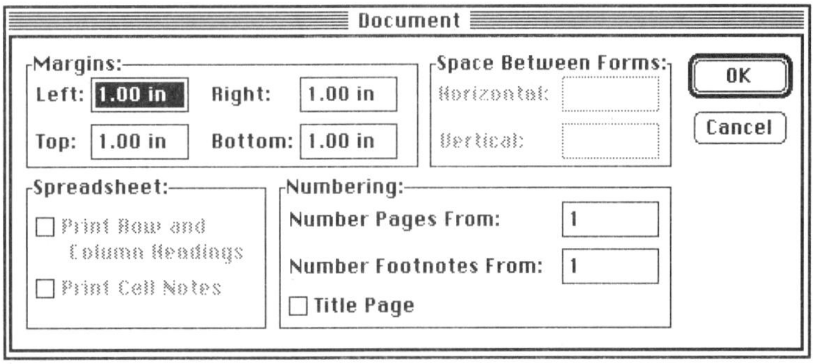

Fig. 3.13
The Document dialog box.

Adding Manual Page Breaks

As you type, Works keeps track of the number of lines and automatically inserts a page break when a page is filled. The page break appears as a thin dotted line running across the page (see fig. 3.14). You cannot remove automatic page breaks, but you can add your own.

To insert a manual page break, place the insertion point on the line immediately below where you want the break. Open the Document menu and choose Insert Page Break. A dotted line, thicker than the one for an automatic page break, appears on the page. You can use the Print Preview command (described in Chapter 2, "Understanding Works Basics") to see the result of your page breaks. Although you cannot remove automatic page breaks, they are realigned to properly match manually placed breaks. To delete a manual page break, place the insertion point on the line immediately below the break and choose Remove Page Break from the Document menu.

Chapter 3
Creating Documents

Fig. 3.14
A manual page break is
indicated by a dotted line.

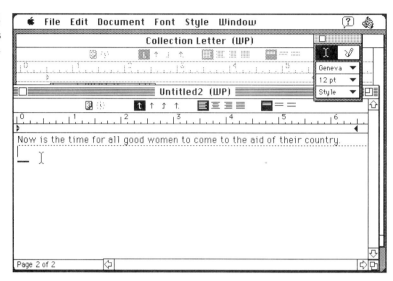

Fig. 3.14
A manual page break is
indicated by a dotted line.

Printing, Saving, and Quitting

Printing, saving, and quitting are generally three operations you will perform at the end of a work session. These topics are covered briefly here, and more fully in Chapter 2.

Printing Your Work

Three commands on the File menu control printing choices: Print Preview, Print, and Print One. You can preview a document with Print Preview before printing to see how it will look on paper. When you print, you can select print quality and the pages you want to print, or you can choose the Print One command to bypass the dialog box and print quickly with the current settings. For more information about printing, refer to Chapter 2.

Saving Your Work

Choose Save As from the File menu to save your document with a name and a file format. After that initial save, you can use the Save command or ⌘-S, to quickly save your document. You also can save a workspace with the Save Workspace command from the File menu. For more information about saving, see Chapter 2.

Part II

Using the Word Processor

Closing and Quitting

When you are finished with a document, you may want to close it and start another or you may want to quit Works.

To close the active document, open the File menu and choose Close or click in the close box in the window's upper left corner. If you have a number of files open, use Close All to close all open documents. If you want to quit Works, you can go directly to Quit. You will be given a chance to save your files. For more information about saving and quitting, see Chapter 2.

Customizing the Word Processor

You can customize certain features of each Works module by choosing the Preferences command from the Edit menu. Figure 3.15 shows the Word Processor Preferences dialog box. You can choose the default font and font size. This choice is reflected in all subsequent word processor documents. You also can choose the separator and placement of footnotes. Use of footnotes is described in Chapter 4, "Enhancing Documents."

Fig. 3.15
Word Processor Preferences enables you to choose default font and size.

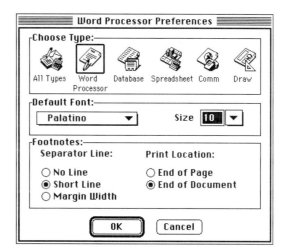

Chapter Summary

This chapter, devoted to the basics of word processing, showed you how to create a simple document. Text entry and editing were explained, with emphasis on the techniques and advantages of selecting text for editing. Page layout features were described, and basic printing techniques were introduced. The chapter concluded with a description of alternatives available for closing files and quitting the program. The following chapter covers document enhancements, including character and paragraph formatting and the use of features such as tabs, headers, and footers.

Enhancing Documents

n the previous chapter, you learned how to enter text and edit a basic document. Those skills may be all you need for many letters and memoranda. However, the era of desktop publishing has prompted an emphasis on a document's appearance. Although elaborate formatting cannot redeem poor writing, a polished appearance can draw attention to well-written material.

In this chapter, you will explore techniques for enhancing the appearance of your document. The process of using these techniques is called *formatting*. You will learn how to change character fonts and sizes, how to control paragraph indents and spacing, and how to change page breaks, margins, columns, and tables. This chapter also introduces the links between the word processor and the Draw module.

Applying Character Formatting

The characters that make up the words in your document have three properties you can alter: font, size, and style. Works provides several ways of changing choices for each of these properties.

USING
MICROSOFT
WORKS

Changing Fonts

A font is a family of type styles that share a basic design, such as Geneva or Times. Figure 4.1 shows a screen containing samples of fonts commonly used with the Macintosh. Your selection may be different depending on the fonts installed in your System file. With System 7, Apple added a font management system called TrueType, which is described in the section called "Choosing TrueType Fonts."

Fig. 4.1
A screen showing samples of installed fonts.

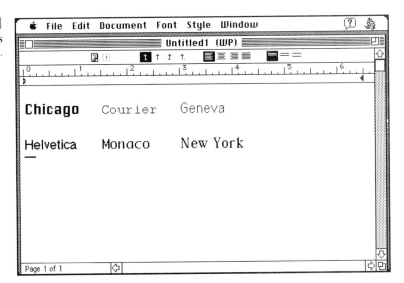

Choosing Standard Fonts

Chapter 3 introduced the concept called *select-do*. In the context of fonts, this concept means that you must have text selected before you can change fonts. If you need a refresher on selection techniques, review the section of Chapter 3 called "Selecting Text."

The Font menu, shown in figure 4.2, lists the fonts installed in your System folder. A check mark appears next to the font of the paragraph that contains the insertion point. To change a font, select the text you want to change, open the Font menu, and click the name of the new font.

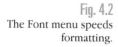

Fig. 4.2
The Font menu speeds
formatting.

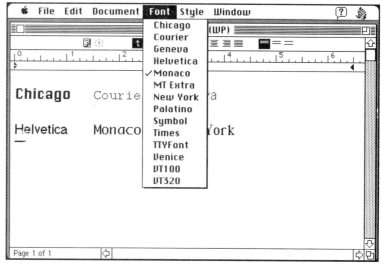

Another way to change fonts is to use the tool palette. To display the
tool palette, shown in figure 4.3, open the Window menu and choose
the Show Tools command. A small window with buttons opens. This
window is the Tool Palette window. The buttons open pop-up menus
containing the same options as the Font and Style menus. Clicking in the
appropriate box opens list boxes of fonts, sizes, and styles. The icons at
the top of the window switch between the word processor and Draw
module, a topic covered later in this chapter.

Because the palette remains open while you work, rather than closing as
a conventional menu, you can make changes to a variety of font properties without repeatedly opening menus. To close the tool palette, click
the close box at the top of its window, or open the Window menu and
choose the command Hide Tools.

Works has a third way to change fonts. If you open the Style menu
and choose the Format Character command, the dialog box shown in
figure 4.4 opens. You can change fonts by clicking the Font box and then
choosing a new font from the list box that appears. An advantage of
using this method is that you can preview the fonts, which are presented
in the sample area at the bottom of the dialog box. The size and style
settings in this dialog box are discussed later in this chapter.

Chapter 4

Enhancing Documents

Fig. 4.3
The tool palette remains
open between commands.

Fig. 4.3
The tool palette remains
open between commands.

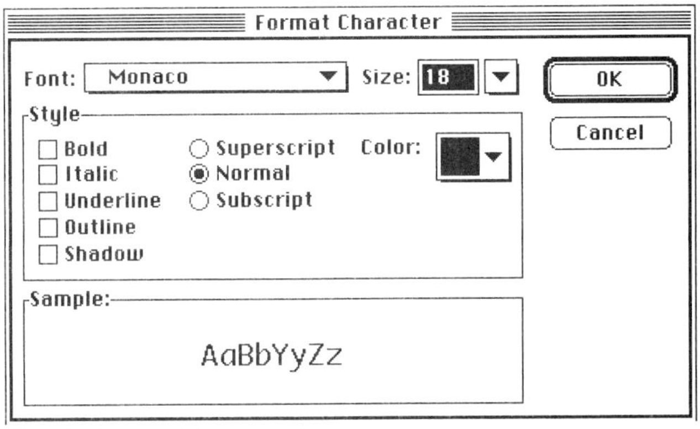

Fig. 4.4
The Format Character
dialog box shows a sample
of the results.

Choosing TrueType Fonts

With System 7, Apple introduced a font management system called *TrueType*. Using a TrueType font, also called a *scalable font*, you can specify any type size and get a smooth result. A single TrueType font can generate all the characters of one font in one style such as Helvetica Bold or Times Italic.

Prior to TrueType, if you wanted smooth printed characters, you had to install a font file for each size and type of character you wanted to use.

Part II

Using the Word Processor

You can distinguish TrueType fonts from fixed-size fonts by examining their icons (see fig. 4.5). If you open a TrueType font icon by double-clicking it, the resulting window (see fig. 4.6) shows multiple size samples. A fixed-size font window displays only one size sample.

Fig. 4.5
Icons for TrueType and
fixed-size fonts.

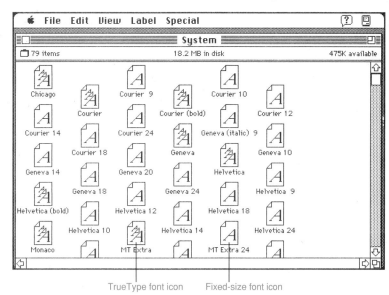

Fig. 4.6
Double-clicking a font icon
opens a sample window.

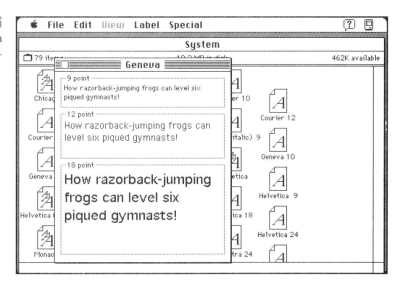

Your choice of TrueType or fixed-size fonts depends on the font variety needed for your documents. If you are creating a standard document with a single type size, any font selection is fine. If you plan to produce a heavily formatted document with a variety of sizes and styles, you have more flexibility with a TrueType font.

Changing Character Sizes

Fonts are sized using a traditional printing unit of measure, the point. An inch equals 72 points. Works uses a default font size of 12 points, about 1/8". Working with points simplifies the mathematics involved in measuring character size and spacing. For example, adding 12 points and 10 points is easier than adding 1/6" and 10/72". The small size of the point enables you to measure easily and precisely.

The Style menu lists the standard sizes available for fixed-size fonts. If the font set you selected has been installed for a listed size, the number showing the size is in an outline font. If you have both fixed-size and TrueType versions of the same font, the Macintosh first checks for a fixed-size font in the size you specify. If one is not available, the Macintosh uses the TrueType version. If you do not have TrueType, the Macintosh builds an approximation of the size you require, but the approximation is not as smooth as an installed font.

To change font size from the Style menu, use these steps:

1. Select the text you want to resize.

2. Open the Style menu.

3. Highlight the desired font size and release the mouse button. Works applies the new size to the selected text.

You can use the Increase Size and Decrease Size commands to change font sizes incrementally, but the commands work differently with fixed-size fonts than TrueType fonts. If you are using fixed-size fonts, choosing one of the commands increases or decreases the font size to the next available fixed-font size. If you are using a TrueType font, the commands increase or decrease font size by one point. The keyboard shortcuts for Increase Size (⌘-]) and Decrease Size (⌘-[) enable you to change font size without entering the Style menu.

Changing Character Size with the Tool Palette

As mentioned earlier in the chapter, the tool palette includes a button that enables you to size characters from a pop-up menu. To change font sizes using the tool palette, follow these steps:

1. Select the characters you want to resize.

2. Open the Window menu and choose Show Tools. The tool palette appears.

3. Point to the box that shows the current text size and hold down the mouse button. A list of fixed-size fonts for the current style appears. Outlined numbers indicate installed font sizes.

4. Move the pointer to the desired size and release the mouse button. Works applies the size to the selected text.

Changing Character Size Using Format Character

With the Format Character command, you can apply nonstandard font sizes. When using TrueType fonts, you can specify point sizes in one-point increments. You also can specify nonstandard sizes for fixed-size fonts, but the resulting font is an approximation if the specified size is not installed. The Format Character dialog box also provides a preview of the resulting change. Follow these steps to change font size using the Format Character command:

1. Select the characters you want to resize.

2. Open the Style menu and choose Format Character. The dialog box shown in figure 4.7 opens.

3. In the Size box, type the point size you want. A preview of the result appears in the Sample box.

4. Click OK to apply changes and close the dialog box.

Applying Styles to Fonts

Styles are effects—such as bold, underline, and italic—that add emphasis to selected text. The methods used to apply styles are similar to the methods used to change point sizes. Figure 4.8 shows the Style menu, which includes samples of the available styles. Not shown are the styles for subscript (H_2O) and superscript (see [3]), which can be applied from the Format Character dialog box.

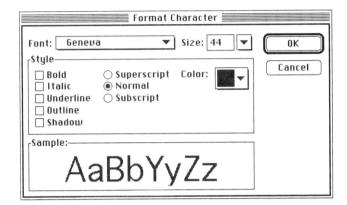

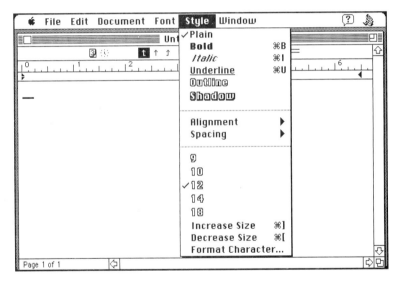

Applying Font Styles with the Style Menu

To change font style using the Style menu, follow these steps:

1. Select the text you want to restyle.

2. Open the Style menu.

3. Highlight the desired style and release the mouse button. Works applies the new style to the selected text.

Applying Font Styles with the Tool Palette

To change font style using the tool palette, use these steps:

1. Select the characters you want to restyle.

2. Open the Window menu and choose Show Tools. The tool palette appears.

3. Click the box that shows the current text style. A list of available styles appears.

4. Highlight the desired style and release the mouse button. Works applies the chosen style to the selected text.

Applying Font Styles with Format Character

You also can change the font style using the Format Character dialog box. You can evaluate the result of your selection in the Sample box. Follow these steps:

1. Select the characters you want to restyle.

2. Open the Style window and choose Format Character.

3. In the check boxes, select the styles you want. You can use combinations such as bold and italic.

4. If you are using a subscript or superscript, click the appropriate button.

5. Click OK to accept changes and close the dialog box.

Removing Font Styles

The Style menu and the tool palette both contain styles named Plain. Applying this style to styled text removes all styles and returns the selected text to an unstyled, or normal, state. In the Format Character dialog box, click to uncheck the boxes that establish the styles. When all the style boxes are unchecked, click OK to return selected text to the normal style.

Applying Paragraph Formatting

In Works, you create a new paragraph every time you press the Return key. Even the blank lines created by pressing Return are empty paragraphs. An important group of formatting commands—used for indenting, aligning, and controlling line spacing—apply to entire paragraphs.

The select-do rule also applies to paragraph formatting, but you can select a single paragraph without dragging the mouse. If the insertion point is within a paragraph, Works assumes that any paragraph formatting commands you choose apply to that paragraph. Just clicking the insertion point into a paragraph is sufficient to select the entire paragraph.

However, if you want to select more than one paragraph, you have to drag a highlight over all the paragraphs you want to select. A convenient way to select multiple paragraphs is to drag the mouse pointer down the selection bar (see fig. 4.9). You can select all paragraphs in a document by choosing Select All (⌘-A) from the Edit menu.

Fig. 4.9
The mouse pointer appears as a bold arrow when the pointer is in the selection bar.

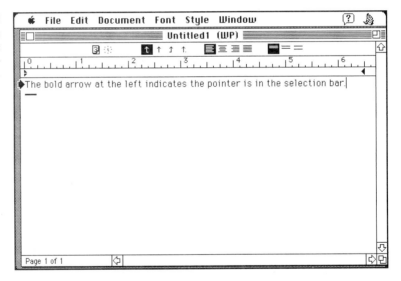

Aligning Paragraphs

In Chapter 3, you learned to establish document margins using the Document dialog box reached through the Page Setup command. When you begin a new document, Works aligns your text down the left margin.

Using the Alignment command on the Style menu, you can align a paragraph left, right, or centered. You also can *justify* a paragraph, which means both left and right edges are aligned evenly. Figure 4.10 shows a screen containing paragraphs that are aligned left, right, centered, and justified. The ruler includes icons that can speed paragraph alignment. For more information, see the section called "Speed Formatting with the Ruler."

Fig. 4.10
Sample paragraphs demonstrating the four possible alignments.

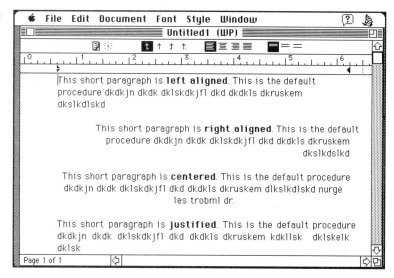

To change paragraph alignment, follow these steps:

1. Select the paragraphs you want to realign.

2. Open the Style menu and choose the Alignment command. A small cascade menu opens to the right.

3. Holding down the mouse button, drag the mouse pointer into the cascade menu.

4. Highlight the alignment you want; then release the mouse button. Works realigns the selected paragraphs.

Controlling Paragraph Indents

To understand indents, think of the document margins acting as a frame for the text. Normally, Works aligns paragraphs down the left margin.

Using commands on the Style menu, you can move paragraphs away from the left or right margins. You also can separately control the first line indent. Indents are measured from the margins, not from the edge of the document. If you have a one-half inch margin and add a one-half inch indent, text begins one inch from the edge of the paper.

Indents are controlled by the triangular symbols at the left and right ends of the word processing ruler (see fig. 4.11). Notice that the left triangle is split into upper and lower sections that can be dragged separately. The upper section controls the first line indent, and the lower section controls the left indent for the remaining lines of the paragraph.

Fig. 4.11
You can drag the triangular symbols to set indents.

Left indent marker

Right indent marker

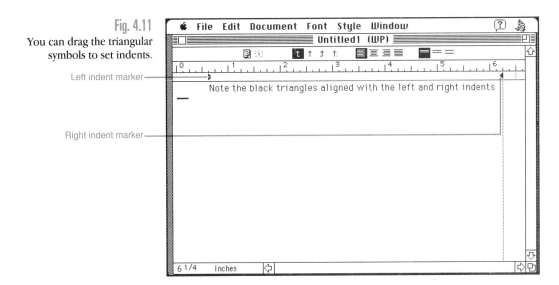

To indent an entire paragraph, use the following steps:

1. Place the insertion point in the paragraph you want to indent. For multiple paragraphs, highlight those you want to indent.

2. Drag the indent marker from the left or right (both upper and lower triangles) to the position you want. A dotted vertical line appears at the document indent as you move the triangle.

3. Release the mouse button. Works indents the selected paragraphs.

Creating First Line Indents

Dragging the upper half of the left indent marker controls the first line indent. Figure 4.12 shows examples of a standard first line indent and a variation called a *hanging indent*. The hanging indent is useful for numbered lists or bulleted items.

Fig. 4.12
A hanging indent is useful for lists.

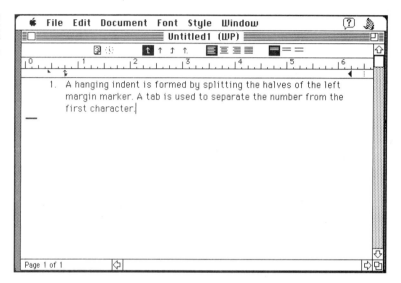

As you drag the indent markers, watch the measurement on the status line at the lower left of the document window. This measurement helps you to align text accurately. Also note that the hanging indent described previously is based on default one-half inch tab settings. When you learn how to manage tabs later in this chapter, you will be able to use any measurement for hanging indents.

To create a standard first line indent, use these steps:

1. Place the insertion point in the paragraph you want to indent. For multiple paragraphs, highlight those you want to indent.

2. Drag the top half of the left indent marker to the desired location.

3. Release the mouse button. The first line indent is established.

To create a one-half inch hanging indent, follow these steps:

1. Place the insertion point in the paragraph you want to indent. For multiple paragraphs, highlight those you want to indent.

2. Hold down the Shift key and drag the bottom half of the left indent marker one-half inch to the right. Release the mouse button. All lines of the paragraph are indented one-half inch.

3. Drag the top half of the left indent marker left one-half inch to create a hanging indent (also called a *negative indent* or *outdent*).

4. Release the mouse button. The first line is placed one-half inch to the left of the remaining lines.

5. To create an indented list, type a number or symbol and press Tab. The standard one-half inch tab aligns the next word with the remaining sentences.

Changing Line Spacing

The distance between text lines is related to character size. The Spacing command, found on the Style menu, enables you to vary line spacing to one-and-a-half lines or double-spacing between each line of text. You also can use the icons on the ruler to change line spacing. See the section called "Speed Formatting with the Ruler."

To change vertical line spacing, use these steps:

1. Place the insertion point in the paragraph where you want to change line spacing.

   For multiple paragraphs, highlight those you want to change. Use Select All for the entire document.

2. Open the Style menu and drag down to the Spacing command. A small cascade menu opens.

3. Drag the mouse sideways into the cascade menu; then select the correct spacing.

4. Release the mouse button. The menu closes, and Works applies the spacing to the selection.

Speed Formatting with the Ruler

The ruler contains buttons that directly apply alignment and spacing choices. Figure 4.13 indicates the alignment and spacing buttons on the ruler and their purposes.

The use of ruler buttons is simple:

1. Place the insertion point in the paragraph you want to change.

   For multiple paragraphs, highlight those you want to change. Use Select All for the entire document.

2. On the ruler, click the appropriate button to change the selected paragraphs.

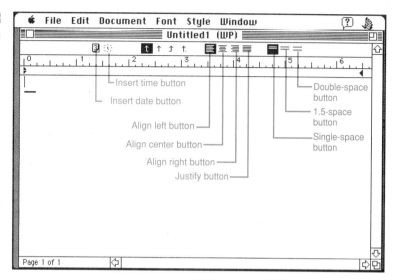

Fig. 4.13
You can use ruler buttons
for alignment and spacing.

Using the Time and Date Buttons

The left end of the ruler contains the Time and Date buttons. You can click these buttons to insert the time and date in a document at the insertion point. The time and date are read from the internal clock of your Macintosh. These buttons provide a shortcut equivalent for the Insert Current Date and Insert Current Time commands found on the Document menu.

Using Tabs

Because tabs in Works are invisible, they are difficult to describe. On the screen, a tab looks like empty space. Although you cannot see tabs, they are an important feature to master. Using tabs is a great improvement over the common practice of aligning text and numbers by pressing the space bar repeatedly. Many printers use *proportional spacing* where the distance between letters and numbers varies to give a better printed appearance. Because a space can have varying sizes, trying to use the space bar to line up a table can be nearly impossible.

To gain a practical understanding of tabs, try the following exercises:

1. Open a new word processor document for practice.

2. Type the following numbers, pressing the Tab key as shown:

[Tab]1000[Tab]2000[Tab]3000[Tab]4000[Tab]50.00[Return]

Be sure to include the decimal point in the last number (50.00).

3. Save the document with the name Tabs, so you can continue using it.

Notice that the left end of each number aligns with the ruler at one-half inch intervals (see fig. 4.14). The default tab in Works is a one-half inch left tab that aligns the left end of the number or word with the position of the tab. You don't see the default tabs on the ruler, but they are there, every one-half inch.

Fig. 4.14

Tab practice exercise aligned with default tabs.

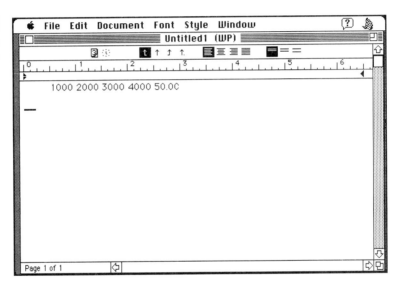

Examine the buttons at the top of the ruler. The four custom tab buttons are shaped as small arrows. From left to right, the buttons represent left, centered, right, and decimal tabs (see fig 4.15). As this section continues, you will use the different tab types.

Fig. 4.15

The tab buttons.

↥	↑	↥	↑.
Left tab	Center tab	Right tab	Decimal tab

Part II

Using the Word Processor

Applying Custom Tabs

The default one-half inch tabs can be replaced by custom tabs at any position on the ruler. You can drag the tab button you want onto the ruler; or you can select a tab button by clicking it, and then point to the ruler where you want the tab and click the mouse button. Using the Tabs document you created in the previous section, practice placing custom tabs by using these steps:

1. Click in the first paragraph.

2. Select the left tab button by clicking it.

3. Point just below the one-inch mark on the ruler and click the mouse button. A left tab stop appears in the area of the ruler between the two indent triangles.

Placing a custom tab stop removes any default tab stops to its left. Your tab stop is now the first one on the ruler, so the left end of the number 1000, preceded by the first (invisible) tab, is aligned with the one-inch tab stop on the ruler.

In the next exercise, you use an alternate way to place a second tab stop:

1. Point to the left tab button, hold down the mouse button, and drag down to the tab area at 2" on the ruler. A copy of the tab symbol is dragged onto the ruler. Note the dotted line you can use to align the tab.

2. Release the mouse button to place the tab. This second custom tab stop controls the (invisible) tab just left of the number 2000.

Understanding Tab Types

So far, you have used only left tab stops. Although left is used most often, there are three other types. The center tab stop centers a word or number. The right tab stop aligns the right end of an entry, and the decimal tab stop aligns numbers around their decimal point. Do the following steps to practice with different tab stop types:

1. Click the center tab button (see fig. 4.15); then drag it down just below the three-inch mark on the ruler.

2. Release the mouse button. The number 3000 is centered below the tab stop.

3. Click the right tab button; then drag it down just below the four-inch mark on the ruler.

4. Release the mouse button. The right end of the number 4000 aligns with the tab stop.

5. Check that the last number in your practice table contains a decimal point (50.00). If it does not, add one now.

6. Click the decimal tab stop button, and then drag down just below the five-inch mark on the ruler.

7. Release the mouse button. The number 50.00 is aligned by its decimal point. If you align text with a decimal tab, the text is right-aligned.

8. Type a zero between the 5 and 0, making the number 500. Notice that the decimal remains aligned with the tab stop.

Figure 4.16 shows the completed table.

Fig. 4.16
The practice table with
alignment completed.

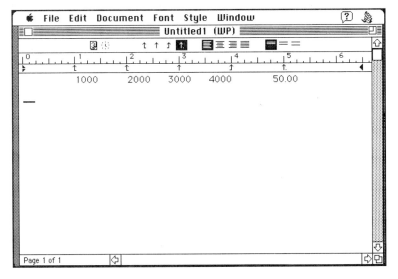

Modifying Tabs

You can both move and remove tab stops easily. To reposition a tab stop on the ruler, drag the tab button to a new position. To remove a tab stop, drag the button downward, off the ruler. When you let go of the button, the tab stop disappears, and Works realigns the paragraph currently selected (containing the insertion point). You also can change the type of a tab, from left-aligned to right-aligned, for example, by repeatedly clicking the tab symbol that you want to modify at the bottom of the ruler until the symbol changes to the type you need.

Creating Tables Using Tabs

Applying tab stops before you begin to type is an effective way to prepare a table. Suppose that you wanted to align rows of numbers an inch apart. Before starting to enter numbers, place tab stops every inch along the ruler. (Decimal or right tab stops work well with numbers.) Press the Tab key after each number you enter, and the insertion point jumps to the next tab stop. When you reach the end of the row, press Return to begin a new row.

When you begin a new paragraph by pressing Enter at the end of a previous paragraph, the new paragraph contains the formatting (fonts, indents, tab, and line spacing) of the previous paragraph. The new paragraph is a "clone" of the previous one.

Working with Specialized Features

You have learned the things you need to know to create and format a conventional document. Works also includes word processing features that can make your documents more accurate and professional. This section covers the use of the spelling checker and thesaurus. This section also explains the use of headers, footers, and footnotes, as well as copying styles.

Using the Spelling Checker

The Works' spelling checker is a flexible and powerful writing assistant. In addition to locating and suggesting replacements for misspelled words, the spelling checker can find repeated words and check words in customized dictionaries.

To begin checking your document, open the Document menu and choose Spelling. The Spelling dialog box opens and the checking process begins (see fig. 4.17).

Fig. 4.17
The Spelling dialog box.

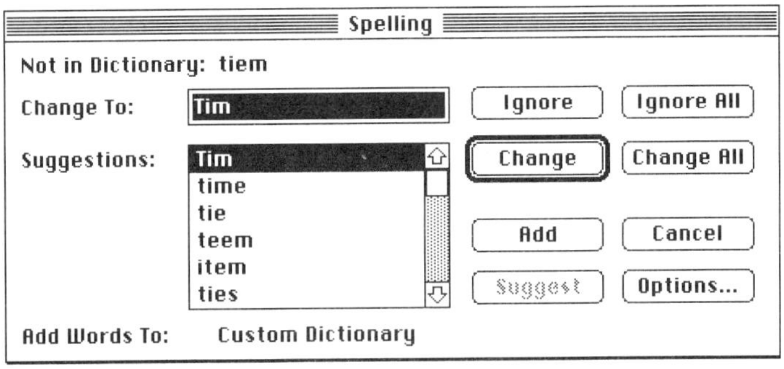

As the checker finds words not in its dictionary, use the buttons in the Spelling dialog box to control the progress and outcome of the check. Table 4.1 describes the spelling checker buttons and their purpose.

Table 4.1
Spelling Checker Buttons

Button	Effect
Ignore	Bypasses the questionable word.
Ignore All	Bypasses all instances of the questionable word. Good during the current check only.
Change	Changes the questionable word to a new spelling typed in the Change To box or highlighted in the Suggestions list.
Change All	Changes all instances of the questionable word to a new spelling typed in the Change To box or highlighted in the Suggestions list. Good during current check only.
Add	Adds the word in the Change To box to a custom dictionary.
Suggest	Activates the Suggestions list if it has been inactivated. (See "Setting Spelling Options.")
Options	Opens the Spelling Options dialog box.

Checking begins from the position of the insertion point and continues through the document until returning to the starting point. You can check part of the document by highlighting the part you want to check before choosing the Spelling command. When the limited check is complete, a dialog box offers the option of continuing the check or choosing OK to quit checking.

Setting Spelling Options

You can open the Spelling Options dialog box (see fig. 4.18) either by clicking the Options button in the Spelling dialog box or by choosing the Spelling Options command from the Document menu. The dialog box contains the tools used to create and edit custom spelling dictionaries and check boxes for controlling the behavior of the spelling checker.

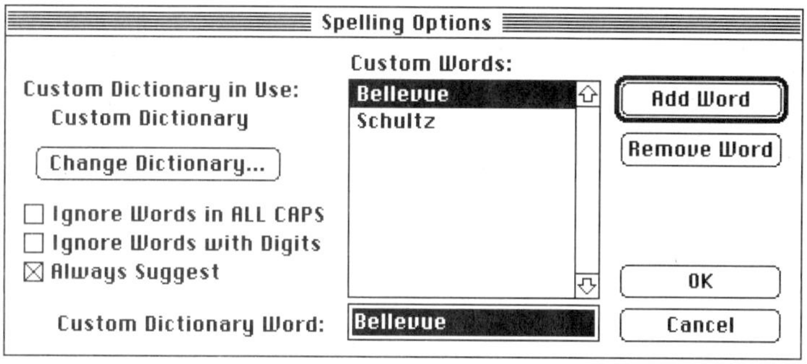

Fig. 4.18
The Spelling Options
dialog box.

The check box labeled Ignore Words in ALL CAPS is inactive by default. You may want to click it to turn it on if you check material with large numbers of acronyms, such as NASA or FBI, which the spelling checker questions. If you check the box, words entirely in capital letters are not checked.

The check box labeled Ignore Words with Digits is also normally inactive. If you check documents that refer to items with part numbers or model designations, you may want to make the spelling checker ignore such words by clicking the check box so that it shows an X.

The check box labeled Always Suggest is active by default. This feature tells Works to present a list of suggested corrections for every question-able word the spelling checker finds. If you are an adequate speller, you may want to inactivate this feature because, depending on the speed of your Macintosh, this feature may slow down your spelling checks. Each time Works prepares a list of suggestions, Works has to churn through large areas of its dictionary, which can be quite time-consuming.

A better alternative for adequate spellers is to turn off this check box by clicking it to remove the X. Then, when the spelling checker is running, click the Suggest button in the Spelling dialog box only when you want a list of suggestions. If you know the correct spelling, simply type it in the Change To box and click Change to replace the questioned word and continue checking.

Creating Custom Dictionaries

Some important words are not in the Works dictionary. You must add specialized technical terms and the names of people, places, and organizations unless you want to put up with the annoyance of having these words questioned each time they appear.

Works includes a custom dictionary that is checked as part of any spelling check. When you click the Add button in the Spelling dialog box, the word in the Change To box is added to the custom dictionary. Use the default custom dictionary (named *Custom Dictionary*) to add important words that do not appear in the main Works dictionary.

If you spell check specialized documents, you may want to create other custom dictionaries to be used for only a certain type of document. For example, a person who worked with medical transcriptions might create a custom dictionary of medical terms to use when spell checking transcriptions.

To create a custom dictionary, click the Change Dictionary button in the Spelling Options dialog box. Another dialog box appears. Type a new dictionary name in the text box in the Select A Custom Dictionary area, and then click New to create the dictionary. Click OK in the Spelling Options dialog box to complete the process. You can add and remove words from a custom dictionary, using the Add Word and Remove Word buttons in the Spelling Options dialog box.

Using the Thesaurus

Works' 190,000-word thesaurus can make your writing clearer and livelier. Incorporating choices from the lists of synonyms, antonyms, and related words is easy (see fig. 4.19).

To activate the thesaurus, use the following steps:

1. Highlight the word you want a synonym for and choose the Thesaurus command from the Document menu. Works presents a list of meanings in the Meanings For list box. Depending on the word, an entry for Close Words or Antonyms may appear.

2. In the Meanings For list, highlight the word for which you want to see synonyms. A list of synonyms appears in the box on the right.

3. Highlight the synonym you want to replace the word in your document.

4. Click Replace to replace the word in your document, or click Cancel to quit.

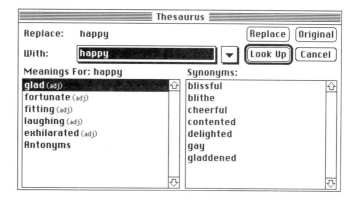

Fig. 4.19
The thesaurus is con-
trolled from this
dialog box.

To look up a new word not in the Meanings For list, type the word into the text box labeled With; then click the Look Up button for a list of meanings and synonyms for the word you typed.

The box labeled With contains a pop-up list of words you have looked up since opening the dialog box. Click the down arrow at the right end to open the list. Drag to highlight and select a word you looked up previously.

If you see the phrase Close To or Antonyms at the bottom of the Meanings For list, you can click the phrase to see a list of similar words (Close To) or words with the opposite meaning (Antonyms). These entries only appear with words for which they are appropriate.

Creating Headers and Footers

Headers and footers are entries printed at the top or bottom of a page. They contain information such as page numbers, chapter names, and the document title. Headers and footers can be as simple as one page number or as complex as a multiline entry including graphics. You can use headers and footers separately or together. Works provides tools that make headers and footers easy to create. For example, there is a tool for making automatic entries that update variable data such as page numbers, time, and date.

Headers and footers are positioned outside the top and bottom page margins. You may need to enlarge your document margins to provide enough room for the headers and footers to fit. If they are placed too close to the edge of the paper, they may fall in your printer's non-printing area. The Print Preview command shows headers and footers in their actual position.

Chapter 4

Enhancing Documents

The Window menu contains the Show Header and Show Footer commands. Each of these commands opens a specialized window; the Header and Footer windows are shown in figure 4.20.

Fig. 4.20
The Header and Footer windows.

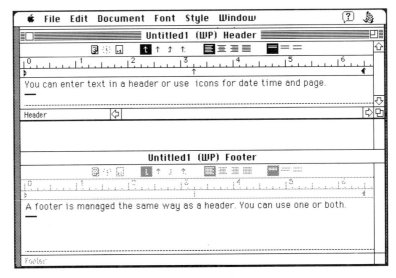

Each Header or Footer window contains its own ruler and buttons. The tab and spacing buttons behave as described in previous sections of this chapter. The three buttons at the left insert the current date, current time, and page number. You can use the buttons in any sequence that suits your purpose. To create a header or footer, follow these steps:

1. Open the document to which you want to add headers or footers.

2. Open the Window menu and choose the Show Header or Show Footer command.

   You can show Header and Footer windows at the same time, if desired.

3. Drag tabs to the locations where you want elements of your footer to be positioned, or you also can use the default tabs at the center and right edge of the ruler.

4. Position the insertion point where you want the time, date, or page number.

5. Click the ruler button for the entry you want. The item represented by the button is put in place.

6. Repeat the process for other elements of the header.

7. Click the close box on the header or footer title bar to record your entries.

You can mix automatic entries like date, time, and page number with text you type. For example, because the page number button inserts only a number, you may want to type the word **Page** in front of the number.

While a Header or Footer window is open, the Document menu contains the command Insert Document Title that, when chosen, inserts the current document name at the location of the insertion point in the header or footer. No button equivalent exists for this command.

Modifying Headers and Footers

Frequently, you will not want headers or footers to appear on the first page of your document. You can suppress them by using these steps:

1. Open the File menu and choose Page Setup.

2. In the Page Setup dialog box, click the Document button. The Document dialog box opens (see fig. 4.21).

3. Click the Title Page check box to select it. Click OK to close the Document dialog box.

4. Click OK to close the Page Setup dialog box.

Your document now has a first page that shows neither header nor footer. If present, the header or footer will begin on the second page. You can check this feature by using the Print Preview command and paging through your document.

Use normal editing techniques to select and modify or delete the elements of your header and footer. You also can have multiline headers and footers if you provide top and bottom margins wide enough to contain them. Margins are adjusted using the Document dialog box. Steps 1 and 2 of the preceding set of steps tell how to open the Document dialog box.

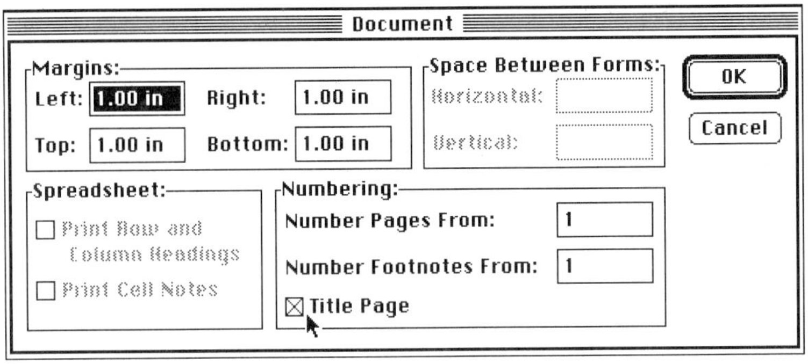

Fig. 4.21
The Document dialog box
contains the Title Page
check box.

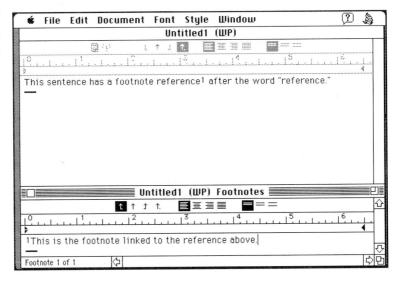

Fig. 4.21
The Document dialog box
contains the Title Page
check box.

Creating Footnotes

The Works word processor contains tools to create footnotes. These tools place a reference number in the text and a numbered entry at the bottom of the page or the end of the chapter. The procedure is similar to the one used for creating headers and footers. A specialized window in which you type footnote text opens on the screen (see fig. 4.22).

Fig. 4.22
The Footnotes window is
used to create and store
footnotes.

Inserting a footnote involves these steps:

1. Position the insertion point where you want the footnote reference to appear in your text.

2. Open the Document menu and choose Insert Footnote. Works places a footnote number in your text, and a Footnotes window opens.

3. Type the text of your footnote. All editing procedures and ruler buttons can be used normally.

4. Open the Document menu and choose the command Go To Reference. The Footnotes window closes, and the screen returns to the text near the reference number. You also can click the close box on the Footnotes window title bar.

Modifying Footnotes

Footnotes are compiled consecutively in the Footnotes window. When you have more than one footnote, the scroll bar at the right end of the window becomes active. You can use the scroll bar to scroll through the footnotes in order to review or edit them.

If the Footnotes window is not open, you can open it to edit its contents by choosing the Show Footnotes command in the Window menu. No new reference is created when you use this command. When the Footnotes window is open, a new command, Go To Footnote, appears on the Edit menu. Choosing this command opens the dialog box shown in figure 4.23. Type in the footnote number you want and click OK to go to its location.

Fig. 4.23
The Go To Footnote
dialog box.

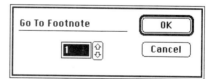

Anytime you are working in the Footnotes window, you can choose the Go To Reference command from the Document menu to go to the reference number of the footnote that currently contains the insertion point.

You can place footnotes at the end of each page or at the end of the document. You also can choose the type of line that divides the footnotes from text. Both choices are made from the Word Processor Preferences dialog box (see fig. 4.24). To establish the settings, use these steps:

1. Open the Edit menu and choose the Preferences command.

2. In the Footnotes section of the Word Processor Preferences dialog box, click a radio button to choose the separator line and the location of your footnotes.

Fig. 4.24

Footnote settings in the Word Processor Preferences dialog box.

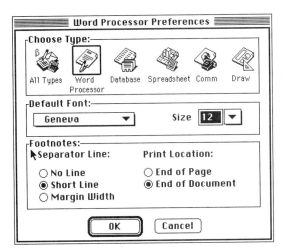

Using Draw with the Word Processor

The tool palette (see fig. 4.25) includes an icon that switches you quickly to the Draw module. Additionally, the command Draw On, on the Window menu, makes the entire set of drawing tools available in the word processor (see fig. 4.26). Obviously, Draw and the word processor have a close connection. Chapter 5, "Creating Drawings," covers Draw completely, including techniques you can use to create enhancements such as borders, graphics, and multiple columns in word processor documents. To close the Draw module, click the close box on the Draw palette window or choose Draw Off on the Window menu.

Fig. 4.25
The tool palette includes an icon for switching to Draw.

Fig. 4.26
Drawing tools are available for use in the word processor.

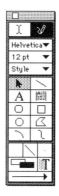

Chapter Summary

n this chapter, you learned to apply enhancements to your documents. Beginning with a basic document, you learned how to apply character and paragraph formatting and change character styles. You also learned how to use the spelling checker and the thesaurus to improve the accuracy and quality of your writing. Finally, this chapter explained the use of tabs, headers, footers, and footnotes.

Using Draw

Includes

USING
MICROSOFT
WORKS

Creating Drawings

The Draw module is a key part of Works. In addition to creating stand-alone illustrations, you can use Draw to enhance documents created by the word processor, database, and spreadsheet modules. The shared "umbrella" of the Works integrated modules lets you easily cut and paste between documents. You can use illustrations created with or imported through Draw wherever some visual interest can make a document more effective. What's more, Draw is fun to use. All of us have a creative streak, and the shapes and colors in Draw can help express some of that creativity, whether for business communication or for personal pleasure.

Basic drawing with Draw is simple and enjoyable. The drawing tools enable you to create and modify any image your drawing skill can handle. If you aren't the world's best artist, you can import or modify clip art from a huge variety of sources. When you use Draw, your letters, spreadsheets, and database reports can have the added impact that graphics provide. And, like a desktop publishing package, Draw enables you to manipulate text and illustrations.

Some major features of Draw include the following:

- A tool palette containing ten different drawing tools
- Powerful features you can use to add and arrange text
- Tools to move, rotate, and stack objects

USING
MICROSOFT
WORKS

■ The capability to automatically create 3-D effects

■ Color drawing and printing (if your Macintosh supports color)

Touring Draw

Think of Draw as an artist's tool kit. In this section, you open the kit and—before plunging into your first masterpiece—look at the different parts. You learn to start the program, examine the main features of the Draw window, and explore the structure of the menu and tool palette. At the end of this section, you will be ready to begin an illustration.

How To Start Draw

When you start Works, the Open dialog box appears. You will see an icon for the Draw module at the right end of the Choose Type box (see fig. 5.1). To choose the module, click the Draw icon. When you do, the files in the scrolling list change as Works applies a filter that shows only Draw files.

Fig. 5.1
You can start Draw from the Open dialog box.

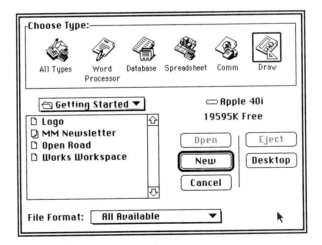

To start the module and open a blank, untitled document, click the New button. A new document appears (see fig. 5.2). You also can double-click the Draw icon. To start with an existing Draw document, select the document in the scrolling list and double-click the file name. Draw starts with the selected file open.

Fig. 5.2
A new file in the Draw
window.

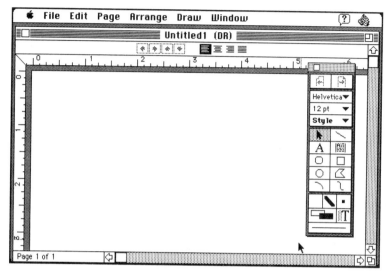

The Draw Window

As you learn more about Works, you will recognize program features that appear in every module. Features common to all Works windows are described at the beginning of Chapter 3, "Creating Documents." If you are not familiar with the title bar, scroll bars, or status bar, review the section of that chapter called "Features Common to All Works Module Screens."

Features new to the Draw window include a different document identifier located beside the document title on the title bar. This abbreviation—DR for Draw—is used by Works to identify which module was used to create a document. With a glance at the title bar, you can identify the document's originating module. Also new are the vertical and horizontal rulers. As you move your mouse, notice the dotted lines moving in the rulers to show the vertical and horizontal location of the mouse pointer. This feature is very helpful in positioning objects precisely in a drawing. The upper area of the ruler contains arrow icons, used to move objects short distances, and text alignment icons similar to those used in the word processing module.

The tool palette is present in all Works modules. In Draw, it includes a variety of drawing tools as well as tools for managing text and object properties. The tools are explained in detail in the section of this chapter called "Using the Tool Palette." You can drag the tool palette by its title bar to a convenient working area on the screen. You can close the palette by clicking the close box on the title bar, or by choosing the command Hide Tools from the Window menu.

An Overview of Draw Menus

Draw has an extensive system of commands, contained in six menus. Table 5.1 describes the menus. The Command Reference in Appendix A contains a complete explanation of all Draw commands.

Table 5.1
The Draw Menus

Menu name	General purpose
File	Create, open, and save files. Print and quit from here.
Edit	Move, delete, undo, and duplicate objects. Set Preferences.
Page	Add, remove, and move through pages.
Arrange	Manipulate graphic objects. Control text formatting and alignment.
Draw	Modify and enhance drawn objects. Fuse and break up object groups.
Window	Show and hide window elements. Get help, perform macros, and select the active window.

Beginning a Drawing

Drawing programs can be intimidating to people who aren't artists. The empty white screen seems so promising until you take the first steps. If you feel discouraged by your first attempts, you're not alone. The following list suggests some solutions that enable you to create quality work without a great deal of expertise:

NOTE

If you use art from other sources—either clip art or scanned images—be sure that you do not violate copyright laws.

Let an artist do the drawing. Clip art illustrations you can use or adapt are widely available. (Be sure the illustrations are bit-mapped or PICT file formats.)

Use a scanner. Scanners are devices that convert pictures into *bit maps* (images made up of electronic bits called *pixels*) you can use on your computer. Scanners are moderately expensive, but you can rent scanner time at a local typographic service bureau. You can scan any sort of picture or photograph, import it into Draw, and modify it to suit your needs. (Be sure to save your files in PICT format because Works does not accept purely scanned images, called *TIFF*.)

Draw with simple shapes. Confine your early illustrations to basic geometric shapes. Draw provides tools to create and apply textures and colors to rectangles, circles, arcs of circles, and polygons (*polygon* means "many-sided"). You can make very effective drawings by sticking to simple yet powerful shapes, textures, and colors.

Opening Existing Stationery and Drawings

Opening one of the Draw stationery documents provided with Works can be an effective way to start a complex project. You can adapt existing components to a new purpose and benefit from layout work already accomplished. You also can open other Draw documents and revise them. If you have a Draw document you want to use repeatedly, turn it into stationery using the instructions in the section of Chapter 2 called "Creating Stationery."

To open a stationery document, follow these steps:

1. Open the File menu and choose New.

   The dialog box shown in figure 5.3 opens.

Fig. 5.3
Select Draw and check Show Stationery in the New dialog box.

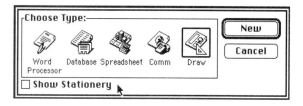

2. Click the Draw icon if it is not surrounded by a square.

3. Click the Show Stationery check box.

   The dialog box expands as shown in figure 5.4.

4. Use the scrolling list to locate the stationery you want to use.

   When you select a file name in the list, the Preview box shows a small image of the Stationery.

TIP

If someone in your organization is an artist, or if you have preexisting boilerplate art, you can convert most Macintosh material to PICT format and then open that material in Draw.

5. Click Open or double-click the file name to open a new document based on the Stationery.

Fig. 5.4
Checking Show Stationery expands the dialog box.

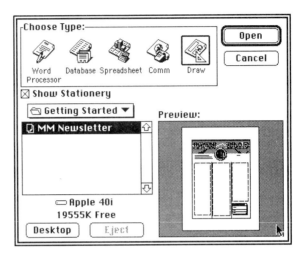

To start from an existing Draw document, use these steps:

1. From the File menu, choose Open.

   The dialog box shown in figure 5.5 opens.

Fig. 5.5
Opening a Draw document.

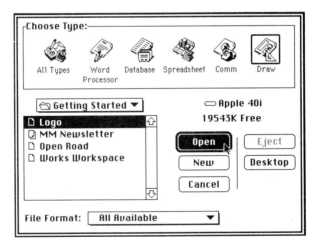

2. In the Open dialog box, click the Draw icon to list Draw files.

3. Select a file from the scrolling list and click Open.

   You also can double-click the file name.

Adding and Deleting Pages

Often when you create business art, such as organization charts or bulleted transparencies, you need to create multipage documents. Draw enables you to add or delete pages through a series of single-step commands. Keeping all the pages for a document together is efficient and helps you avoid misplacing them. This handy feature is not always available on drawing programs.

Add pages to your publication with these steps:

1. Open the document.

2. Open the Page menu and choose the Add Pages command.

   Figure 5.6 shows the Add Pages dialog box.

Fig. 5.6
The Add Pages dialog box lets you specify page quantity and location.

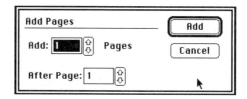

3. Type the number of pages to add and the page after which you want to add them.

   You can click the arrows to the right of the text boxes to change numbers.

4. Click Add to insert the new pages.

   The status bar in the lower left corner of the screen reflects the additional pages.

The process of deleting pages is similar to that of adding pages. Follow these steps:

1. Open the document you want to change.

2. Open the Page menu and choose Delete Pages.

Chapter 5
Creating Drawings

Figure 5.7 shows the Delete Pages dialog box.

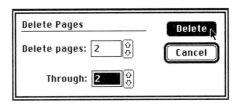

3. Enter the page range to delete.

   Remember that the page in the Through text box is included in the deletion.

4. Click Delete to remove the pages.

   There is no confirmation. Be sure that you want to remove the pages.

Moving through a Multipage Document

You can move through a multipage document by clicking the page icons at the top of the tool palette, or by opening the Page menu and choosing either the Next Page or Previous Page command. To go to a specified page, choose Go To Page, which opens the dialog box shown in figure 5.8. Type in the destination page and click OK or press Return.

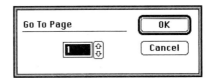

Using the Grid

An alignment grid can be extremely helpful in obtaining precise alignment of objects such as text columns. The grid is an invisible mesh of horizontal and vertical lines at a chosen spacing. Although you can't see the grid, objects on the screen "snap" to it as though it were magnetic. The idea may seem strange at first, but you should try it. Perfect alignment gives a professional look to your work.

To open and modify a grid, use these steps:

1. Open the Arrange menu and choose Grid Settings.

   The dialog box shown in figure 5.9 opens.

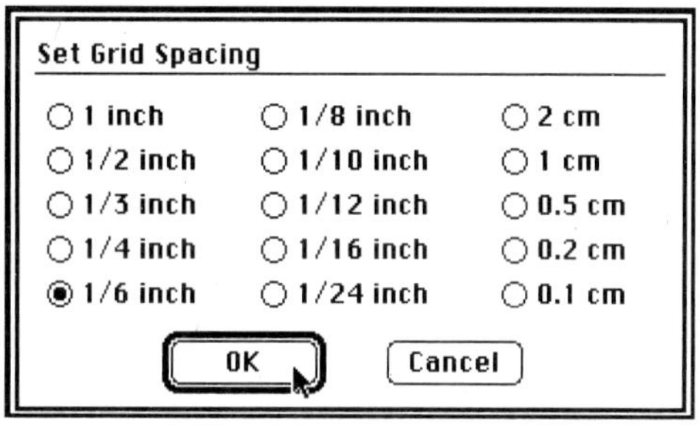

Fig. 5.9
The Grid Settings dialog box enables you to specify grid widths.

Set Grid Spacing

○ 1 inch	○ 1/8 inch	○ 2 cm
○ 1/2 inch	○ 1/10 inch	○ 1 cm
○ 1/3 inch	○ 1/12 inch	○ 0.5 cm
○ 1/4 inch	○ 1/16 inch	○ 0.2 cm
● 1/6 inch	○ 1/24 inch	○ 0.1 cm

[OK]   [Cancel]

2. Click the radio button for the spacing you want.

3. Click OK to set the spacing and return to the screen.

   The grid is not yet active.

4. Open the Arrange menu a second time and choose Snap To Grid.

   A check mark appears next to the command on the menu.

After you choose Snap to Grid, notice that objects dragged across the screen seem to move in small jumps. This behavior occurs as they "snap" to the nearest vertical or horizontal grid lines. Create two or three small rectangles, and practice aligning them vertically and horizontally. To turn off the Snap to Grid feature, choose the command again.

Creating Headers and Footers

You can apply headers and footers (entries printed at the top and bottom of every page) to Draw documents by using the Show Header and Show Footer commands from the Window menu. Chapter 4, "Enhancing Documents," contains complete instructions for creating headers and footers.

TIP

If you frequently work with multipage documents, you can move through your document faster using these keyboard shortcuts for page changing:

Next Page ⌘-=
Previous Page ⌘--
Go To Page ⌘-K

Double-clicking the status bar (where the page numbers are) is another shortcut to the Go To Page dialog box.

Using the Tool Palette

TIP

Because headers and footers are individual windows linked to your Draw document, you can use the Draw Copy and Paste commands to put graphics into headers and footers.

The Draw tools are the equivalent of a painter's brushes. You use the tools to create and revise your drawings. When you start to work with the tools, you may feel awkward, particularly if you are new to the mouse. If you get frustrated, ask yourself whether you would expect to pick up real paints and brushes and immediately be productive. Be kind to yourself. Enjoy experimenting with Draw.

The Draw tool palette contains 21 items (see fig. 5.10). Table 5.2 lists the tools and briefly describes their functions. The pages that follow describe the function of each drawing tool in detail.

Fig. 5.10
The Draw tool palette.

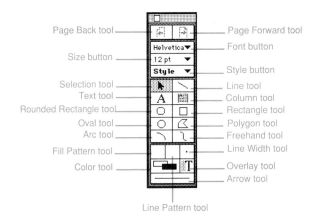

Table 5.2
Tools in the Draw Tool Palette

Tool	Function
Page Back tool	Turns to preceding page. Dimmed if no preceding page.
Page Forward tool	Turns to next page. Dimmed if no following page.
Font button	Opens pop-up menu for choosing fonts.
Size button	Opens pop-up menu for choosing font sizes.
Style button	Opens pop-up menu for choosing font style.
Selection tool	Selects objects.
Line tool	Draws lines.
Text tool	Creates and manipulates text.

Tool	Function
Column tool	Creates columns of text.
Rounded Rectangle tool	Draws squares and rectangles with rounded corners.
Rectangle tool	Draws squares and rectangles.
Oval tool	Draws circles and ovals.
Polygon tool	Draws shapes comprised of straight lines.
Arc tool	Draws segments of circles.
Freehand tool	Draws freehand lines and shapes.
Fill Pattern tool	Chooses pattern for filled objects.
Line Pattern tool	Chooses pattern for lines.
Line Width tool	Chooses line width, from hairline to 10 points.
Color tool	Sets foreground and background colors.
Overlay tool	Controls overlay effects.
Arrow tool	Places arrow heads on lines.

NOTE

Although you can import scanned images as PICT files, remember that scanned images are bit-mapped images (pictures of bits of data) and cannot be scaled, rotated, or generally manipulated like Draw's own objects.

You use the drawing tools to create what Draw refers to collectively as *objects*. Squares, circles, lines, and squiggles are all objects. You can scale objects (change their size or proportions), move objects around as required, and print them. Whatever tool you use, the object you draw shares certain properties with other objects in your drawing.

To select a tool, click it. Or you can double-click the tool to use it repeatedly without having to reselect it. When permanently selected, the tool turns black. Click another tool to deselect the first tool.

The Selection Tool

The mouse pointer represents the Selection tool. This tool is the default selection on the tool palette.

After you finish drawing, objects have small squares on their borders. These squares are *handles* that you use to move and reshape the objects. If you click the screen outside the object, the handles disappear. To make the handles reappear, click the object with the Selection tool. You

Chapter 5
Creating Drawings

can use the Selection tool to surround, and thus select, multiple objects and cause handles to appear on all those objects. You also use the Selection tool to select and drag objects. The section of this chapter called "Managing Graphic Objects" includes more details on the use of the Selection tool and handles.

The Line Tool

You use the Line tool to draw straight lines.

To draw a single straight line:

1. Click the Line icon on the tool palette.

    The pointer changes to a cross-hair drawing tool.

2. Place the cross hair where you want the line to begin.

3. Hold down the mouse button and drag the mouse to where you want the line to end.

    Before you release the mouse button, you can pivot the line around its starting point to draw at any angle.

4. When the line is complete, release the mouse button.

    The line, with handles, appears (see fig. 5.11).

Fig. 5.11
A line drawn with the
Line tool.

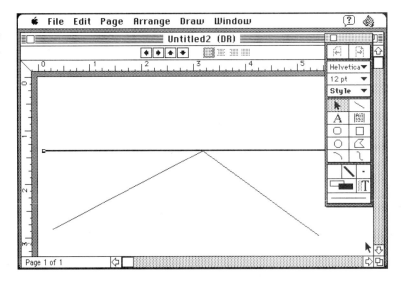

The Line tool is very versatile when combined with the Arrow tool and Join command. The combination enables you to draw complex figures using simple forms.

The Text Tool and Column Tool

An entire section of Chapter 6, called "Using Text in Draw," addresses the many facets of creating, managing, and enhancing text and text columns in Draw. Please turn there for details on the use of the Text and Column tools.

The Rounded Rectangle and Rectangle Tools

The Rounded Rectangle (also called a *fillet*) tool and Rectangle tool work identically, differing only in the shapes of their rectangles' corners. Figure 5.12 displays a plain rectangle and a rounded rectangle.

Fig. 5.12
Examples of a plain rectangle and a rounded rectangle.

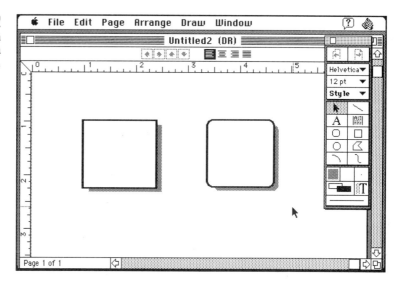

To create either type of rectangle, follow these steps:

1. Click the tool you want to use.

   The tool icon turns dark to indicate its selection.

2. Place the cross hair where you want a corner of the rectangle.

Chapter 5

Creating Drawings

3. Hold down the mouse button and drag diagonally away from the starting point.

   An outline of the rectangle appears.

4. When the rectangle is the size and shape you want, release the mouse button.

   The rectangle, with its handles, appears.

To constrain a rectangle into a square, hold down the Shift key while using the tool.

The Oval Tool

The Oval tool enables you to draw ovals and circles. Figure 5.13 displays two objects drawn with the Oval tool.

Fig. 5.13
Examples of an oval and
a circle.

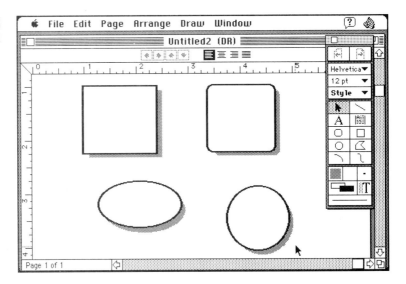

To draw an oval or a circle, follow these steps:

1. Click the Oval tool.

   The tool icon turns dark to indicate its selection.

2. Click where you want one side of the oval.

3. Hold down the mouse button and drag diagonally away from the starting point.

An outline of the oval appears.

4. When you have created the figure you want, release the mouse button.

The oval, with its handles, appears.

To constrain the oval into a circle, hold down the Shift key while using the Oval tool.

The Polygon Tool

The Polygon tool draws objects composed of straight line segments. You can close the objects and fill them, or leave them open (see fig. 5.14). You learn how to control color and fills in the section of this chapter called "Changing Object Properties."

Fig. 5.14
Open and closed polygons.

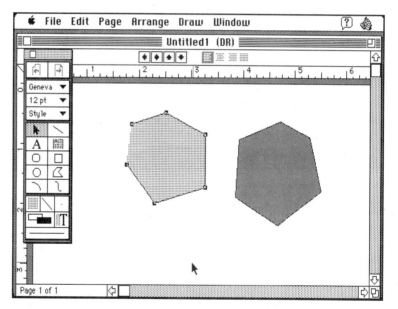

Use these steps to create a polygon:

1. Click the polygon icon to select the tool.

2. Click where you want to anchor the first segment of the object.

3. Move to the end of that segment and the beginning of the next, and then click.

4. Continue moving and clicking to draw additional segments.

5. To end a figure without closing it, double-click at the end of the last segment.

6. To close a figure, click the end of the final segment on top of the starting point.

To constrain a polygon into one with 45-degree angles, hold down the Shift key while using the tool.

The Arc Tool

With the Arc tool, you can draw segments of circles or ovals. When you first use the tool, a quarter-circle segment appears (see fig. 5.15 and fig. 5.16). When you complete the drawing, you can use the Selection tool to drag the straight lines to any angle around a circle, thus drawing any type of partial circle.

To draw an arc, follow these steps:

1. Select the Arc tool by clicking its icon.

2. Drag the cross hair diagonally to draw a 90-degree arc.

Fig. 5.15
Segment drawn with the Arc tool.

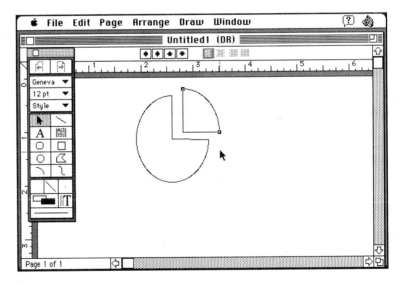

3. Release the mouse button to finish drawing.

4. To increase or decrease the angle of the segment, drag the handles at the end of the straight line segments.

As with the Oval tool, you need to hold down the Shift key while using the Arc tool to constrain the object into a true circle.

Fig. 5.16
Examples of arcs.

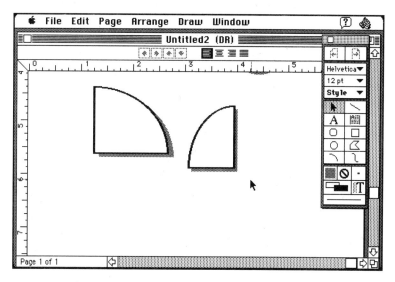

The Freehand Tool

TIP

The direction you drag controls which 90-degree segment of a circle you draw. For instance, dragging up and to the left produces the lower left segment. Dragging down and right produces the upper right segment. Experiment—you will catch on quickly.

The Freehand tool is for those of us with steady hands and ambitious plans. When chosen, this tool follows your mouse's path exactly. Most of us don't possess a hand steady enough to draw well with the mouse; but sometimes you may need an unusual shape and only the Freehand tool will do. The section called "Changing Object Properties" presents some tools to help spruce up shaky freehand work.

To make a freehand drawing, follow these steps:

1. Select the Freehand tool by clicking its icon.

2. Position the cross hair at the beginning of your object.

3. Hold down the mouse button and draw the object.

4. Release the mouse button to quit drawing.

Chapter 5
Creating Drawings

When you release the mouse button, your line shows many handles. You drag these handles to change the line. The number of handles can become excessive in a complex line.

You can choose Remove Handles from the Draw menu to remove every other handle. See more on this topic in the "Changing Object Properties" section.

The Object Properties Tools

The bottom segment of the tool palette contains six tools for changing the properties of objects. These tools are dealt with in the section of this chapter called "Changing Object Properties."

Managing Graphic Objects

In the previous section you learned to create different types of objects using the tools on the tool palette. In this section, you learn techniques such as selecting, moving, grouping, resizing, and deleting objects. In most cases, the techniques apply to all types of objects: circles, rectangles, polygons, text blocks, and so on. Objects you handle differently are mentioned as exceptions.

Selecting Objects

All the objects in figure 5.17 are selected. The small squares surrounding the objects are the handles you use to reshape the objects. You can select an object two ways: by clicking the object, or by dragging a selection rectangle around it. Both methods use the Selection tool.

To select an object by clicking, point to it with the Selection tool and click the mouse button. If handles appear, you have selected the object. Clicking a different object selects it, but deselects the first one. To select additional objects while keeping the first one selected, hold down the Shift key and click the others.

You also can select an object or group of objects by dragging a selection rectangle around them. This method enables you to select multiple objects rapidly.

Fig. 5.17
A complex arrow with all of its pieces selected on all layers.

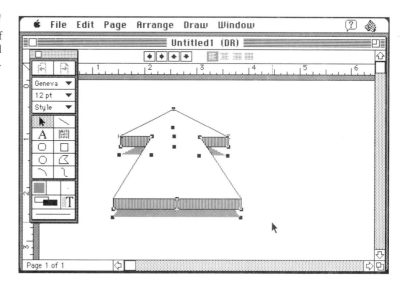

To select objects by dragging, follow these steps:

1. Click the Selection tool on the tool palette.

2. Place the pointer outside the objects you want to select.

3. Hold down the mouse button and drag diagonally until all the objects you want to select are within the dotted rectangle.

4. Release the mouse button.

   The rectangle disappears, and handles appear indicating you have selected all the objects that were within the rectangle.

Grouping and Ungrouping Objects

You may create a complex drawing made up of many objects, such as an organizational chart balloon with text, border, and shadow. How do you move it without dragging the objects apart and reassembling them again? One approach is to group the component objects together so that they become a single object. Then you can move the objects as a unit with no fear of leaving a part behind. If you need to edit the object, an Ungroup command reduces it to component parts again.

To group objects, use these steps:

1. Choose the Selection tool from the tool palette.

2. Hold down the Shift key while clicking the objects to be grouped, or select the objects by drawing a selection rectangle around the entire group.

3. Open the Arrange menu and chose the command Group.

   Notice how the multiple handles become one set (see fig. 5.18).

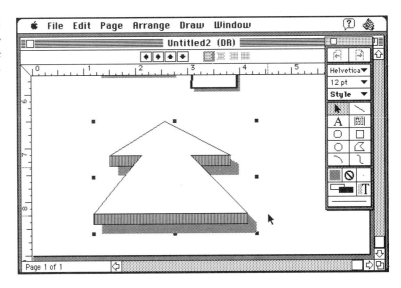

Fig. 5.18

The complex arrow grouped reveals only one set of handles.

To break grouped objects apart again, select them and open the Arrange menu. Then choose Ungroup.

Joining and Breaking Up Objects

TIP

Use the Vertex Snap command from the Arrange menu (or hold down the N key while selecting) to align the objects' end points before using the Join command.

Using the Join command, you can draw portions of a graphic using simple shapes and join the pieces into a whole—for example, the Olympic symbol out of a series of arcs and circles. The benefit of this command is that you can manipulate, fill, and color the resulting object as a whole; whereas you cannot treat grouped pieces this way because the program still considers them separate entities.

Follow these procedures to join pieces of a graphic into a whole:

1. With the Selection tool, select the objects you want to join.

2. Select Join from the Draw menu.

   The lines that intersect at the end points (where the handles are located) become polygons.

You can break up a joined object by following this procedure, but replacing the Join command in step 2 with the Break Up command. The resulting graphic consists of a series of line segments broken at their intersections.

Locking and Unlocking an Object

Keeping a specific object in place is often helpful when you are working with several different objects. Perhaps, for example, a background shape keeps getting dragged inadvertently when you rearrange objects on top of it. You can freeze the object, so you can neither move nor change it, by selecting the object and then choosing the Lock command from the Draw menu.

Choose Unlock All from the Draw menu to unfreeze all locked objects in your drawing. You must Unlock every locked object; you cannot unlock a single object.

Moving Objects

To move an object to a new location, drag it with the mouse. A dotted outline of the selected object follows the mouse pointer while you move that object. When you release the mouse button, the program redraws the object in its new location. You can cancel a drag by replacing the outline around the object and then releasing the mouse button.

When you move an object, grab it by its border or somewhere inside the shape. Do not drag it by a handle. You use handles for resizing—dragging its handle stretches the object out of shape.

A way of moving objects very short distances involves the four arrows on the ruler (see fig. 5.19). When you select an object, the arrows become active. Clicking an arrow moves, or *nudges*, the object one pixel in the direction of the arrow. A pixel, short for *picture element*, is one of the tiny dots on your computer screen that make up the image. Your screen has roughly 72 pixels per inch (or more, depending on the monitor), so a movement of a pixel is very short. You can use the arrows to perfect the alignment of objects you have roughly aligned.

Fig. 5.19

Arrows on the ruler can nudge an object one pixel.

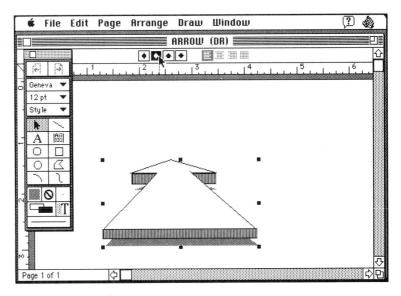

Fig. 5.19

Arrows on the ruler can nudge an object one pixel.

Don't forget the invisible grid you can activate to align text and objects. When you choose Snap To Grid from the Arrange menu, objects you drag automatically align to the grid. This feature is indispensable for aligning complex documents like newsletters.

Copying, Duplicating, and Pasting Objects

The capability to duplicate objects is very helpful when you are creating an illustration. Recurring patterns or duplicate shapes may need to appear in your work more often than you expect. The Copy, Duplicate, and Paste commands make it easy to clone useful elements of your work.

To copy and paste objects in your illustration, use these steps:

1. Choose the Selection tool from the tool palette.

2. Select the object you want to copy.

3. Choose Copy from the Edit menu.

4. Click where you want the object pasted.

5. Choose Paste from the Edit menu.

Works pastes your copied object where you specified, and the object appears on-screen.

TIP

With Snap To Grid turned on, Duplicate places the objects in a row, aligned with the first object, and distributed evenly across the row.

Works temporarily holds the object you copy or cut in a part of memory called the *Clipboard*. You can therefore continue pasting that object in other places until you copy or cut another object, which replaces the preceding one on the Clipboard.

The Duplicate command is a convenient version of Copy and Paste that saves you from having to perform two commands for a single task. To use this command, select the object to duplicate and choose Duplicate from the Edit menu. Works copies the selected object and pastes the duplicate below and to the right of the original. You can duplicate an object only once per command, however, because Works does not place duplicated objects on the Clipboard.

Resizing Objects

Dragging the handles located on the edges of an object enables you to make the object larger or smaller. You also can use the handles to alter an object's proportions by changing it in one direction but not another. Selected objects typically have six handles in a rectangular arrangement. The exceptions are arcs and lines, with only two.

Corner handles and those at the midpoints of the sides are different from one another. You can drag a corner handle two directions at once, but handles on the sides only at a 90-degree angle to the side. In other words, you can drag the handle on the vertical side of a rectangle only to the left or right, not up and down.

To resize an object, choose the Selection tool and click an object to select it. Place the tool on one of the handles and drag in the direction you want to resize (see fig. 5.20).

Rotating Objects

Graphic artists prize drawing programs with the capability to rotate objects. When you examine quality advertising, you see examples of the effective use of object rotation. Although Works cannot rotate some objects, such as text objects and imported bit-map illustrations, it can rotate other objects to any desired angle (see fig. 5.21).

Chapter 5

Creating Drawings

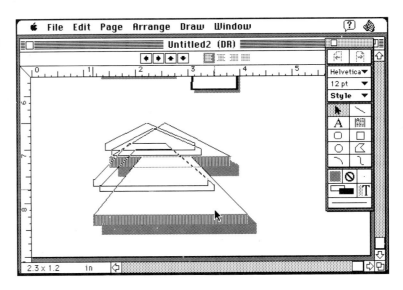

Fig. 5.20
Rectangle being dragged to resize.

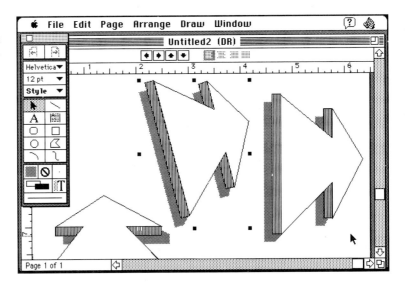

Fig. 5.21
Examples of object rotation.

To rotate an object, perform the following steps:

1. Select an object by clicking it.

2. Choose Rotate from the Draw menu.

   The dialog box in figure 5.22 opens.

Part III

Using Draw

Fig. 5.22
The Rotate dialog box.

Fig. 5.22
The Rotate dialog box.

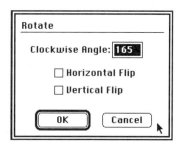

3. Enter the degrees of the clockwise rotation you want.

4. Click OK.

Flipping Objects

Flipping means rotating an object 180 degrees around its horizontal or vertical axis. You can use this technique when you need a left-hand and right-hand version of an object, or to produce reflected effects like that in figure 5.23, which was produced by flipping and rotating identical objects. To flip an object, click it and choose the Rotate command from the Draw menu. In the dialog box that opens, click the check box for Vertical Flip or Horizontal Flip, or both.

Fig. 5.23
Identical objects, flipped and rotated.

Flipped object _____

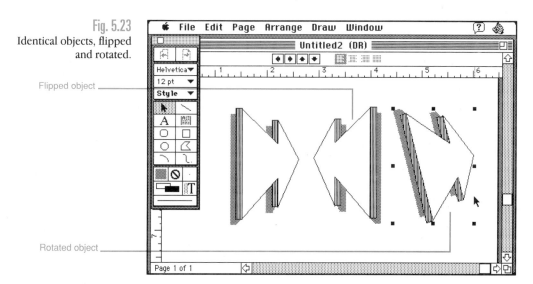

Rotated object _____

Changing Handles

When you draw a freehand object, Works adds a handle to the line you draw every time you change direction, even slightly. These additions can result in a finished drawing with lines almost obscured by the profusion of handles (see fig. 5.24). On the other hand, you may want to make complex adjustments on a line or object that has too few handles.

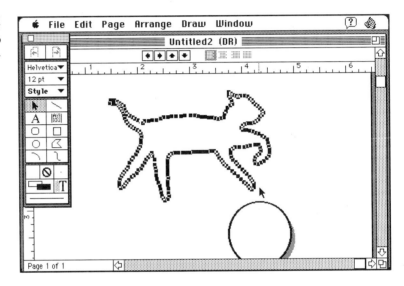

Fig. 5.24
Freehand object with too many handles.

Multiple handles are useful on a complex curved object because you can drag them to make subtle adjustments to curves and angles. Working with too many handles, however, becomes awkward and difficult. Keeping track of many handles also taxes your computer's memory and slows its performance. Works provides a command to reduce the number of handles.

To reduce handles, first select the object, and then open the Draw menu and choose Remove Handles (see fig. 5.25). Works halves the number of handles in the selected object. If you still have too many, choose the command again. Each time you choose the command, you halve the number of handles.

To increase the number of handles in an object, select the object and open the Draw Menu. Then choose Add Handles. The number of handles doubles. You can repeat the command until you have the quantity you want.

Fig. 5.25
Handles reduced using the
Remove Handles
command.

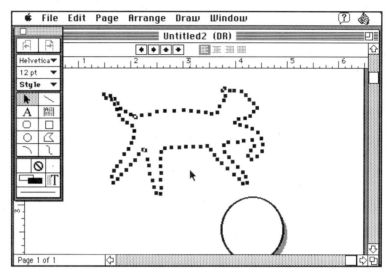

Fig. 5.25
Handles reduced using the
Remove Handles
command.

Smoothing Objects

Unless you are deft at manipulating handles, creating a smooth curve is difficult. Works can help through its Smooth command, which turns straight lines in an object such as a polygon into smoothly flowing curves (see fig. 5.26). To use the command, select the object, and then open the Draw menu and choose the Smooth command.

Fig. 5.26
The effect of applying the
Smooth command to a
polygon.

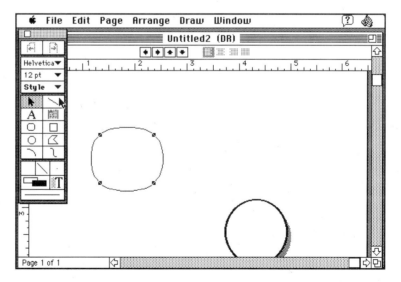

You can drag the handles on the smoothed object to further alter its shape. You also can unsmooth a smoothed object by deselecting the command.

Changing Object Properties

The term *properties* is used here to encompass the fill patterns, line widths, and colors that you can apply to objects created in Draw. The six icons at the bottom of the tool palette enable you to control and apply these properties.

Tearing Off Menus

The six object-property icons at the bottom of the tool palette have a novel feature. You can "tear" these tool icons off the tool palette and place them anywhere on-screen. The tool window then stays open until you click its close box. Because these tear-off tool windows remain open, you can make multiple selections or experiment with settings without having the window close each time. You can see the effects you choose, while the tear-off window remains open.

To tear off a window, point to the icon for the tool you want to use. Hold down the mouse button and drag away from the tool palette. A dotted outline of the tear-off window follows the pointer (see fig. 5.27). Position the outline where you want the window, and release the mouse button. The window appears.

Using Line and Fill

All graphic objects created in Draw, other than lines and arrows, have two components: the line that defines their boundary and the pattern or color inside the boundary. Because objects can have white or transparent lines and fills, sometimes you may not see these components, but both are always present. You also can apply a pattern to a line. Figure 5.28 shows the same square with several patterns and line thicknesses.

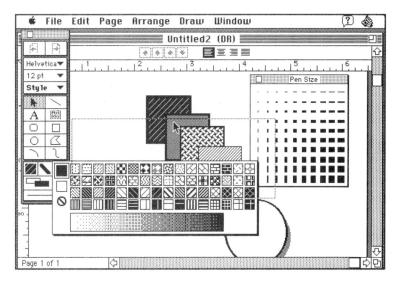

Fig. 5.27
One tear-off window open,
a second being dragged
into position.

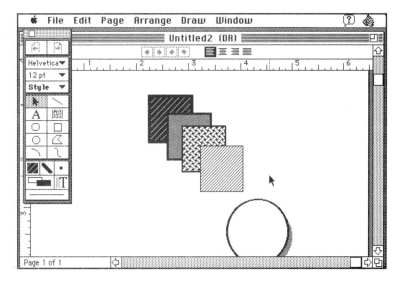

Fig. 5.28
Identical squares with
different lines and
patterns.

Chapter 5
Creating Drawings

Controlling Line Width

The Line Width tool looks like a small dot or rectangle, depending on the thickness of the line currently chosen. If you hold down the mouse button while pointing to the tool, a pop-up menu of width selections appears (see fig. 5.29). Clicking a width selection changes the line width for any selected object. The new line width also applies to all objects drawn after the new width is set.

Fig. 5.29
The pop-up list for
selecting line width.

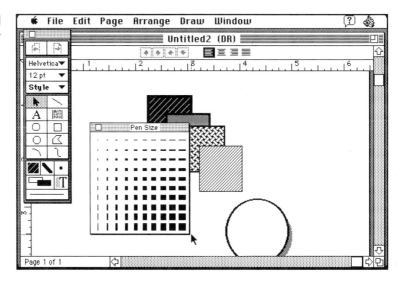

Drawing Arrows

At the bottom of the tool palette is the tool for drawing arrows. This tool attaches arrowheads to the right or left end of lines you draw. To use the tool, follow these steps:

1. Select the Line tool from the tool palette.

2. Point to the Arrow tool and hold down the mouse button.

   A cascade menu with three selections (right arrow, left arrow, and no arrow) opens.

3. Drag the mouse down the menu and highlight the arrowhead you want, or click the desired arrowhead from the tear-off menu.

   Notice that the tool on the palette changes to reflect your choice.

TIP

You also can add an arrowhead to or delete an arrowhead from an existing line by selecting the line and clicking an arrowhead type from the menu.

Part III

Using Draw

4. Release the mouse button, and then draw a line.

   The line has an arrowhead at one end.

Using Color

Because not all Macintosh monitors support 256 colors, Draw provides fill patterns and masks—percentages of gray filler—to represent shading. Monitors that support 256 colors or grays cause Draw to replace the percentages of gray filler with actual shades of gray or colors. The following sections discuss the available patterns. Notice that Draw's foreground and background colors or grays can be applied to these patterns to modify their appearance, providing even more variety for you as an artist. Colors are discussed separately.

Controlling Line Patterns

The Line Pattern tool enables you to change the appearance of straight lines or lines that border objects by applying as many as 100 shades of gray and up to 64 different patterns. To see the choices, point to the tool and hold down the mouse button. A pop-up pattern menu appears (see fig. 5.30). Keeping the mouse button down, slide the pointer onto the pattern you want or slide across the gray scale at the bottom of the pop-up menu to choose a percentage of gray. Releasing the mouse button selects the pattern or gray. By opening the menu a second time, you can add a percentage of gray or a pattern.

Fig. 5.30
The line pattern selection box.

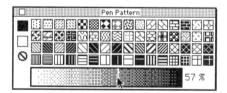

The pattern or gray percentage you select becomes the default for all lines you subsequently draw until you change the selection. A sample of the current setting appears in the Line Pattern tool on the tool palette.

Three icons, separated from the rest at the left end of the pop-up menu, set the line colors based on the color selected in the Foreground or Background Color tool. The black square applies the current foreground color to lines. The white square applies the current background color to lines. The circle with a slash makes lines transparent.

Controlling Object Fills

The procedure for changing object fills and gray percentages is identical to the procedure described previously for lines.

The Fill Pattern tool enables you to change the appearance of objects' interiors by applying as many as 100 shades of gray and up to 64 different patterns. To see the choices, point to the tool and hold down the mouse button. A pop-up pattern menu appears (see fig. 5.31). Keeping the mouse button down, slide the pointer onto the pattern you want or slide across the gray scale at the bottom of the pop-up box to choose a percentage of gray. Releasing the mouse button selects the pattern or gray.

Fig. 5.31
The fill pattern selection box.

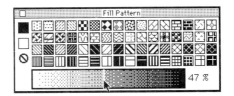

The pattern or gray percentage you select becomes the default for all objects drawn. A sample of the current setting appears in the Fill Pattern tool icon.

Three icons, separated from the rest at the left end of the pop-up menu, set the fill pattern for solid objects or lines based on the color selected in the Foreground or Background Color tool. The black square applies the current foreground color to object fills. The white square applies the current background color to object fills. The circle with a slash makes object fills transparent.

Setting a fill pattern to white or transparent can make the object seem to disappear if its borders also are white or transparent. One way to find such lost objects is to choose the Select All command from the Edit menu. All objects then show visible handles that help you to locate them.

Setting Line and Fill Colors

Depending on the display capability of your Macintosh, you can apply up to 256 colors to lines, objects, and text. If you have a black and white monitor, you still can apply colors that drive a color printer, but you see them as shades of gray on your screen. The number of colors or gray shades you have to work with depends on the video system of your Macintosh and monitor settings in the Control Panel.

You can change the foreground and background colors of objects and text with the Foreground and Background Color tools. You can work most easily by tearing off each of these color palettes. Open each palette by pointing to the tool icon and then dragging the palette on-screen. The palette stays open until you click its close box.

To apply a color to an object, click on the object, and then choose a color from a palette. To apply a color to text, click the Text tool, highlight the text, and then select a color. When no object or text is selected, you can set the default colors for foreground and background by selecting them from the palettes.

Using the Overlay Tool

You can vary the visual interaction of objects stacked on one another by using the Overlay tool. Because several interactions are possible, you can work most easily by tearing off the Overlay menu. Open the menu by pointing to the Overlay tool icon and then dragging the menu on-screen. The pop-up menu turns into a small window that stays open until you click its close box.

To apply the Overlay effects, click an object and choose an effect from the Overlay menu. Experimentation is in order because the effects vary with the object selected and the relative position and patterns of the layers. Figure 5.32 shows some of the various possible effects.

Applying Three-Dimensional Effects

You can apply 3-D effects to any object except text and imported images. Select the object, and then choose the 3-D Effect command from the Draw menu. The dialog box shown in figure 5.33 opens. Enter the desired thickness, in points, and the degrees of rotation around a horizontal axis. Click OK to apply the effect.

Applying Shadows

Draw can apply an effect sometimes called a *drop shadow*. You create this sort of shadow by duplicating an object, and then putting the duplicate behind and slightly offset from the original (see fig. 5.34). To

Chapter 5

Creating Drawings

do this automatically in Works, select an object and then choose the Shadow command from the Draw menu. Initially, the shadow is a medium gray. You can select it as a separate object and change its color or pattern.

Fig. 5.32
Effects of various Overlay choices.

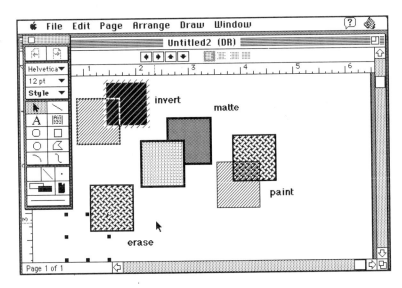

Fig. 5.33
3-D dialog box with a 3-D object behind it.

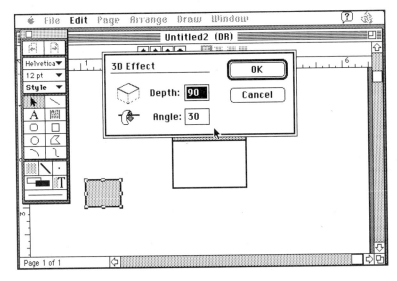

Part III

Using Draw

Fig. 5.34
A drop shadow effect
produced with the Shadow
command.

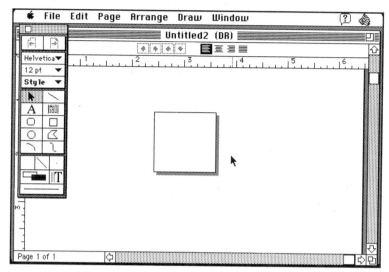

Fig. 5.34
A drop shadow effect
produced with the Shadow
command.

Chapter Summary

his chapter described the basic features of the Draw module. You
learned how to start a drawing—including using the grid—and
how to use the tools in the Draw tool palette. You also learned
how to select, group, and join objects, and how to move, resize, rotate,
and flip objects. This chapter described object properties, such as line
width and object filling, and taught you how to change these properties.
In the next chapter, you will learn how to enhance with Draw the
documents you create in other modules.

Chapter 5
Creating Drawings

Enhancing Documents with Draw

You can use Draw for more than just creating drawings. Draw also has tools you can use to enhance the effectiveness of other documents. You can organize text in boxes or columns, import drawings from other applications, and exchange material between Draw and other Works modules. This chapter explains how to do all these things, and concludes with sections on printing, saving, closing, and quitting Draw.

Using Text in Draw

Draw can enhance text in both traditional and unexpected ways. For example, Draw's features can help you put text into side-by-side and newspaper columns or spread text along a curve for striking design effects. To create attention-getting documents, you simply move text enhanced in Draw into the word processor, spreadsheet, or database reports.

USING
MICROSOFT
WORKS

Creating Text Objects

Text has a dual nature in Draw. You can enter and edit text much as you do in the word processor, but when you create a text block, you also can move and reshape the text as you would a graphic object. To create a text block in Draw, follow these steps:

1. Click the Text tool in the tool palette (the Text tool resembles a capital A). The mouse pointer changes into a cross hair.

2. Position the cross hair where you want to start entering text, and click. The outline of a text box appears.

3. Enter your text. Text wraps to the next line as you reach the right end of the text box. The box enlarges vertically to hold the text.

4. Click outside the box when you finish entering text.

After you create a text block, you can move and resize it like a graphic object. Use these steps:

1. Choose the Selection tool (arrow) from the tool palette.

2. Click the text block to select it. Handles appear around the block.

3. To move the block, click anywhere in the block *except* on a handle. Drag the block to the desired location.

4. To resize the block, drag a handle as you would to resize a graphic. You cannot resize a block so that it is too small to contain its text.

Editing Text in Draw

Text editing is the same in Draw as it is in the word processor. Table 6.1 summarizes the principal editing procedures. For detailed instructions, see Chapter 3, "Creating Documents," and Chapter 4, "Enhancing Documents."

Table 6.1
Text Editing Summary

Activity	Procedure
Add text	Click Text tool in the text. Type new material.
Copy text	Select text to copy. From Edit menu, choose Copy.
Cut text	Select text to cut. From Edit menu, choose Cut.

Part III

Using Draw

Activity	Procedure
Paste text	Click Text tool at destination. From Edit menu, choose Paste.
Move text	Cut from source. Paste at destination.
Clear text	Select text. From Edit menu, choose Clear.
Change alignment	Select paragraph. Click Alignment icon on ruler.
Change font	Select characters. Click Font tool. Select font.
Change size	Select characters. Click Size tool. Select size.
Change style	Select text. Click Style tool. Select style.
Change text color	Select text. Click Color tool (foreground). Select color.
Change background color	Click Color tool (background). Select color.

You also can select the font, size, and style from the Arrange menu by choosing the Format Character command. Procedures are identical to those in the word processor.

Creating Text Columns

A document with text arranged in columns conveys a professional appearance. Columns are more inviting to read than full-page paragraphs. Creating and manipulating text is easy with Works, so try a columnar layout in some of your documents.

Setting Up Columns

The Column tool helps you draw text columns. Using the Column tool (it resembles a single column), you drag the pointer to draw a rectangle of the proper column dimensions. Depending on the size of your Macintosh screen, you may not be able to see your entire page at once, which hinders your ability to lay out columns accurately. Sketching your column layout with pencil and paper before beginning in Draw is strongly recommended. You can measure columns accurately, and then use the on-screen ruler to duplicate the measurements precisely. If you use identical columns, select and copy the first column; then paste copies in place.

Use the invisible grid, described in the section of Chapter 5 called "Using the Grid." With the Snap to Grid feature turned on, you can align your columns precisely. You also can position text blocks within the column on the grid.

Unlike text blocks, columns do not expand to accommodate text as you type. Consequently, you need to watch for when you enter more text that the column can hold. Extra text scrolls upward, out of sight, somewhat like the list of files in a scrolling list. If more room exists, you can drag the column boundaries to enlarge the space for text. See the section called "Linking Columns" to learn how to let surplus text flow to another column.

Follow these steps to create a two-column layout on a blank page:

1. Sketch out and measure your column layout before starting with Draw.

2. Open a new Draw document.

3. Click the Column tool to select it from the tool palette.

4. Carefully drag the pointer to create the column outline. Use the ruler and the measurements on the status line to guide you.

5. Switch to the Selection tool. Click the column to select it. Handles appear at the corners of the column.

6. Open the Edit menu and choose Copy.

7. Click the window at the center of the area where you want the pasted column.

   Otherwise, the column will be pasted after the first column, requiring more realignment.

8. Choose Paste from the Edit menu. The second column is pasted in place.

9. Drag the pasted column into position. Use Snap to Grid to help align the columns.

Placing Text in Columns

You can choose the Text tool and type text directly into columns or copy text from another Works module. Use these steps to copy text from outside Draw:

TIP

In Chapter 2, "Understanding Works Basics," you learn how to create Stationery documents, which you can use in Draw. These reusable templates are an excellent way to store blank multicolumn pages. When needed, you can quickly open a copy and save the work of recreating the layout.

1. Switch to the document containing the text you want to copy. Use the Open command from the File menu, or switch to an open document using the Window menu.

2. Select the text you want to copy. From the Edit menu, choose Copy.

3. Switch to the Draw document with columns. If the document is open, use the Window menu.

4. Select the Text tool from the tool palette.

5. Click the Text tool in the column where you want to paste the copied text.

6. Open the Edit menu and choose Paste. The text is inserted with its original formatting.

Linking Columns

You can arrange paragraphs side by side in adjacent columns as you might for a table, but there are times when you want text to flow from one column to another as text does in a newspaper. This arrangement, sometimes called *snaking* columns, can be created by linking adjacent columns. Works provides three tools to assist with the process.

When you complete drawing a column or select a column by clicking it with the Selection tool, three tools (see fig. 6.1) appear below the column. Two of the tools are arrows used for navigating from column to column. The icon for the Link tool, which is between the two arrows, changes depending on the linking situation.

When a selected column is empty or when the text it contains fits within the column, the Link tool is shaped like a stop sign. If the column contains more text than can be seen, the Link tool changes to three dots (...) called *ellipses*. If the ellipses are present, clicking the Column tool turns the mouse pointer into a movable icon that resembles the Column tool icon in the tool palette.

When you move the pointer icon over a column to which you can link, the symbol turns into a bold arrow (see fig 6.2). When you move the pointer icon to a column containing text—or one that is already linked—the pointer changes to an X. When you move the pointer outside a column, the pointer becomes a question mark. If you click the mouse button when the question mark shows, you cancel the current linking process.

Fig. 6.1

The tools appear below
the selected column.

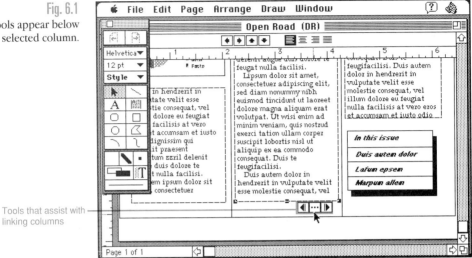

Tools that assist with
linking columns

Fig. 6.2

This pointer icon indicates
that you can link columns.

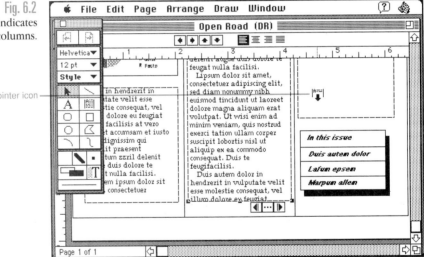

Pointer icon

To link two columns, follow these steps:

1. Create the columns. See "Creating Text Columns."

2. Paste the desired text in the first column. You must have more text than will fill the column.

3. With the Selection tool, click the column. Three tools appear at the bottom of the column.

4. Click the ellipses (...) in the center. If there are no ellipses, the column does not contain enough text.

5. Click the pointer in the adjacent column. The columns are linked. Text flows from the first to the second column.

6. Move the pointer icon away from any column, and then click to end the linking process. You also can click in another column to continue linking.

Moving between Columns

To understand linked columns, you need to learn what comprises a story. In terms of columns, a story is a continuous block of text. For example, if you type several paragraphs of text in a single column, you have one story that can flow from one column to another. If you type paragraphs in one column, then switch to another column and type more paragraphs, you have two stories. You cannot link columns with different stories.

The linking arrows furnish a quick way to move between columns that share a single block of text. To move to a previous linked column, click the left arrow. To move to a subsequent linked column, click the right arrow. If your columns do not contain elements of a single story, you cannot use the navigation arrows. You still can use the Text tool and edit the text as separate blocks, but such blocks will not snake from one column to another as you lengthen or shorten them.

Modifying Links

As you edit, you may want to modify or break the links between columns. For example, you may shorten a story or want to link it to a different column. Use these steps:

1. With the Selection tool (arrow), click the column you want to unlink.

2. Click the Link tool at the bottom of the column. The column is unlinked from an adjacent column.

3. Move the pointer away from all columns and click the mouse button to end the linking procedure.

4. If you want to link to a different column, move the pointer into a different blank column and click.

Chapter 6

Enhancing Documents with Draw

Importing Drawings

TIP

If an imported image is a bit map, the image can be cropped. Open the Arrange menu and choose Crop. Drag the pointer to draw a box around the section of the drawing you want to see. Click outside the crop box to complete the process.

Works can use drawings created by other Macintosh programs. Often, such drawings have been created or can be changed to the PICT format, a common denominator for images on the Macintosh. Importing a PICT image involves the Clipboard. To import a drawing, follow these steps:

1. Copy the image from a source program onto the Clipboard, using the Copy command on the Edit menu.

2. Switch to (or start) Works.

3. Open a Draw document.

4. From the Edit menu, choose Paste to insert the image.

5. To move the image, select it and drag its handles.

Using Draw with Other Works Modules

You have learned to draw objects, create text, and manage columns in Draw. Using these skills, you can create complex documents without ever leaving Draw. The integrated environment of Works also enables you to combine the specialized capabilities of the various modules to achieve more than you could with any one alone.

Draw has special links to the word processor, database, and spreadsheet. The tool palette in all three of these modules has an icon that switches on a Draw layer. Think of this layer as a sheet of transparent plastic covering your basic document. A Draw menu is added to the module menu bar, and Draw tools appear in the tool palette (see fig 6.3). You also can activate Draw by choosing Draw On from the Window menu.

You can add borders, illustrations, text blocks, or any other object you can create in Draw. These objects occupy a layer on top of your document, spreadsheet, or database. You can change these objects without altering the underlying layer. When you are through with the Draw layer, click an icon to return to the host module.

Instead of adding a Draw layer to a document, spreadsheet, or database report, you also can copy material from these modules into a Draw document so that you can take advantage of Draw's column features or use the alignment grid and rulers for a complex multipart document.

Fig. 6.3
Choosing the Draw icon
adds a Draw menu item
and drawing tools.

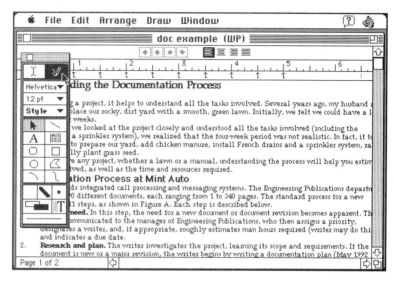

Customizing Draw

Like the Edit menus in all Works modules, the Edit menu in Draw has a
Preferences command that enables you to set the default font and other
features for all documents. In the Draw Preferences dialog box, you can
choose Snap to Grid and Vertex Snap (covered in Chapter 5) for all
documents by checking their respective check boxes (see fig. 6.4).

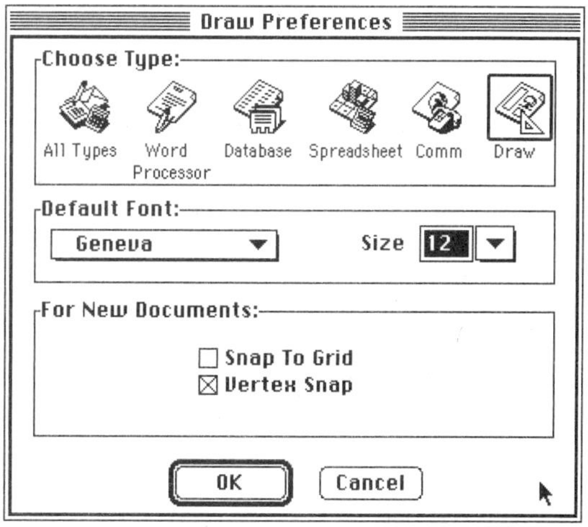

Fig. 6.4
The Draw Preferences
dialog box.

Normally, the Selection tool is the default setting for tools. However, if you hold down the Shift key while clicking a tool in the tool palette, that tool temporarily becomes the new default until you select a different one. You still can select other tools by clicking, but unless you hold down Shift again, the Selection tool becomes the default tool when you finish.

Printing, Saving, and Quitting

Printing, saving, and quitting are three operations you usually perform at the end of a work session. These topics are covered briefly here and more fully in Chapter 2.

Printing in Draw

Three commands on the File menu control printing choices: Print Preview, Print, and Print One. You can preview a drawing with the Print Preview command before printing to see how the drawing will look on paper. When you print, you can select print quality and the pages you want to print, or you can choose the Print One command to bypass the dialog box and print quickly with the current settings. For more information about printing, refer to Chapter 2.

Saving Your Work

Choose Save As from the File menu to save your drawing with a name and a file format. After that initial save, you can use the Save command or ⌘-S to quickly save your drawing. You also can save a workspace with the Save Workspace command from the File menu. For more information about saving, see Chapter 2.

Closing and Quitting

When you are finished with a drawing, you may want to close it and start another, or you may want to quit Works. To close the active drawing, open the File menu and choose Close, or click the close box in the window's upper left corner. If you have a number of files open, use Close All to close all open files. If you want to quit Works, you can go directly to the File menu and choose Quit. You will be given a chance to save your files. For more information about closing and quitting, see Chapter 2.

Chapter Summary

This chapter focused on the ways that Draw can enhance documents. Complete instructions for creating and managing text blocks and columns were included. Other sections showed you how to import PICT images and how to use Draw with other Works modules. Printing, saving, closing, and quitting were explained briefly. In the next chapter you will learn to create spreadsheets.

P A R T

IV

Using
Spreadsheets

Creating Spreadsheets

The electronic spreadsheet was the application that made businesses see early computers as more than hobbyists' toys. Spreadsheets brought number-crunching power, which previously was available only to companies wealthy enough to own mainframe computers, within reach of an individual computer user or business professionals. The spreadsheet's importance continues today; spreadsheet applications rank second only to word processors as the most used type of PC software.

The Works spreadsheet is excellent for the home and small business. If you have experience with Macintosh spreadsheets, you will appreciate the advanced features packed into the program. Three chapters of this book are devoted to spreadsheet issues. This chapter shows you how to create a basic spreadsheet. Chapter 8, "Applying Spreadsheet Functions," explains and lists the powerful preprogrammed mathematical tools called *functions*. Chapter 9, "Working with Charts," explains how to use charts to present and clarify your data.

USING
MICROSOFT
WORKS

Touring the Spreadsheet

Spreadsheets are composed of similar elements; when you have mastered one, you quickly recognize the common features in another. If you are new to spreadsheets, this section will introduce you to basic spreadsheet features. If you have used a spreadsheet before, you may want to skim to the section called "Editing Your Spreadsheet" where new features of the Works spreadsheet are introduced.

Opening a Spreadsheet

When you first start Works, an icon for the spreadsheet module appears among those in the Choose Type box (see fig. 7.1). To start the module and open a blank, untitled document, double-click the Spreadsheet icon; or click the Spreadsheet icon, and then click the New button.

Fig. 7.1

Starting a new spreadsheet
using the New button.

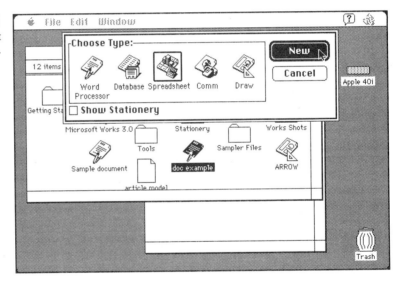

To start with an existing spreadsheet, click the Spreadsheet icon. The files in the scrolling list change as Works applies a filter that shows only spreadsheet files (see fig. 7.2). Find the spreadsheet you want in the scrolling list, and double-click the file name. The spreadsheet module starts with the selected file open.

Fig. 7.2
The File Open dialog box,
showing spreadsheet files.

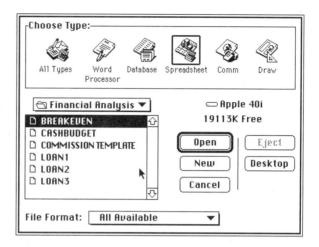

Fig. 7.2
The File Open dialog box,
showing spreadsheet files.

Understanding the Spreadsheet Window

When the module opens, a *spreadsheet* (sometimes called a *worksheet*) appears on-screen (see fig. 7.3). Like its paper counterpart, the computer spreadsheet is a grid of vertical columns and horizontal rows. The section you see on your screen is only a small portion of the entire spreadsheet. The complete sheet is 256 columns wide and 16,382 rows deep. Few users ever use more than a portion of this vast area, but if your computer has enough memory, the potential to create massive spreadsheets exists.

Understanding Spreadsheet Cells

A *cell* is the intersection of a row and column. Cell outlines create a grid on the screen. Each cell is a unique working area that the program can track and manipulate. With so many possible cells to use, you need to specify a distinct location (address) for each cell. To determine a cell's address, you combine the column letter and row number of the cell. The cell in the tenth row of column B has the address B10, for example. Because the spreadsheet is 16,382 rows deep, the last cell in column B has the address B16382.

The Works spreadsheet has 256 vertical columns named by letters of the alphabet. When the lettering passes Z, it begins again with AA, AB, AC, and so on. Beyond AZ, the series continues BA, BB, BC, and so forth.

The 256th column is IV (not the Roman numeral four, but the letters I and V). The rows of the spreadsheet are identified by their row numbers. If you want to see the outer reaches of your spreadsheet, drag the scroll boxes all the way down or all the way to the right.

Fig. 7.3
The spreadsheet window.

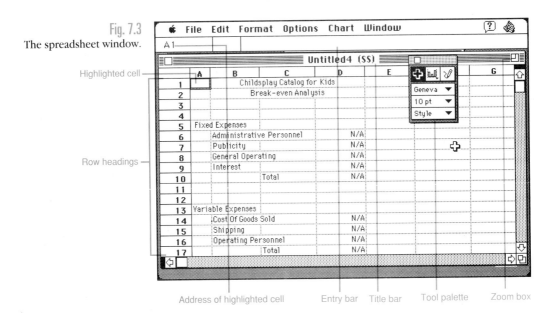

Before you get the impression of unimaginably vast spreadsheets, remember that the maximum number of cells you can use in a single spreadsheet depends on the amount of memory in your computer. The memory capacity is usually far smaller than the total number of cells, but this discrepancy usually is not a problem. In fact, a majority of the spreadsheets you create probably fit on a single screen (about 160 cells).

Using the Active Cell

As you work on a spreadsheet, the cell in which you are working is the *active cell*. You can identify the active cell by its thick outline.

The address of the active cell appears at the left end of the entry bar, just above the close box (see fig. 7.4). As you enter data or create formulas, knowing the location of the active cell is important. You move the active cell location by using keyboard arrow keys or clicking a new location with the mouse. In this chapter, moving the active cell marker—the thick outline—to a cell also is called *highlighting* the cell.

Fig. 7.4
The active cell is identified
by a surrounding thick line.

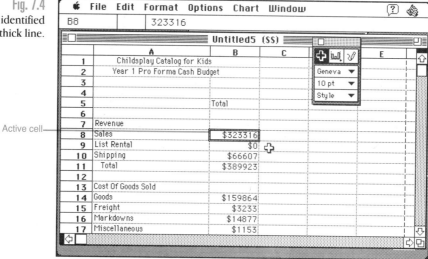

Active cell—

Reviewing the Spreadsheet Menus

Spreadsheet commands are contained in six menus. Table 7.1 describes
the menus in general terms. For more information about the spreadsheet commands, refer to the command reference in Appendix A.

Table 7.1
The Spreadsheet Menus

Menu name	General purpose
File	Controls creating, opening, and saving files. Prints and quits.
Edit	Cuts and pastes text, numbers, and functions. Moves, selects, and inserts cells. Fills areas. Sets preferences.
Format	Formats characters, cells, and column widths. Splits the screen.
Options	Establishes display of grid, values, formulas, and notes. Sets calculation.
Chart	Accesses charting tools and menus.
Window	Displays or hides tool palette. Controls headers, footers, macros. Switches active window. Displays help.

Acquiring Basic Spreadsheet Skills

A spreadsheet is comprised principally of numbers, with text added to label the numbers. This section explains ways to enter information and how the spreadsheet interprets what you enter.

Using Labels

How the spreadsheet interprets what you type is an important concept to understand. Consider the entry, 1992. If this entry is the number of dollars in your paycheck, you would want the spreadsheet to treat the entry as a value and add that amount to your bank balance. If you intended 1992 to stand for the year, you might want to use it as a title for your spreadsheet. In this case, 1992 should be treated as text rather than a number, and excluded from spreadsheet calculations. In spreadsheets, text entries are usually called *labels*.

The spreadsheet needs to distinguish between numbers and labels in order to process cell contents correctly. Normally, the distinction is clear, but, as illustrated in the 1992 example, sometimes the program may need help distinguishing a number from a numeric label. To designate any entry as a label, start the entry with a double quotation mark (") as you type. Anything you enter after the double quotation mark is considered text, not a value. After you have entered your text, end the label with a double quotation mark.

Using Numbers and Formulas

You need to recognize two types of values: numbers and formulas. *Numbers* are simply digits or groups of digits. When entering numbers, use decimal points when appropriate, but do not type commas to divide a number. Commas are an element of cell formatting, a topic explained in the section called "Establishing Cell Formats."

Formulas are a combination of data and symbols, called *operators*, that produce a result. This is a formula: =2+2. The twos are data, and the plus sign is the operator. The result, of course, is 4. The equal sign marks the entry as a formula in the same way that a double quotation mark indicates a label. When you enter a formula in a spreadsheet, you type the entire formula in the entry bar, but only the result appears in the cell.

Typing in the Entry Bar

When you type information into your spreadsheet, the information appears first in the *entry bar*. The entry bar, located just below the menu bar, is the only area of the spreadsheet where you directly enter or edit cell contents (see fig. 7.5). When you highlight a cell with the active cell marker, the cell's contents are displayed in the entry bar. If a cell shows the result of a formula, you can see the formula in the entry bar by selecting the cell.

Clicking the mouse pointer in the entry bar displays an editing tool—like the insertion point in the word processor—you can use to delete or insert new material. Editing capabilities are the same as those found in other modules: Delete removes characters, typing inserts text, and dragging the mouse selects material.

When you enter or edit material in the entry bar, two icons appear near the left end of the entry bar. You can activate these icons with the mouse to enter or remove contents. Clicking the X deletes everything in the entry bar if you have not yet entered the material in a cell. Clicking the check mark enters the contents of the entry bar into the active cell. You also can enter material by pressing Return, or exit without making changes by pressing the Esc key.

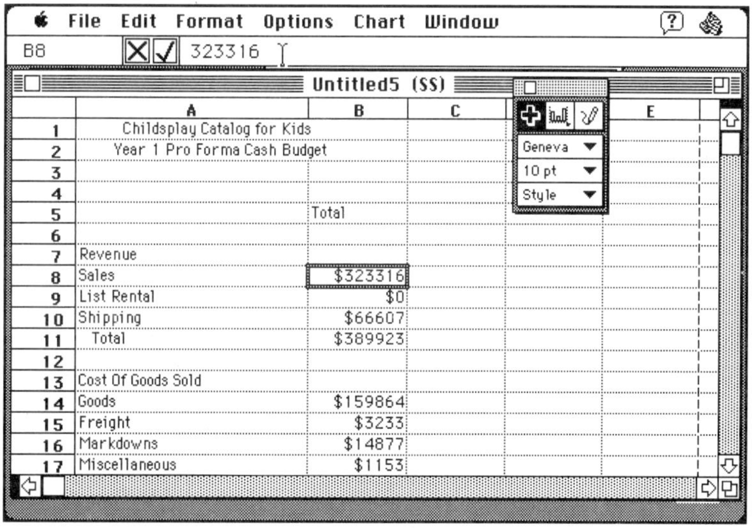

Fig. 7.5
The entry bar is used to enter and edit cell contents.

	A	B	C		E
1	Childsplay Catalog for Kids				
2	Year 1 Pro Forma Cash Budget			Geneva	
3				10 pt	
4				Style	
5		Total			
6					
7	Revenue				
8	Sales	$323316			
9	List Rental	$0			
10	Shipping	$66607			
11	Total	$389923			
12					
13	Cost Of Goods Sold				
14	Goods	$159864			
15	Freight	$3233			
16	Markdowns	$14877			
17	Miscellaneous	$1153			

Chapter 7

Creating Spreadsheets

Creating a Simple Spreadsheet

The following steps describe the process used to create a simple
spreadsheet. You may need to adapt the steps for a specific situation, but
they represent a basis for beginning:

1. Open the File menu and choose New. A blank spreadsheet opens.

2. Move the active cell pointer where you want your first entry. Use
   arrow keys or click the desired cell.

3. Type a value or a label. Your typing appears on the entry bar.

4. Press Return to place your entry in the active cell and move down
   one cell. You also can click the enter box (the check mark) on the
   entry bar.

5. If necessary, move the pointer to a new cell and repeat steps 3 and
   4. Continue to enter your data.

6. Open the File menu and choose Save As. Name and save the
   spreadsheet (see fig. 7.6).

Fig. 7.6
Using Save As to name and
save a spreadsheet.

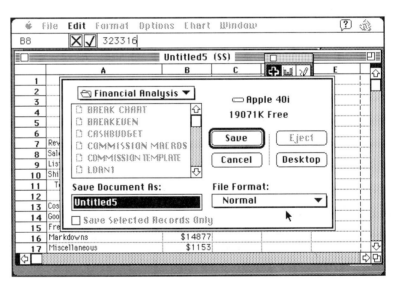

This simple process is the basis of spreadsheet construction. As you
continue this chapter, you will learn additional ways to organize and
enhance this core of information.

Moving the Active Cell

In addition to pressing Return to enter information in the active cell and move down, you can use the keys in table 7.2 to both enter data and move to another location, saving time and keystrokes. You also can use the keyboard arrow keys to enter data and move to a new location.

Table 7.2
Movement Keys

Key(s)	Result
Return	Enters data and move down one cell.
Shift-Return	Enters data and move up one cell.
Tab	Enters data and move right one cell.
Shift-Tab	Enters data and move left one cell.

Editing Cells

NOTE

You also can use the Cut command to remove cell contents to the Clipboard so that you can paste the contents into a new location. To bypass the Clipboard, use the Clear command on the Edit menu.

Until you press Return or click the check mark to enter data in a cell, you can edit the information on the entry bar. You can even delete the information entirely by clicking the X. The following steps explain the principal editing procedures after data has been entered in a cell:

To delete the contents of a cell, follow these steps:

1. Highlight the cell.

2. Type the new data.

3. Press Return to enter the new information and replace the old.

To change the contents of a cell, follow these steps:

1. Highlight the cell.

2. Click in the entry bar and insert or delete text.

3. Press Return to enter the edited information and replace the old.

To remove the contents of a cell, follow these steps:

1. Highlight the cell.

2. Press Delete to remove the cell contents from the entry bar.

3. Press Return to remove the entry from the cell.

Using Formulas

A spreadsheet consisting of rows of raw information is of limited use. The power of computer spreadsheets to rapidly and accurately perform mathematical operations is the reason for their popularity. In order for the spreadsheet to process numbers, you must give it instructions in the form of formulas. This section describes methods for creating and applying formulas.

Understanding Formulas

To review briefly, a formula consists of *data,* usually numbers, and mathematical *operators,* which describe what to do to the data. In the formula =2+2, the twos are the data and the plus sign is an operator. The *result* of the formula, 4, is the outcome of the interaction between the operators and the data.

In a spreadsheet, you can designate data by entering either numbers or cell addresses. In other words, if cell A1 and B1 both contain the number 2, you create a formula to add the contents of the cells by typing **=A1+B1** on the entry bar. Notice the equal sign (=) that begins the formula. This symbol tells Works that what follows is a formula. Otherwise, the letter A in this example might be mistaken for a text label. *Formulas always begin with an equal sign.*

Adding by Pointing

Works has an easy shortcut for adding a row or column of numbers. Try this method:

1. Highlight the cell where the total should appear.

2. Type an equal sign (=).

3. Click each cell you want to add.

4. When the formula is complete, press Return.

As you click each cell to be added, Works inserts the cell address and an addition operator, building the formula for you (see fig. 7.7). Later in this chapter you will learn an even more efficient way of adding that uses a function, but the pointing method is quick and effective for small groups of cells.

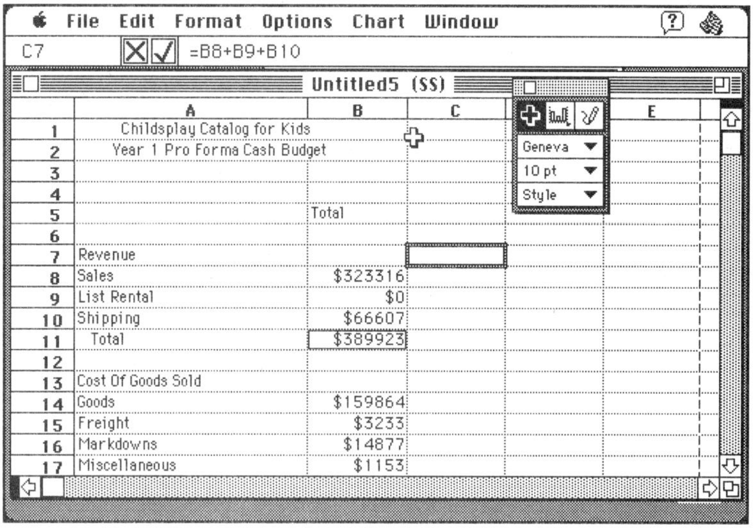

Fig. 7.7
As you point, Works builds
the formula on the
entry bar.

Fig. 7.7
As you point, Works builds
the formula on the
entry bar.

Using Operators in Works

Table 7.3 lists the mathematical operators available in Works. Don't be concerned if some are not familiar to you. You can learn new ones as needed. If you are new to computers, note that the symbols for multiplication and division are not the ones traditionally used in print.

To use an operator in a formula, type the operator between two values or cell references. For example: **=2 / 2** or **=B5 * A6**.

Table 7.3
Works' Mathematical
Operators

Symbol	Purpose
+	Addition
–	Subtraction
*	Multiplication
/	Division
=	Equal to
<	Less than
>	Greater than
<=	Less than or equal to
>=	Greater than or equal to
<>	Not equal to

Chapter 7
Creating Spreadsheets

Using Relative and Absolute Addresses

One of the features that makes spreadsheets so useful is the capability to automatically adjust *relative addresses*. You can create a formula in one cell, and when you copy it to another cell, the addresses in the formula are adjusted relative to the new location. This feature saves you from having to manually change all the addresses to adjust for a formula's new location.

Imagine a formula that adds the contents of the active cell to the contents of the cell two cells to the right. The phrase "two cells to the right" is a relative address. If you copy the example formula to a new location, a different cell will now be located "two cells to the right." In other words, addresses in the formula are relative to the cell containing the formula. Relative addresses are the default in the Works spreadsheet. They are adjusted as you move them to new addresses.

Sometimes you need to specify an *absolute address*. Perhaps you have an inflation rate in cell A1, and you want certain formulas in your spreadsheet to always refer to A1 for inflation information, even if the formulas are moved or copied on the spreadsheet. You do so by entering the cell reference as an absolute address.

To create an absolute reference, put a dollar sign ($) before the address you want to make an absolute address. For example, the formula =A1+A2 is relative, but in the formula =$A1+A2, the address for A1 has been made absolute. Note, however, that A2 is still a relative address.

The reference to A2 will be adjusted if the formula is relocated. In the formula =$A1+$A2, both addresses are absolute. The formula will always look at the same cells regardless of where it is copied or moved in the spreadsheet.

Introducing Functions

A *function* is a preprogrammed mathematical procedure. Working with values you provide, called *arguments*, a function quickly can calculate complex results such as loan payments or averages. This short section only introduces the concept and provides one simple example. Chapter 8, "Applying Spreadsheet Functions," is devoted entirely to explaining the 64 functions furnished with Works.

As an example, consider the most frequently used function: Sum( ). To add a group of cells using this function, type **=Sum( )** on the entry bar, and then insert your arguments—a reference to the cells you want to add, a list of numbers, or a list of cell references—between the parentheses. When you press Return, the function rapidly calculates the total of the cells specified in the argument (see fig. 7.8). You will learn more about cell references later in this chapter and more about functions in Chapter 8.

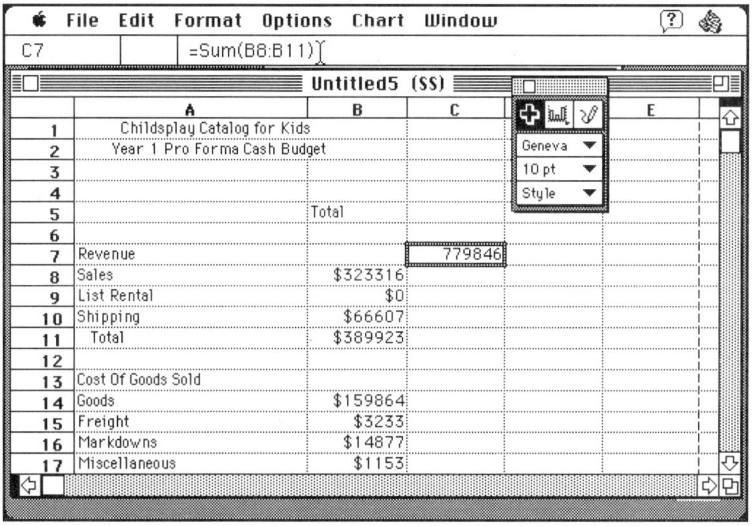

Fig. 7.8
A column of numbers added by the function shown on the entry bar.

Editing Your Spreadsheet

Unless you create only the simplest spreadsheets, your ability to edit a spreadsheet is as important as your ability to enter information. Editing tools help you work on groups of cells, view the cells in different ways, and make the spreadsheet easier to view and understand. In this section, you will learn how editing tools increase your spreadsheet control and effectiveness.

Using Ranges

Perhaps you need to remove a whole row of information, or you decide to change the font for every cell in a spreadsheet. Both of these tasks can be done a cell at a time, but working with a block of cells would be much faster. You need to work with a *range*. A range is a block of cells selected together so that they can be changed together (see fig. 7.9).

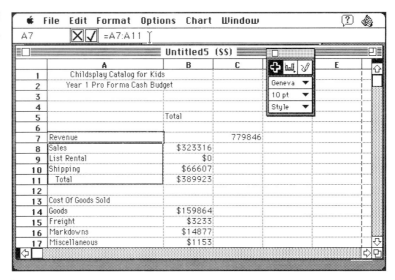

To specify a range in a formula or command, use the addresses of the starting and ending cells in the block. Separate the addresses with a colon. To describe a range that begins at cell A1 (upper left) and ends at D6 (lower right), type **A1:D6**, for example.

A range can be sized from a single cell to an entire worksheet, but it must be a continuous rectangular block. In other words, you cannot have L-shaped ranges or hollow squares. With a range selected, you can affect all its cells at the same time—formatting them alike or using them in formulas, for instance.

To select a range, place the mouse pointer at one corner of the block, hold down the mouse button, and drag the pointer to the corner diagonally opposite the beginning cell. The area is highlighted. To remove a range highlight, simply click the mouse outside the range.

Shortcuts available for several types of range selection are listed in table 7.4.

Table 7.4
Range Selection Shortcuts

Selection	Action
To select a row	Click the row number at the left edge of the spreadsheet.
To select a column	Click the column letter at the top of the spreadsheet.

Part IV

Using Spreadsheets

Selection	Action
To quickly highlight an area	Click the first cell, move to the last cell, and hold down Shift while clicking the mouse button. The range between the two cells will be highlighted.
To adjust a range	Hold down Shift and drag from a corner of the range to extend or reduce its size.
To highlight all used cells	Open the Edit menu, choose Select, and then drag to Select All in the small cascade menu that opens.
To highlight the last active cell	Open the Edit menu, choose Select, and then drag to Select Last Cell in the small cascade menu that opens.

Establishing Cell Formats

Cell formats control the format type, alignment, number format, and number of decimal places displayed in a cell. You can change alignment and other formats using the Format Cells dialog box (see fig. 7.10). Cell formats remain when cell contents are deleted or changed. The steps below explain how to change formats using the Format Cells command.

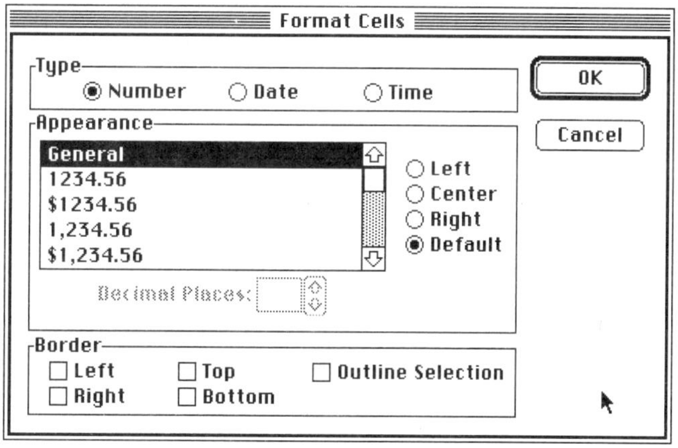

Fig. 7.10
The Format Cells
dialog box.

Alignment refers to the position of cell contents to the left, center, or right of the cell. The Default choice places values to the right and text to the left of a cell. Use the following steps to change alignment:

1. Select the cells to be changed.

2. From the Format menu, choose Format Cells. The Format Cells dialog box appears.

3. In the Appearance area, click the radio button for the alignment you want.

4. Click OK to apply the setting and close the dialog box.

Three options exist for format types: Number, Date, and Time. Choosing a type for selected cells opens a list in the Appearance list box that shows examples of the type (see fig. 7.11). Choosing a format and clicking OK applies the format to the selected cells. Any entry in the cell is displayed in the chosen format. The format is attached to the cell, not the data. If you move the data to another location, the data's format may change.

Fig. 7.11
The Appearance list box provides examples of formats for the type you choose.

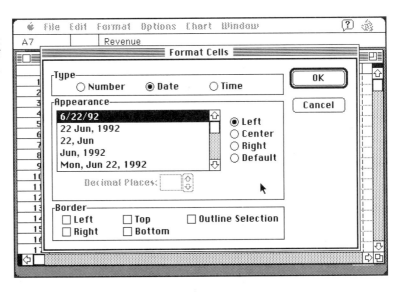

You also can set the number of decimal places shown in a cell from the Format Cells dialog box using these steps:

1. Select the cells to be changed.

2. Open the Format menu and choose Format Cells. The Format Cells dialog box appears.

TIP

A quicker way to get the Format Cells dialog box is to double-click a cell.

Part IV
Using Spreadsheets

3. Choose Number in the Type selection box.

   Decimals apply only to number entries.

4. Choose a format other than General in the Appearance list box.

   The General format enters exactly the number of decimals you type.

5. In the Decimal Places text box, type the number of places desired.

   You also can click the up or down arrows to choose the number of places.

6. Click OK to set the number of decimal places and close the dialog box.

Editing Cell Contents

Using ranges, you can apply editing techniques to groups of cells as well as individual cells. In this section, you learn to copy, move, and delete information. These techniques apply to either ranges or single cells.

Copying

Copying data creates a duplicate of the information in the selected cells. If the cells contain formulas, they are copied as well. Works also adjusts any cell references in copied formulas to fit their new location. To copy data, use these steps:

1. Select the cell(s) you want to copy.

2. Open the Edit menu and choose Copy. A copy of the highlighted information is placed in the Clipboard.

3. Click the destination cell.

   If copying a range, click the cell at the upper left of the destination area.

4. Open the Edit menu and choose Paste. The information in the Clipboard is placed at the destination.

Moving

Moving information is almost like copying, except that you remove the source information from the spreadsheet. As with copying, formulas are moved as well, and cell references are adjusted if needed. To move data use these steps:

1. Select the cell(s) you want to move.

2. Open the Edit menu and choose Cut. The highlighted information is removed and placed in the Clipboard.

3. Click the destination cell. If copying a range, click the cell at the upper left of the destination area.

4. Open the Edit menu and choose Paste. The information in the Clipboard is placed at the destination.

Adding Information

Adding information to a cell involves editing the cell contents.

1. Select the cell you want to edit.

2. Edit the contents on the entry bar to add the desired information.

3. Enter the edited information in the cell by clicking the check button or pressing Return.

Deleting Information

The three ways to delete information differ in how they affect the cell containing the information. The following steps explain the different deletion methods:

1. Select the cell(s) you want to edit.

2. Open the Edit menu and choose Clear. Clear removes cell contents and cell formatting permanently.

3. Open the Edit menu and choose Cut. Cell contents move to the Clipboard. Cell formatting is unchanged.

4. Press the Delete key on the keyboard. Cell contents are removed permanently. Cell formatting is unchanged.

Changing Column Width

The standard column width in the spreadsheet is 12 characters. When you enter labels or data with more characters than the cell can hold, the excess will spill into the adjacent cell on the right—but only if that cell is empty.

TIP

To copy or move information without including underlying formulas, use the preceding steps, but when you are ready to paste, open the Edit menu and choose Paste Special. The Paste Special dialog box opens. Choose Values Only and click OK.

NOTE

If you realize you have cleared or deleted information you want to keep, immediately open the Edit menu and choose Undo. You usually can undo your last action if you have not used any other commands since the clear or deletion.

If the adjacent cell is used, the contents of the first cell will be cut off at the cell boundary. To solve this problem, you can widen the column. You also may want to narrow columns that contain only a few numbers (see fig. 7.12).

Fig. 7.12
Column widths can range from 1 character to 40.

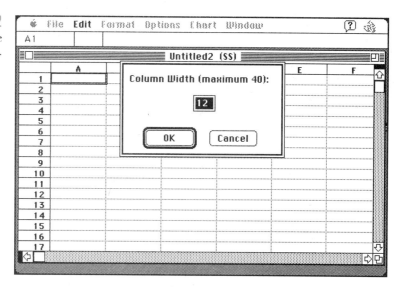

Change column width using either the mouse or the menu by performing the following steps:

Using the mouse

1. Position the mouse pointer at the right edge of the column heading. The pointer changes to a vertical bar with arrows pointing left and right.

2. Drag the boundary of the column left or right to the desired width.

    Notice the vertical, dotted line that represents what your new column width will be when you release the mouse button.

Using the menu

1. Place the active cell anywhere in the column you want to change.

2. Open the Format menu and choose Column Width.

3. In the dialog box that opens, type the number of characters for column width. Maximum width is 40 characters.

4. Click OK to implement the new width.

TIP

You can select several columns by dragging across their column headings; then change the width of all the selected columns at one time by using the Column Width command on the Format menu.

Chapter 7
Creating Spreadsheets

Locating Cells

On a large spreadsheet, moving to a particular cell using arrow keys or the mouse can be a slow process. The Find command takes you directly to a cell that contains the text, address, or numbers you specify.

1. Open the Edit menu and choose Find. The dialog box shown in figure 7.13 appears.

Fig. 7.13
The Find dialog box.

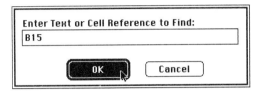

```
Enter Text or Cell Reference to Find:
B15
              [    OK    ]    [  Cancel  ]
```

2. Enter the cell address or information you want to find, and click OK. The active cell marker moves to the cell containing the material.

3. To repeat the search quickly with the same target, press ⌘-F to reopen the Find dialog box, and then click OK.

   Works finds specified information even if it is embedded in other information. If you are searching for the number 222, for example, the Find command locates 45222, 382.22, or any other number or text containing three consecutive 2s.

NOTE

The Find command finds *exactly* what you specify. Be careful about capitalization and spacing in text. Numbers are found on the basis of their stored value, not the displayed value, which may be modified by cell formatting.

Sorting Cells

Sometimes you may want to sort the items in your spreadsheet either alphabetically or numerically. You can sort in ascending (A–Z) or descending (Z–A) order. To sort the spreadsheet, you use a sorting feature similar to the one found in the database module. In fact, if you need to sort frequently or to extract and reorganize sorted elements, consider moving your data to the database module where you can use specialized tools. The database module is covered in Chapter 10, "Creating Databases."

Sorting is simple if you understand the concept of a *key column*. The data in table 7.5 will help explain:

	Col. A	Col. B
Table 7.5 Sorting Sample	Sandy	Smith
	Beulah	Smith
	Ellis	Smith
	Albert	Jones

If you used the Sort command on the data in table 7.5, you would need to specify the first key column name in the box shown in figure 7.14. To sort by last name, you would enter **B** to use Column B as the first sort key.

Fig. 7.14
The Sort dialog box.

```
┌─────────────────────────────────────────────────┐
│ Sort                                  ( ▶ OK )    │
│                                                   │
│ 1st Key Column: [B▮]   ◉ Ascending   [ Cancel ]   │
│                        ○ Descending               │
│                                                   │
│ 2nd Key Column: [  ]   ◉ Ascending                │
│                        ○ Descending               │
│                                                   │
│ 3rd Key Column: [  ]   ◉ Ascending                │
│                        ○ Descending               │
└─────────────────────────────────────────────────┘
```

Assume you sorted in ascending (A–Z) order. When the sort was done, Albert Jones would be at the top of the list because J comes before S, but the first names of the Smiths would still be in the original nonalphabetic order because no second sort key was specified to sort the first names.

To sort by last, then first, names, you would specify Column B as the first sort key, and then specify Column A as a *second* sort key. After the sort, the Column B would be in alphabetic order and Column A would be rearranged alphabetically within the last name groupings. In other words, the Smiths would now be alphabetized by first name as well as last. You might use a third sort key column if the names included middle initials.

Works sorts only selected information. Be sure to highlight all the material you want sorted. Failure to do so can scramble data by sorting selected data but not sorting related adjacent data that is not selected. If this happens, immediately open the Edit menu and choose Undo to reverse the sort.

Use the following steps to perform a sort:

1. Select the cells you want to sort.

2. Open the Options menu and choose Sort. The Sort Key dialog box appears.

3. In the Sort Key dialog box, enter the letters of the columns you want to make key columns.

4. Click a radio button to select ascending or descending order.

5. Click OK to complete the sort.

Showing Formulas

Normally, only the results of a formula show in the cell where the formula is located. You can see the formula in a single highlighted cell on the entry bar. But if you want to examine all the formulas in your spreadsheet at the same time or display and print them, use the Show Formulas command.

When you open the Options menu and choose Show Formulas, formulas and unformatted numbers show in the cells (see fig. 7.15). You probably will need to widen columns to see all the information. Only material visible on-screen will print.

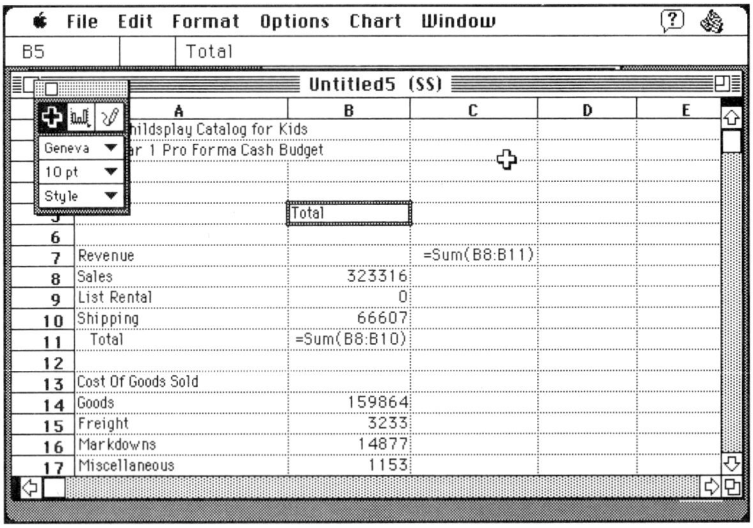

Fig. 7.15

The Show Formulas command reveals formulas and unformatted numbers.

To restore the spreadsheet to its normal appearance, choose Show Values from the Options menu.

Changing Recalculation

By default, Works recalculates the formulas in your worksheet every time you enter or change a value. While the program is recalculating, you cannot continue your work.

If you want to prevent automatic recalculation, open the Options menu and choose the Manual Calculation command. A check mark appears next to the command. To begin calculation manually, open the Options menu and choose Calculate Now.

To restore automatic recalculation, choose the Manual Calculation command a second time. The check mark disappears and automatic calculation resumes.

Protecting Cells

When you get complex data and formulas just right, you may want to protect them from alteration by accident or by others using the spreadsheet. Select the range of cells you want to protect, open the Format menu, and choose Protect Cell. A check mark appears next to the command, and the selected cells are protected from further change.

To unlock cell protection, choose the Protect Cell command a second time. The check mark disappears, and you can edit the cells again.

Controlling Display Options

In this section, you learn ways of controlling how information is displayed on your screen. For example, you can choose to view or remove the grid that defines cell boundaries. You also can choose whether you see formulas or results, change column widths to accommodate data, and sort cells in alphabetic or numeric order.

Changing the Grid

Normally, a grid is present on the screen to show cell boundaries, but you may want to view your data without the grid. When you remove the grid from the screen, the grid disappears from printed output as well. This technique creates spreadsheet printouts resembling those in publications. The result can be quite effective with relatively simple spreadsheets (see fig. 7.16).

Fig. 7.16
A simple spreadsheet with the grid removed.

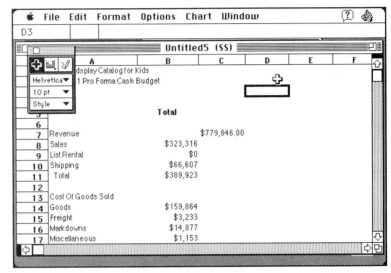

To remove the grid from the screen, follow these steps:

1. Open the Options menu.

   A check mark is next to the Show Grid command.

2. Choose Show Grid, which removes the check mark.

   The grid disappears from the screen.

To restore the grid, choose the command again.

Attaching Notes

Cell notes can be helpful in explaining to others (or reminding yourself) of the purpose or procedure associated with a cell's contents. Think of attaching cell notes as taping a small slip of paper to the cell, except that the electronic note appears and disappears on command (see fig. 7.17).

Fig. 7.17
An electronic note
associated with its cell.

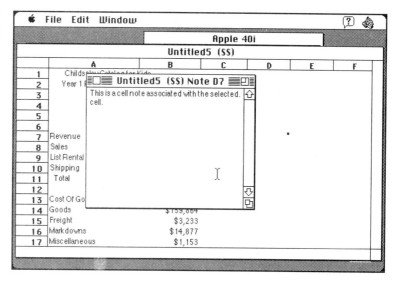

To create a note, use these steps:

1. Select the cell to contain the note.

2. Open the Options menu and choose Open Cell Note. A text window opens on the screen.

3. Type the note contents.

4. Click the close box in the note window to finish. A small rectangle appears in the upper right corner of the cell.

Viewing a note is simple. Follow these steps:

1. Select a cell containing a note.

2. Open the Options menu and choose Open Cell Note.

   You also can double-click the cell while holding down the ⌘ key.

Cell notes can be printed as the spreadsheet is printed. They appear separately, identified by their address. To print cell notes, follow these steps:

1. Open the File menu and choose Page Setup.

2. Click the Document button to open a secondary dialog box.

3. Click the Print Cell Notes check box.

4. Choose OK twice to exit both dialog boxes.

Chapter 7
Creating Spreadsheets

Splitting the Display

With a large spreadsheet, you sometimes need to see parts that won't fit on the display at the same time. By splitting the display into multiple windows, you can put a different part of the spreadsheet in each window. You could look at a range of data in one window and the totals from the bottom of the spreadsheet in another, for example.

You can split a window either horizontally or vertically, producing either two or four *panes*—screen sections that scroll independently.

Because the contents of each pane scroll independently, you can view as many as four different areas at the same time. The tool used to split windows is the *split bar*, a small black rectangle found at the end of both the vertical and horizontal scroll bars (see fig. 7.18).

Fig. 7.18

A split bar is at the end of each scroll bar.

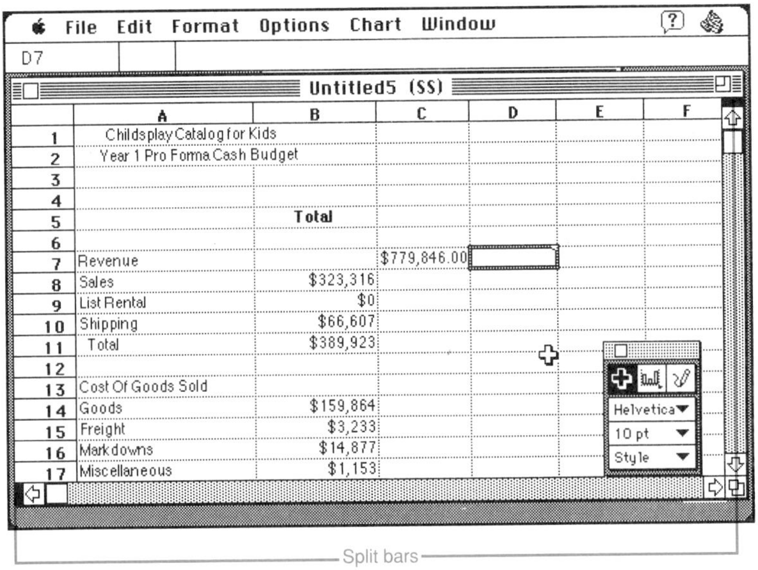

To split a window, use the following steps:

1. Place the mouse pointer precisely on the split bar. The pointer changes into up and down arrows.

2. Drag the split bar to the edge of the column or row where you want the split.

Part IV

Using Spreadsheets

You can split a window horizontally, vertically, or both ways. When the window is split, each pane has a scroll bar, and the contents of each pane scroll independently (see fig. 7.19). To close a split window, drag the split bar back to the extreme end of its scroll bar.

Fig. 7.19
A vertical and horizontal split produces four independent panes.

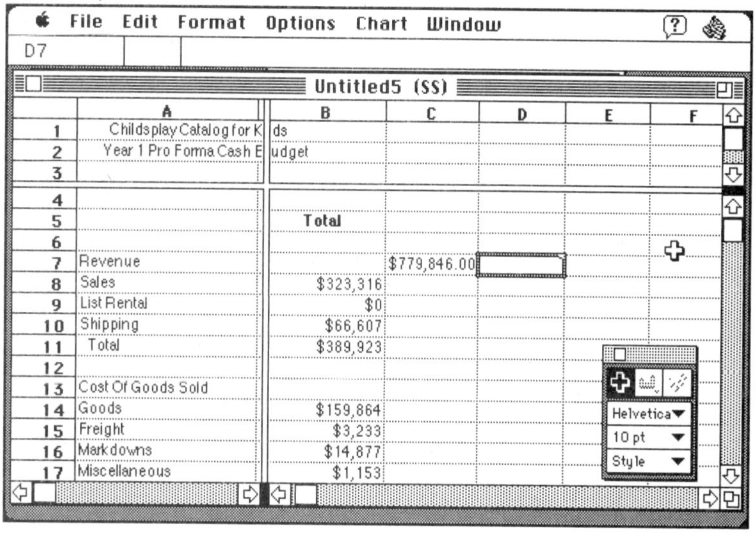

Freezing Split Panes

If you have a spreadsheet taller or wider than the screen, row and column titles move out of sight when you scroll to view another area. You can split the display window in two panes, show titles in one pane, and then "freeze" the titles while the other pane scrolls. Freezing removes the scroll bar from the frozen pane and keeps labels in view while you move to any part of the spreadsheet in the other pane.

You also can split the screen vertically, to freeze row labels, or both horizontally and vertically if you want to freeze both row and column labels (see fig. 7.20).

Use these steps to freeze rows:

1. Drag the split bar in the horizontal scroll bar into position.
2. Open the Format menu and choose Freeze Titles Vertical.

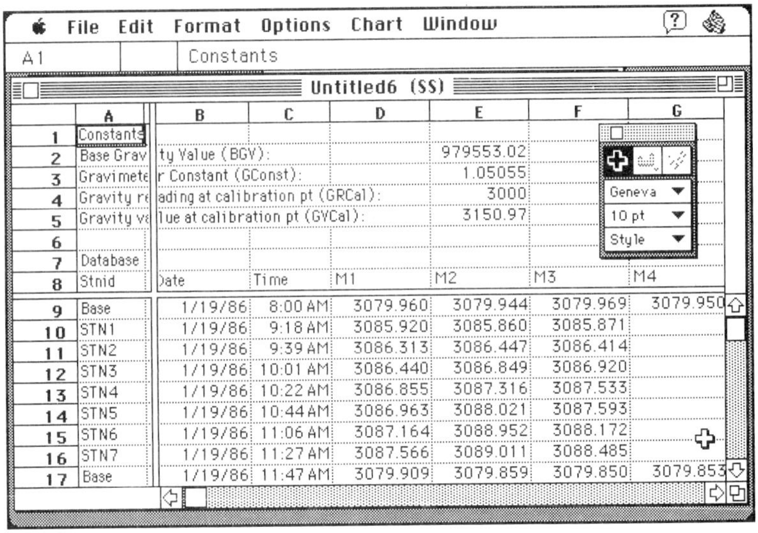

Fig. 7.20

You can split a screen both
vertically and horizontally
to freeze the labels on the
rows and columns.

The procedure for freezing columns is similar:

1. Drag the split bar in the vertical scroll bar into position.

2. Open the Format menu and choose Freeze Titles Horizontal.

To unfreeze either rows or columns, open the Format menu and choose
the appropriate Freeze command a second time.

Enhancing Your Spreadsheet

Polishing a spreadsheet with enhanced fonts, colors, and annotations
can give the spreadsheet a greater impact. In this age of desktop publishing and multimedia presentations, users of visual information have
higher expectations. A polished presentation gets more attention than a
crude one.

Works gives you the ability to enhance many aspects of your spreadsheet. Several features are built into the spreadsheet. You also can
create a Draw layer on top of your spreadsheet and apply additional
enhancements.

Using the Tool Palette in the Spreadsheet

The tool palette is available in all Works modules, although its contents vary slightly from module to module. In the spreadsheet, the palette contains three icons across the top that you can use to switch between the spreadsheet, the charting module, and the Draw layer (see fig. 7.21).

The remaining elements of the palette are identical to those found in other modules. There are three buttons that open menus used for choosing fonts, font sizes, and type styles. If you choose Draw On from the Window menu, or click the Draw icon, the drawing tools are added to the tool palette. The drawing tools are explained in Chapter 5, "Creating Drawings."

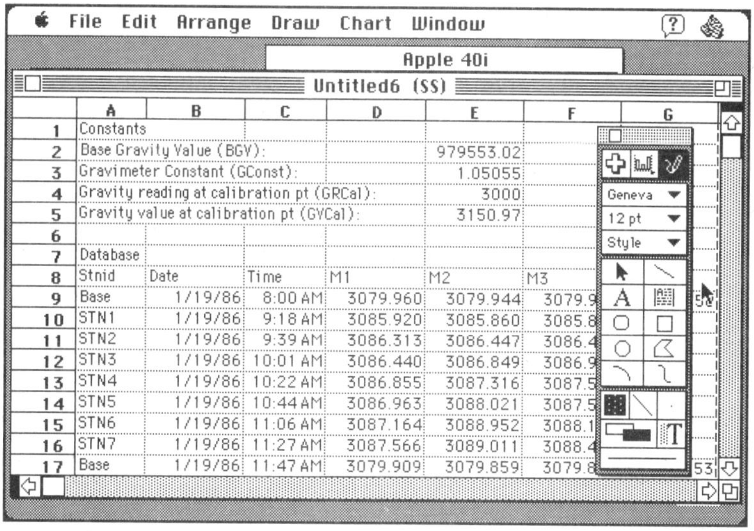

Fig. 7.21
The tool palette as it appears in the spreadsheet.

Enhancing Cell Contents

The spreadsheet font or font size can be changed using either the Font and Size pop-up menus opened by buttons on the tool palette or the dialog box opened by choosing Format Character. When you change the font or font size for *any* cell, the font or font size is altered for *every* cell in your spreadsheet.

Bold, italic, or underline formats can be applied to the contents of individual cells or ranges. You also can add outlines or shadow effects.

Select the cells you want to format; then click the arrow on the Style tool on the tool palette, or choose Format Character from the Format menu. Select the style you want, and click OK or close the pop-up menu. Figure 7.22 shows style formats applied.

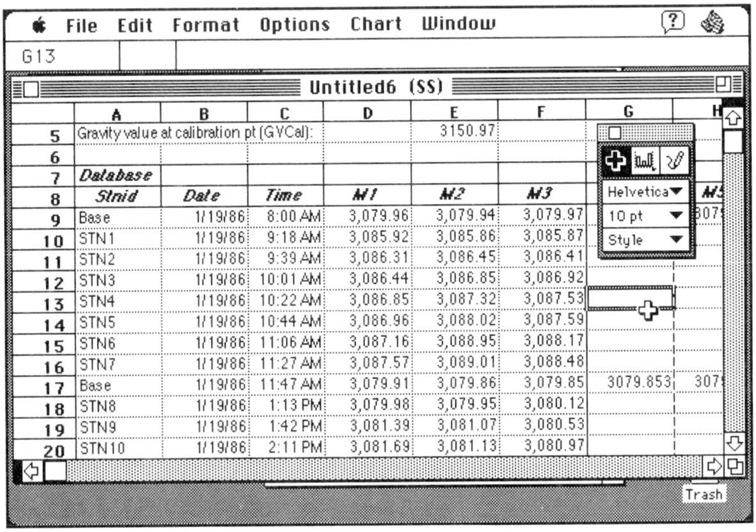

Fig. 7.22
Style formats can be applied to both text and numbers.

You can apply color to individual cells or ranges. Select the desired cells, and then choose Format Character from the Format menu, or double-click the cell or range. Open the pop-up list under Style, and choose the color you want.

Borders can be applied to single cells or ranges. With options, you can put a border on any edge of the selection or surround the whole selection. Use these steps:

1. Select the cell or range you want to border.

2. Open the Format menu and choose Format Cells, or double-click the cell or range.

3. In the Border section of the dialog box, choose the options you want.

4. Click OK to apply the borders and close the dialog box.

Saving Your Work

Choose Save As from the File menu to save your spreadsheet with a name and a file format. After that initial save, you can use the Save command or ⌘-S to quickly save your spreadsheet. You also can save a workspace with the Save Workspace command from the File menu. For more information about saving, see Chapter 2, "Understanding Works Basics."

Printing Your Spreadsheet

Three commands on the File menu control printing choices: Print Preview, Print, and Print One. You can preview a spreadsheet before printing to see how it will look on paper. When you print, you can select both print quality and the pages you want to print, or choose the Print One command to bypass the dialog box and print quickly with the current settings.

Some printing choices depend on the capabilities of the printer you use. Use the Chooser desk accessory, found under the Apple menu, to specify your printer. If your printer does not appear in Chooser, you need to install a *printer driver* in your Macintosh System folder.

A printer driver is a small software utility that tells your computer how to communicate with your brand and model of printer.

Drivers for most popular Apple printers are included with system software, but if yours is not, it is usually packed with the printer. For additional information on this topic, consult your system software manual or your printer documentation.

Setting Page Size and Orientation

To print the entire active area of your spreadsheet, print with a single cell highlighted.

If you want to print part of your spreadsheet, select the part by highlighting cells. When you print, only the highlighted cells are included.

Because specifying correct document size and orientation is critical for printing, the Page Setup command, found on the File menu, links both printer and page information. When you choose Page Setup, a dialog box for the printer you have selected appears. Figure 7.23 shows the dialog box for a LaserWriter printer. The dialog box contains radio buttons used to select paper size and check boxes to choose printer-specific effects such as image reduction. Two buttons under the heading Orientation choose vertical (often called *portrait*) or horizontal (*landscape*) printing.

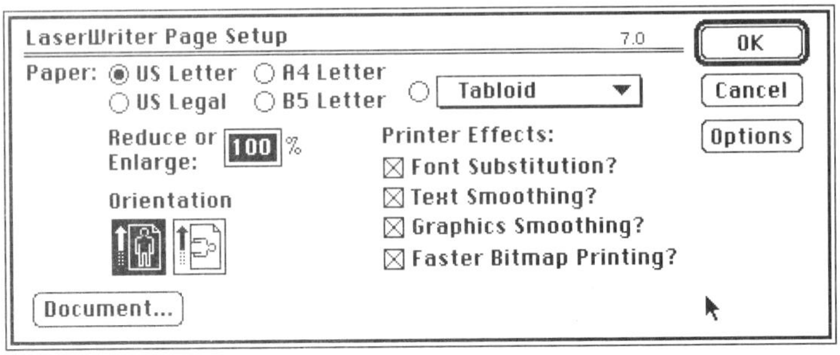

Fig. 7.23
The Page Setup dialog box
for a LaserWriter.

Setting Up the Document

The Document button at the bottom of the Page Setup dialog box opens the secondary dialog box (see fig. 7.24). This dialog box contains Margins, Spreadsheet, and Page Numbering sections for spreadsheet document settings. The following sections explain these document settings.

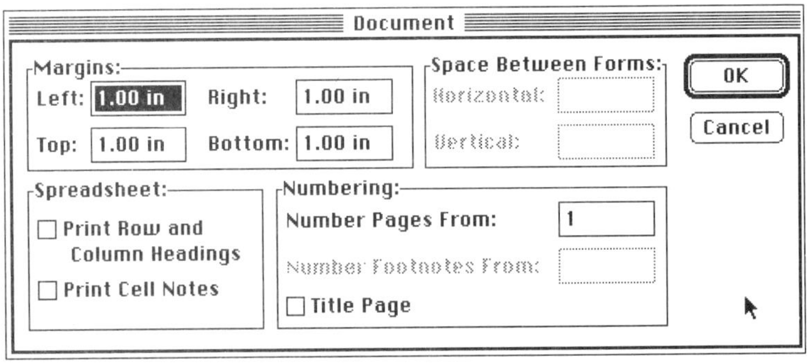

Fig. 7.24
The Document dialog box.

Setting Margins

Each spreadsheet margin—left, right, top, and bottom—has a text box in the Document dialog box. To change document margins, type new measurements in these margin text boxes. The default measurement is in inches.

Numbering Pages

Starting numbers for pages are entered in the Document dialog box. This feature enables you to start with a number other than 1. For example, you may need consecutive page numbering for multiple documents. If the Title Page check box is selected, Works does not print a page number on the first page. Numbering begins with 2 printed on the second page.

Printing Headings and Notes

The Spreadsheet section of the Document dialog box contains two check boxes, one for printing row and column headings and another for printing cell notes. Choosing the check box for headings tells Works to print any row or column headings with the spreadsheet. To print your cell notes with the spreadsheet, choose the second check box.

After entering all the settings in the Document dialog box, click OK. Works then applies the settings to the spreadsheet document.

Adding Manual Page Breaks

As you create a spreadsheet, Works keeps track of its size and, when a page is filled, automatically inserts a page break. In spreadsheets, you can have vertical as well as horizontal page breaks. You can see how your spreadsheet has been paginated by choosing the Page Preview command from the File menu. Although you cannot remove automatic page breaks, you can add your own.

To insert a manual page break, follow these steps:

1. Click the cell you want to appear in the upper left corner of a new page.

2. Open the Format menu and choose Set Page Break.

   Vertical and horizontal dashed lines appear to indicate the boundaries of the new page.

   Works resets the previous automatic page breaks to reflect the new manual page break.

To remove a manual page break, perform the following steps:

1. Select the row below the page break for horizontal breaks, or the column to the right of the page break for vertical breaks.

2. Choose Remove Page Break from the Format menu.

   Works removes the break, and the dashed line disappears.

Chapter 7

Creating Spreadsheets

Previewing a Spreadsheet

You can save substantial amounts of time and paper by using the Print Preview command. Choosing this command from the File menu opens a display similar to the one shown in figure 7.25. Although you cannot see individual words—unless you use large type—you can get a sense of the spreadsheet layout and page breaks. If you have more than one page, use the Previous and Next buttons to flip through the spreadsheet.

To see an enlarged view of the spreadsheet, move the cursor, which now looks like a magnifying glass, across the page and click an area to magnify it. You can drag the magnified document with the cursor, which now looks like a hand. If you are satisfied with the spreadsheet, click the Print button to open the Print dialog box. If you need to make changes, choosing Cancel or clicking the close box returns you to the spreadsheet.

Fig. 7.25
The Print Preview window shows layout and page breaks.

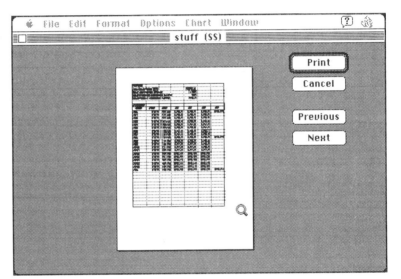

Controlling the Print Settings

The Print dialog box is part of the Macintosh system software, which controls printing for all Macintosh applications. The exact appearance of the dialog box depends on the printer you are using. Figure 7.26 shows a print dialog box for a LaserWriter.

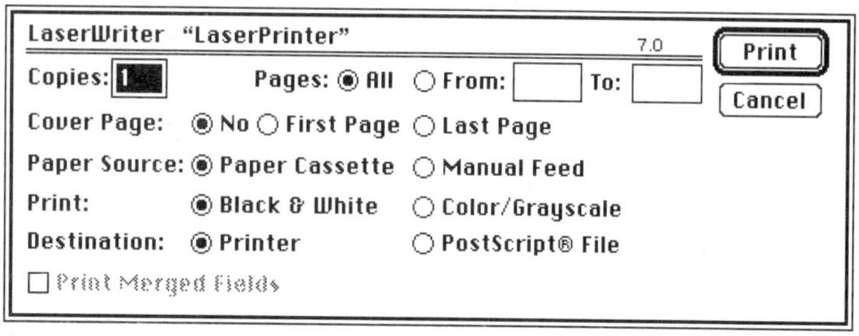

Fig. 7.26
The Print dialog box for a
LaserWriter.

The LaserWriter has settings for number of copies, page range, paper feed, color, and output destination. If you are using a different printer, a different selection of choices is offered in the dialog box.

Printing a Spreadsheet Directly to the Printer

The handy Print One command sends the current spreadsheet directly to the printer, using the settings presently in the Print dialog box. Use this command if you don't need to make any adjustments in printer settings.

Using Spreadsheets with Other Works Modules

You can copy all or part of a spreadsheet into a Works word processing or database document by selecting, copying, and pasting from one module to another. The procedure includes the following steps:

1. Select the material you want to copy.

2. Open the Edit menu and choose Copy. Works copies the selected material to the Clipboard.

3. Open the File menu and choose New.

   If you want to use an existing document, choose Open.

4. Click the icon for the type of the destination document, and then click New.

   With an existing document, double-click its name.

5. Open the Edit menu and choose Paste to insert the spreadsheet material as text.

NOTE

Spreadsheet formulas do not function when pasted into a nonspreadsheet document. You can no longer change figures and have formulas recalculate the results.

Customizing Spreadsheets

You can customize certain features of each Works module by choosing the Preferences command from the Edit menu. Figure 7.27 shows the Spreadsheet Preferences dialog box. You can choose the default font and font size, a choice that is reflected in all subsequent spreadsheet documents. You also can choose the default chart type Works uses when you create a new chart. Charting is discussed in Chapter 9, "Working with Charts."

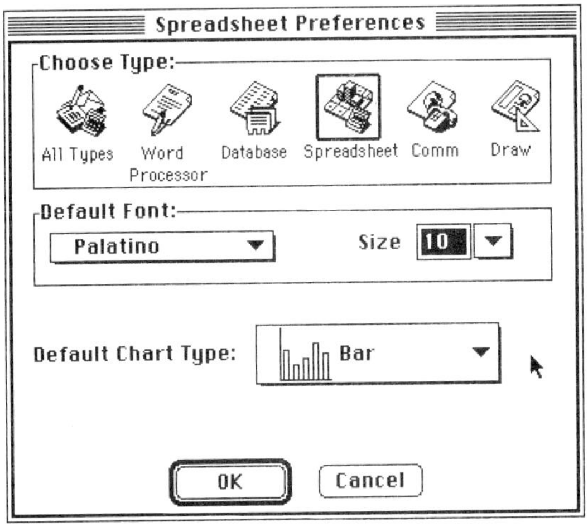

Fig. 7.27

The Spreadsheet Preferences dialog box enables you to choose font, font size, and chart type.

Closing and Quitting

When you are finished with a spreadsheet, you may want to close it and start another, or you may want to quit Works. To close the active spreadsheet, open the File menu and choose Close, or click the close box in the window's upper left corner. If you have a number of files open, use Close All in the File menu to close all open files. If you want to quit Works, you can go directly to Quit in the File menu. You are given a chance to save your files. For more information about saving and quitting, see Chapter 2.

Chapter Summary

n this chapter, you learned the basics of working with the Works spreadsheet module. You learned screen layout and terminology, how to navigate the spreadsheet, and how to enhance your work. You learned methods of selecting and using ranges and ways to control display options. Finally, you learned to preview and print your spreadsheet and how to use spreadsheets with other Works modules.

The two chapters that follow also cover spreadsheet issues. Chapter 8 contains a complete list of functions, and Chapter 9 explains how to use charting features.

Applying Spreadsheet Functions

unctions are built-in calculations that increase the speed and accuracy with which you can create both spreadsheets and databases. Version 3 of Microsoft Works for the Macintosh provides 64 functions. Using all or even a majority of these functions would be unusual, but even if you use only a few, you will find them extremely useful. Functions will save you time otherwise spent writing complex formulas, and increase the accuracy of your work.

The functions divide into broad groups. Some functions help with time and date calculations, and others are specialized for trigonometric or statistical calculations. An important group aids financial modeling. Logic functions enable you to add decision-making capabilities to your documents, and lookup functions can retrieve and reorganize complex information.

Understanding the Structure of Functions

Functions consist of the function *name* and a set of *arguments* surrounded by parentheses (see fig. 8.1). The function name tells Works what type of action to perform, and the arguments specify the values acted upon. The number of arguments can range from none to several. Arguments can be numbers, references to cells and ranges, or even other functions. Commas separate multiple arguments from each other.

When you enter a function and its argument into a cell by pressing Return, you see the result of the function in the cell as you do with formulas. The value in the cell is said to be the value *returned* by the function.

Fig. 8.1
A function in the entry bar.

Sum function —

Function argument —

Fig. 8.1
A function in the entry bar.

Sum function —

Function argument —

	A	B	C	D	E	F	G	H
1	Constants							
2	Base Gravity Value (BGV):				979553.02			
3	Gravimeter Constant (GConst):				1.05055			
4	Gravity reading at calibration pt (GRCal):				3000		Geneva	
5	Gravity value at calibration pt (GVCal):				3150.97		12 pt	
6							Style	
7	*Database*							
8	*Strnid*	*Date*	*Time*	*M1*	*M2*	*M3*	*M4*	*M5*
9	Base	1/19/86	8:00 AM	3,079.96	3,079.94	3,079.97	3079.950	307
10	STN1	1/19/86	9:18 AM	3,085.92	3,085.86	3,085.87		
11	STN2	1/19/86	9:39 AM	3,086.31	3,086.45	3,086.41		
12	STN3	1/19/86	10:01 AM	3,086.44	3,086.85	3,086.92		
13	STN4	1/19/86	10:22 AM	3,086.85	3,087.32	3,087.53		
14	STN5	1/19/86	10:44 AM	3,086.96	3,088.02	3,087.59		
15	STN6	1/19/86	11:06 AM	3,087.16	3,088.95	3,088.17		
16	STN7	1/19/86	11:27 AM	3,087.57	3,089.01	3,088.48		

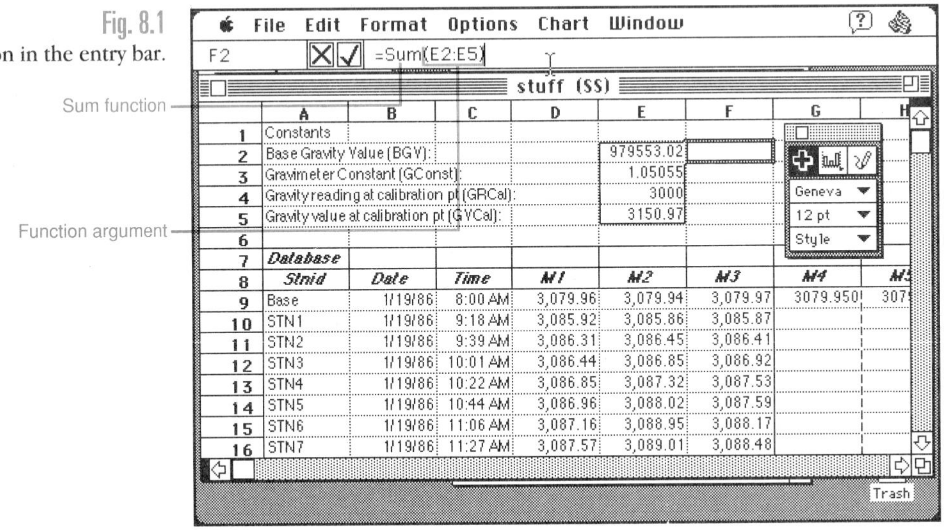

Understanding the Syntax of Functions

Observe a few rules when creating or editing functions. Although these rules are not difficult, they are precise. If you have problems with a function, check first for an error in the way you entered the function.

- Precede a function with an equal sign if it is the first entry in a cell.

- Spell the function name properly.

- Do not space between a function name and the left parenthesis that follows it.

- Do not space within a formula or function.

- Be sure all arguments are provided and in the specified order.

- Use the proper separator: the comma.

Like the functions of which they are a part, arguments also have rules of usage. Arguments can consist of values, ranges that include values, and references to cells containing values. Other important rules include the following:

Part IV

Using Spreadsheets

- An argument should not refer to an empty cell or one containing text.

- Separate multiple arguments with commas.

- Leave no spaces between arguments.

- Leave no space between surrounding parentheses and arguments.

Entering Functions

You can type functions into the entry bar, but the most accurate way to insert them is to use the Paste Function command found on the Edit menu. Pasting includes place holders for the arguments, which helps ensure that you have the right number in the right sequence. Use the following steps to paste a function on the entry bar:

1. Select the cell to receive the function.

2. Open the Edit menu and choose Paste Function.

   The Paste Function dialog box appears (see fig. 8.2).

3. Click the button that selects the function category you want to use.

   The list in the list box changes.

4. Scroll the list, if necessary, to locate the function name.

5. Double-click the function name or click OK.

   The function is pasted on the entry bar.

6. Select the argument place holders and replace them with the correct references.

Editing Functions

When you make an unnoticed syntax error while entering a function, Works finds it and opens a special dialog box for editing the function (see fig. 8.3). You can edit the function in the dialog box and click OK to enter the change, or you can click the Treat As Text button to put the function back in the edit bar. After choosing Treat As Text, click the cell containing the function to select it. In the edit bar, double quotes (") precede the function, indicating it is text. When you have made the necessary corrections, delete the quotes and press Return to enter the corrected function or formula.

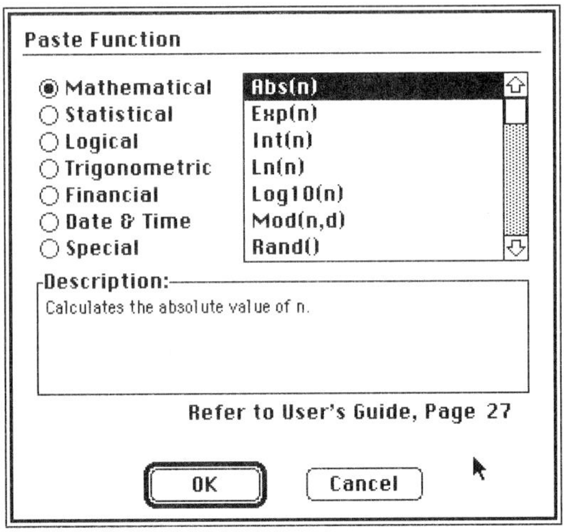

Fig. 8.2
The Paste Function
dialog box.

Fig. 8.2
The Paste Function
dialog box.

Paste Function

- ⦿ Mathematical
- ○ Statistical
- ○ Logical
- ○ Trigonometric
- ○ Financial
- ○ Date & Time
- ○ Special

| Abs(n) |
| Exp(n) |
| Int(n) |
| Ln(n) |
| Log10(n) |
| Mod(n,d) |
| Rand() |

Description:
Calculates the absolute value of n.

Refer to User's Guide, Page 27

[OK]   [Cancel]

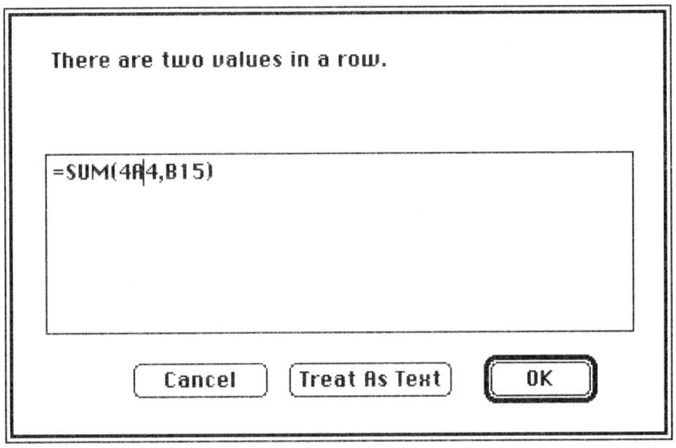

Fig. 8.3
The Edit Function
dialog box.

There are two values in a row.

=SUM(4A4,B15)

[Cancel] [Treat As Text] [OK]

The remainder of this chapter consists of listings and examples of the 64 Works functions. A table precedes each section and lists briefly the functions discussed in that section and their purposes or results. Within sections, the functions are arranged alphabetically.

Using Mathematical Functions

Twelve mathematical functions serve purposes that vary from furnishing random numbers to rounding. Several functions generate logarithms.

Part IV

Using Spreadsheets

Another important group raises numbers to a specific power and derives square roots. Not to be overlooked is Sum, the most frequently used function. Table 8.1 describes the mathematical functions.

Function	Result
Abs(*number*)	Returns the absolute value of *number*.
Exp(*number*)	Raises *e* to the power of *number*.
Int(*number*)	Returns the integer part of *number*.
Ln(*number*)	Returns the natural logarithm, base *e*, of *number*.
Log10(*number*)	Returns the logarithm, base 10, of *number*.
Mod(*number,divisor-number*)	Returns remainder of *number* divided by *divisor-number*.
Rand( )	Returns a random number between 0 and 1.
Round (*number,number of digits*)	Rounds *number* to *number of digits*.
Sign(*number*)	Returns the sign of *number*.
Sqrt(*number*)	Returns square root of *number*.
SSum(*value-1,value-2,...*)	Adds *values* to precision displayed on-screen.
Sum(*value-1,value-2,...*)	Adds *values* to precision entered.

Abs

Syntax: Abs(*number*)

Purpose: Abs lists the absolute value of *number* or reference used as its argument. An absolute value is a number without a positive or negative sign.

Example: =Abs(6-8) and =Abs(2) both equal 2.

Exp

Syntax: Exp(*number*)

Purpose: The Exp function returns *e* raised to the power of *number*, where *e* is 2.71828, the base number of natural logarithms.

Example: =Exp(1) equals 2.71828.

Int

Syntax: Int(*number*)

Purpose: Int yields the integer portion of *number*, rounding down any numbers to the right of the decimal point. Note that other spreadsheets commonly truncate to the right of the decimal.

Example: =Int(5.6) equals 5, but =Int(-5.6) equals -6 due to rounding down.

Ln

Syntax: Ln(*number*)

Purpose: Ln computes the natural logarithm (to the base *e*) of a positive *number*, which is the power to which the base is raised to equal the number.

Example: =Ln(2.71828) equals 1.

Log10

Syntax: Log10(*number*)

Purpose: Log10 computes the base 10 logarithm of a positive *number*. Log10 is the inverse of base 10 exponentiation.

Example: =Log10(10) equals 1.

               =Log10(100000) equals 5.

Mod

Syntax: Mod(*number,divisor*)

Purpose: The Mod function returns the remainder after *number* is divided by *divisor*. *Number* and *divisor* should have the same signs.

Example: =Mod(5,3) equals 2.

Rand

Syntax: Rand( )

Purpose: The Rand function generates a random number from 0 up to but not including 1. A new random number is generated every time the spreadsheet or database is recalculated.

The parentheses are required.

Round

Syntax: Round(*number,number of digits*)

Purpose: The effect of Round depends on the entry for *number of digits*. If the entry is positive, this function rounds *number* to that many decimal places. If *number of digits* is zero, the function rounds *number* to the nearest integer. And, if *number of digits* is negative, the function rounds *number* to the left of the decimal point.

Example: =Round(24.06,1) equals 24.1.

=Round(24.06,0) equals 24.

=Round(375,-2) equals 400.

Sign

Syntax: Sign(*number*)

Purpose: Sign is a test for positive or negative numbers. Positive numbers generate a 1, negative numbers a -1, and zero quantities a 0.

Example: =Sign(44) equals 1.

=Sign(-44) equals -1.

=Sign(0) equals 0.

Sqrt

Syntax: Sqrt(*number*)

Purpose: Sqrt calculates the square root of a positive *number*. If *number* is negative, the system generates an error message.

Example: =Sqrt(25) equals 5.

SSum

Syntax: SSum(*value-1,value-2,...*)

Purpose: SSum adds the *values* in a range exactly as they appear on-screen rather than using the underlying values in the cell.

Example: If you enter 1.888 in a cell formatted to display two decimals, the cell shows the value 1.89. SSum adds 1.89 into a total, whereas the Sum function adds the underlying value (1.888) to the total.

Sum

Syntax: Sum(*value-1,value-2,...*)

Purpose: Sum adds the *values* in a range based on the underlying value entered in the cell. The function treats blank cells or text entries as zero. Compare with the SSum function which adds values as they appear on-screen.

Using Statistical Functions

Statistical functions can save enormous amounts of time that are needed otherwise to calculate standard deviation, variance, and averages. Other statistical functions count entries and find maximum and minimum values.

Table 8.2 Statistical Functions		
Function	*Result*
Average(*value-1,value-2,...*)	Returns average of values in *values*.
Count(*value-1,value-2,...*)	Returns the count of values in *values*.
Max(*value-1,value-2,...*)	Returns maximum value in *values*.
Min(*value-1,value-2,...*)	Returns minimum value in *values*.
StDev(*value-1,value-2,...*)	Returns standard deviation of *values*.
Var(*value-1,value-2,...*)	Returns variance of *values*.

Average

Syntax: Average(*value-1,value-2,...*)

Purpose: Average adds the *values* in a range then divides the sum by the number of values. The function ignores blank cells and text entries.

Example: If cells A1 to A4 contain the values:12, 10, 5, and 5, then =Average(A1:A4) equals 8.

Count

Syntax: Count(*value-1,value-2,...*)

Purpose: Count gives the number of cells in the list of arguments. The function ignores cells containing text and blank cells.

Example: If cells A1 to A4 contain the values 12, 10, 5, and 5, then =Count(A1:A4) equals 4.

Max

Syntax: Max(*value-1,value-2,...*)

Purpose: Max returns the largest number in the range specified by the arguments. The function ignores cells containing text and blank cells.

Example: If cells A1 to A4 contain the values 12, 10, 5, and 5, then =Max(A1:A4) equals 12.

Min

Syntax: Min(*value-1,value-2,...*)

Purpose: Min returns the smallest number in the range specified by the arguments. Min ignores cells containing text and blank cells.

Example: If cells A1 to A4 contain the values 12, 10, 5, and 5, then =Min(A1:A4) equals 5.

StDev

Syntax: StDev(*value-1,value-2,...*)

Purpose: StDev gives a sample standard deviation of the arguments. The function ignores cells containing text and blank cells. In calculating standard deviation, Works uses the following formula:

=Sqrt(Var(value-1, value-2,...))

Example: If C5:C10 contains 18, 21, 6, 8, 14 and 30, then =StDev(C5:C10) equals 8.86.

Var

Syntax: Var(*value-1,value-2,...*)

Purpose: The Var function returns the variance of the numbers in the list of arguments. Var ignores cells containing text and blank cells. You can compute true population variance by including an average of the entire population in the calculation, as in the following example.

Example: =Var(Population,Average(Population))

Using Logical Functions

Logical functions return only true (1) or false (0) answers. Arguments must be values or references to cells containing values. These functions ignore text arguments.

Table 8.3 Logical Functions	Function	Result
	And(*value-1,value-2,...*)	Returns 1 (true) if all arguments are true. Returns 0 (false) otherwise.
	False( )	Returns 0 (false).
	If(*number,value-if-true,value-if-false*)	Returns *value-if-true* if *number* is true. Returns *value-if-false* if number is *false*.
	IsBlank(*value-1,value-2,...*)	Returns 1 (true) if all *values* are blank or text; otherwise returns 0 (false).
	IsError(*value*)	Returns 1 (true) if *value* is *Error*; otherwise returns 0 (false).
	IsNA(*value*)	Returns 1 (true) if *value* is N/A; otherwise returns 0 (false).
	Not(*number*)	Returns 1 (true) if *number* is 0 (false). Returns 0 (false) if *number* is 1 (true).
	Or(*value-1,value-2,...*)	Returns 1 (true) if any logical value in values is 1 (true); returns 0 (false) if all values are 0 (false).
	True( )	Returns 1 (true).

And

Syntax:	And(*value-1,value-2,...*)
Purpose:	The And function tests the list of *values* in the arguments. If any value is false, the function returns the value 0 (false). If all values are true, the function returns the value 1 (true).
Example:	=And(2*2=4,3*2=6) returns 1 (true).
	=And(2*2=6,3*2=6) returns 0 (false).

Chapter 8

Applying Spreadsheet Functions

False

Syntax: False( )

Purpose: The False function is primarily for testing spreadsheet logic. This function enables you to place a False entry in a specific location. The function takes no arguments, but you need the parentheses.

If

Syntax: If(*number,value-if-true,value-if-false*)

Purpose: The If function enables you to write a branching instruction equivalent to the verbal statement "If something is true, do this; otherwise, do that." Effective use of the If function can give your spreadsheet decision-making power.

Example: If cell A1 contains the number 39, then the function =If(A1>40,A2,A3) returns the value in cell A3.

IsBlank

Syntax: IsBlank(*value-1,value-2,...*)

Purpose: If all cells specified in the arguments are blank, the IsBlank function returns the value 1 (true). If any cell contains a number, IsBlank returns 0 (false). The function treats cells containing text as blanks.

Example: If cells A1 through A4 are empty, then =IsBlank(A1:A4) equals 1 (true).

IsError

Syntax: IsError(*value*)

Purpose: If any single cell specified in *value* contains an *Error* message, the IsError function returns the value 1 (true). If no *Error* message is present, IsError returns a 0 (false). You can use this function to test the components of a formula for errors that may cause an *Error* message.

IsNA

Syntax: IsNA(*value*)

Purpose: N/A is the *Not Available* warning message. If any cell specified in *value* contains the N/A message, the IsNA function returns the value 1 (true). If no N/A warnings are found, the function returns a 0.

Not

Syntax: Not(*number*)

Purpose: The Not function returns a truth value opposite to that of *number*. In other words, if *number* is 1 (true), then the function returns 0 (false). Or, if *number* is 0 (false), the function returns 1 (true).

Example: =Not(5+5=10) equals 0 (false).

Or

Syntax: Or(*value-1*,*value-2*,...)

Purpose: The Or function returns a 1 (true) if *any value* in the argument is true. If *all* arguments are false, the function returns 0 (false).

Example: =Or(2+2=5,4+4=8) returns a 1 (true).

            =Or(2+2=5,4+4=9) returns a 0 (false).

True

Syntax: True( )

Purpose: True returns the value 1 (true) in any cell where you place it. The True function is primarily for testing. You do not use arguments, but you do need the parentheses. See the related False function.

Example: If A1 contains True( ), then =A1 returns 1 (true).

Using Trigonometric Functions

Works' trigonometric functions greatly ease the burden of computing the angular measurements associated with geometric analysis. Functions derive sines, cosines, and tangents and convert between degrees and radians.

Table 8.4
Trigonometric Functions

Function	Result
ACos(*number*)	Returns arccosine of *number*.
ASin(*number*)	Returns arcsine of *number*.
ATan(*number*)	Returns arctangent of *number*.
ATan2(*x-number*, *y-number*)	Returns arctangent of point (*x-number*, *y-number*).
Cos(*number*)	Returns cosine of *number*.
Degrees(*number*)	Converts *number* from radians to degrees.
Pi( )	Returns value of *pi* to 17 places.
Radians(*number*)	Converts *number* from degrees to radians.
Sin(*number*)	Returns sine of *number*.
Tan(*number*)	Returns tangent of *number*.

ACos

Syntax: ACos(*number*)

Purpose: ACos returns the arccosine of the argument, that is, the angle for which *number* is the cosine. The function returns the result in radians.

Example: Because the cosine of 45 degrees is 0.707, =ACos (0.707) returns 0.785, which equals the radians in 45 degrees.

ASin

Syntax: ASin(*number*)

Purpose: ASin returns the arcsine of the angle whose sine is the function argument. The arcsine is the angle whose sine is *number*. The function presents the result in radians.

Example: Because the sine of 90 degrees is 1, =ASin (1) returns 1.570, which equals the radians in the sine.

ATan

Syntax: ATan(*number*)

Purpose: The ATan function returns the arctangent of *number*. The arctangent is the angle whose tangent is *number*. The function presents the result in radians.

Example: Because the tangent of 45 degrees is 1, =ATan (1) returns the value .785, which equals the radians in 45 degrees.

ATan2

Syntax: ATan2(*x-number, y-number*)

Purpose: The ATan2 function returns the arctangent of the angle defined by *x-number* and *y-number*. The arctangent is the angle, in radians, defined by the point described by *x-number* and *y-number*.

Example: The point (3,4) defines an angle of 53.13 degrees (or .927 radians). Thus, =ATan2(3,4) returns the value .927, which equals the radians in 51.13 degrees.

Cos

Syntax: Cos(*number*)

Purpose: The Cos function returns the cosine of an angle measured in radians.

Example: =Cos(1.047) returns 0.5.

Degrees

Syntax: Degrees(*number*)

Purpose: The Degrees function converts radians to degrees. The equation used is as follows: Degrees = Radians * 180/π.

Example: A circle contains 360 degrees or 2 radians.
Therefore,=Degrees(2*(π)) returns 360 degrees.

Pi

Syntax: Pi( )

Purpose: The Pi function returns the value of 3.14159. You do not use arguments, but do need the parentheses.

Example   If cell A1 contains =Pi( ), then the value in the cell is 3.14159.

Radians

Syntax: Radians(*number*)

Purpose: The Radians function converts degrees to radians.

Example: A circle contains 360 degrees or 2 radians. Therefore, =Radians(180) returns 3.14159.

Sin

Syntax: Sin(*number*)

Purpose: The Sin function returns the sine of *number*, when *number* is entered in radians.

Example: =Sin(Pi( )/2) equals 1.

Tan

Syntax: Tan(*number*)

Purpose: The Tan function returns the tangent of *number*, when *number* is entered in radians.

Example: =Tan(0.785)=.999.

Part IV

Using Spreadsheets

Using Financial Functions

The financial functions principally deal with present and future values of investments. Other functions compute periodic payments and the number of even payments for given terms.

Table 8.5
Financial Functions

Function	Result
FV(*rate,nper,pmt,pv,type*)	Calculates future value of an investment.
IRR(*range,guess*)	Calculates internal rate of return of *range*.
MIRR(*range,safe,risk*)	Calculates modified internal rate of return of *range*.
NPer(*rate,pmt,pv,fv,type*)	Calculates number of payments for an investment.
NPV(*rate,value-1,value-2,...*)	Determines net present value of *values*.
Pmt(*rate,nper,pv,fv,type*)	Calculates period payments for an investment.
PV(*rate,nper,pmt,fv,type*)	Calculates present value of an investment.
Rate(*nper,pmt,pv,fv,type,guess*)	Calculates the growth rate of an investment.

FV

Syntax: FV(*rate,nper,pmt,pv,type*)

Purpose: The FV function gives the future value of an investment of equal payments at a fixed interest rate over a specified term. The function takes several arguments:

rate   Interest rate in percentage points

nper   Number of payment periods

pmt   Payment per period (entered as a negative number)

pv   Present value

Chapter 8

Applying Spreadsheet Functions

This entry is optional. If nothing is entered, the function assumes 0.

type   Time of payment
Enter 1 for payments made at the end of each period, or 0 for payments made at the beginning of a period. This entry is optional. If it is omitted, the function assumes 0.

Example: The following example computes the future value of a $1000 account earning 7% annual interest for 25 years when $300 payments are added each month. Note that the annual rate and number of years were divided by 12 to yield monthly rates.

Assume the following arguments for the function:

rate   7.0/12 = monthly rate

nper   25*12 = number of months

pmt   -300 = monthly payment

pv   -1000 = present value

type   1 = payment at end of period

The function is written as follows: =FV(7%/12,25*12, -300,-1000,1).

The future value of the investment is $250,164.

IRR

Syntax: IRR(*range,guess*)

Purpose: The internal rate of return is the interest rate that gives a cash flow series a net present value of zero. The result is produced by an iterative process that starts with a guess and cycles through twenty tries at a solution. The argument range specifies the series of cash flows to be analyzed. The argument *guess* gives the function a starting value. Try a value between 0 and 1, or try another value if a *guess* in that range returns an *Error* message. (Spreadsheets only.)

Example: The *range* A1:F1 contains cash flows of -7000, 2000, 2000, -3000, 2000, and 6000 dollars. You guess that the yield from this income should be around 10%. You want to know the actual internal rate of return.

The formula is =IRR(10%,A1:F1).

The resulting IRR value is 10%.

MIRR

Syntax: MIRR(*range,safe,risk*)

Purpose: The MIRR function computes the modified internal rate of return of a series and cash flows. The *safe* and *risk* arguments modify the computation. *Safe* is the rate required to finance negative cash flows. *Risk* is the income rate from reinvestment of positive cash flows. (Spreadsheets only.)

Example: The *range* A1:A5 contains cash flows of -40000, 20000, -4000, 30000, and 6000 dollars. You believe you will have to borrow at 14% to finance negative cash flows, and you think you can earn 16% by reinvesting your positive cash flows.

The formula is =MIRR(A1:A5,14%,16%).

The resulting MIRR value is 13.71%.

NPer

Syntax: NPer(*rate,pmt,pv,fv,type*)

Purpose: The NPer function computes the number of payment periods required to liquidate an investment with constant payments. The function takes several arguments:

rate   Interest rate in percentage points

pmt   Payment per period (entered as a negative number)

pv   Present value

fv   Future value (optional) If this entry is omitted, the function assumes 0.

type   Time of payments Enter 1 for payments made at the end of each period, or 0 for payments made at the beginning of a period. This entry is optional. If it is omitted, the function assumes 0.

Example: The following example computes how long it would take to repay a $15,000 car loan, assuming an annual interest rate of 8% and monthly payments of $200. Note that the annual rate and number of years were divided by 12 to yield monthly rates.

Assume the following arguments for the function:

rate   8%/12 = monthly rate

pmt   -200 = monthly payment

pv   -15000 = present value

fv   0

type   1 = payment at end of period

The function is written as follows: =NPer(8%/12, -200,15000,0,1).

The loan would be repaid in 103.35 months.

NPV

Syntax: NPV(*rate,value-1,value-2,...*)

Purpose: The NPV function computes the net present value of future cash flows given a constant *rate* of interest. The *values* in the argument must be numbers or references to numbers.

Example: You are considering an investment that provides a 12% yield (1% per month) and monthly, end-of-month payments of 700, 1200, 1400 and 1800 dollars. What should you pay for such an investment?

The function is written as follows: =NPV(1%,700,1200,1400,1800).

The present value of the investment is $4958.02.

Pmt

Syntax: Pmt(*rate,nper,pv,fv,type*)

Purpose: The Pmt function returns the periodic payment necessary for a loan or investment. The function takes several arguments:

rate   Interest rate per period

nper   Total number of payment periods

pv   Present value

fv   Future value (optional)
            If this entry is omitted, the function assumes 0.

type   Time of payments
            Enter 1 for payments made at the end of each period, or 0 for payments made at the beginning of a period. This entry is optional. If it is omitted, the function assumes 0.

Example: The following example computes the monthly payment required to retire a 30-year (360-month), $100000 mortgage with an interest rate of 12% (1% per rates).

Assume the following arguments for the function:

rate   1% = monthly rate

nper   360 monthly payments

pv   -100000 = present value

fv   0

type   1 = payment at end of period

The function is written as follows:
=Pmt(1%,360,100000,0,1).

The monthly payment on the loan would be $1018.43.

> **TIP**
>
> Be careful to enter numbers without formatting (such as commas), because Works will incorrectly interpret them as argument separators.

PV

Syntax: PV(*rate,nper,pmt,fv,type*)

Purpose: The PV function calculates the present value of an investment. The function takes several arguments:

rate   Interest rate per period

Chapter 8
Applying Spreadsheet Functions

nper	Total number of payment periods
pmt	Payments paid (a negative number) or received (a positive number)
fv	Future value (optional) If this entry is omitted, the function assumes 0.
type	Time of payments Enter 1 for payments made at the end of each period, or 0 for payments made at the beginning of a period. This entry is optional. If it is omitted, the function assumes 0.

Example:
You feel you can make $1000 monthly mortgage payments. If interest rates are 12% and you want a 25-year mortgage, what will the mortgage amount be?

Assume the following arguments for the function:

rate	1% = monthly rate
nper	300 monthly payments
pmt	1000 payment amount
fv	0
type	1 = payment at end of period

The function is written as follows: =PV(1%,300,1000,0,1).

You could take a $95896 mortgage.

Rate

Syntax: Rate(*nper,pmt,pv,fv,type,guess*)

Purpose: The Rate function determines the probable interest rate for an investment based on its initial value and probable value at the end of a specified time period. The function takes several arguments:

nper	Total number of payment periods
pmt	Payments paid (a negative number) or received (a positive number)
pv	present value

| *fv* | future value (optional) |

| *type* | Time of payments
Enter 1 for payments made at the end of each period or 0 for payments made at the beginning of a period. This entry is optional. If it is omitted, the function assumes 0. |

| *guess* | A starting estimate of the probable interest rate (optional) |

Example:

You plan to purchase a condominium for $85000 and sell it in 5 years for $100000. You collect annual rent of $9600. You guess that your investment has an 8% annual rate of return.

Assume the following arguments for the function:

nper	60 monthly rent periods
pmt	800 monthly payment
pv	-85000 present value
fv	100000 future value
type	0 = payment at beginning of period
guess	8%/12 for a monthly rate.

The function is written as follows: =Rate(60,800, -85000,100000,0,8%/12).

The proposal yields 1.2% per month or 14.4% per year.

Using Date and Time Functions

In Works, dates have consecutive serial *numbers*, from 0 (January 1, 1904) to 49710 (February 6, 2040), which enable you to perform mathematical operations on dates. You can add and subtract these serial numbers in formulas to generate results such as the number of days between two dates or the date 478 days in the future.

Decimals attached to date serial numbers represent time. For example, the serial number 49710.5 is noon on February 6, 2040. You can use date and time functions to convert serial numbers to dates and vice versa. Other functions extract parts of the serial number to produce results like the time, the day of the week, or the year.

Table 8.6
Date and Time Functions

Function	Result
Date(*year,month,day*)	Gives the serial number of the specified date.
Day(*cell-reference*)	Extracts the day of the month from the date.
Hour(*cell-reference*)	Extracts the hour from a time value.
Minute(*cell-reference*)	Extracts the minutes from a time value.
Month(*cell-reference*)	Extracts the month from the date value.
Now( )	Returns the current date and time.
Second(*cell-reference*)	Extracts the seconds from a time value.
Time(*hour,min,sec*)	Returns the serial number of the specified time.
Weekday(*cell-reference*)	Returns the day of the week from a date value.
Year(*cell-reference*)	Extracts the year from a date.

Date

NOTE

A serial number will not appear in a cell with the date format. To see a numeric result, change the cell format to number.

Syntax: Date(*year,month,day*)

Purpose: The Date function returns the date as a serial number. The argument *year* must be in the range from Jan. 1, 1904 to Feb. 6, 2040. The argument for *month* must be a number from 1 to 12. The argument for *day* must be a number from 1 to 31.

Example: =Date(1993,4,5) returns the serial value 32602.

Day

Syntax: Day(*cell-reference*)

Purpose: The day function extracts the day portion of the serial number. The *cell-reference* must contain a date, either as a serial number or in a date format.

Example: Cell A1 contains the date 4/5/1993. Therefore, =Date(A1) returns the value 5.

Hour

Syntax:	Hour(*cell-reference*)
Purpose:	The Hour function extracts the decimal portion of the time and expresses it as a numeral between 1 and 24.
Example:	Cell A5 contains the time 6:15:24 p.m. Therefore, =Hour(A5) returns 18, which represents 6 p.m.

Minute

Syntax:	Minute(*cell-reference*)
Purpose:	The Minute function extracts the minutes portion of the time and expresses it as a numeral between 1 and 60.
Example:	If the current time is 10:50:30, then =Minute(Now( )) returns the value 50.

Month

Syntax:	Month(*cell-reference*)
Purpose:	The Month function extracts the month portion of the date serial number and returns an integer between 1 and 12.
Example:	If A2 contains the serial number 32445, then =Month(A2) returns the value 10 (representing October).

Now

Syntax:	Now( )
Purpose:	The Now function returns the current date and time as a serial number based on your computer clock. Every recalculation of the spreadsheet then updates the number.

Second

Syntax: Second(*cell-reference*)

Purpose: The Second function extracts the seconds from a serial number located in *cell-reference*. The value is returned as an integer between 0 and 60.

Example: If, in cell D6, the function =Now( ) returns the time 12:29:30, then the function =Second(D6) returns 30.

Time

Syntax: Time(*hour,min,sec*)

Purpose: The Time function converts the numbers entered as arguments into the fractional part of a serial number.

Example: =Time(6,0,0) returns the value .25, representing one-quarter of a day.

Weekday

Syntax: Weekday(*cell-reference*)

Purpose: The Weekday function extracts the weekday portion of the serial number. The values returned range from 1 (Sunday) to 7 (Saturday).

Example: If cell C2 contains the date 5/7/93, then =Weekday(C2) returns the value 6, representing Friday.

Year

Syntax: Year(c*ell-reference*)

Purpose: The Year function extracts the year portion of a serial number.

Example: If cell A1 contains the serial number 32250, then =Year(A1) returns the value 1992.

Using Special-Purpose Functions

Works also contains a group of *special-purpose functions*, used primarily for locating information.

Table 8.7
Special-Purpose Functions

Function	Purpose
Choose (*index,value-1,value-2,...*)	Chooses the value located at *index* from a list of values.
Error( )	Places the value *Error* in a cell.
HLookup(*lookup-value,compare-range,index-number*)	Searches for and retrieves a value from a table.
Index(*range,row,column*)	Extracts the value where a column and row in a range intersect.
Lookup(*lookup-value,compare-range,result-range*)	Finds the item in *compare-range* which is less than or equal to *lookup value* and returns the result in *result-range*.
Match(*lookup-value,compare-range,type*)	Compares *lookup-value* with *compare-range* and locates a matching value which fits *type*.
NA( )	Places N/A value in a cell.
Type(*value*)	Returns the type of cell entry in *value*.
VLookup(*lookup-value,compare-range,index-number*)	Searches for and retrieves a value from a table.

Choose

Syntax: Choose(*index,value-1,value-2,...*)

Purpose: The Choose function returns the value found at the position *index*.

Example: =Choose(3,10,20,30) returns 30, the third value.

Error

Syntax: Error( )

Purpose: The Error function enables you to place an intentional
           error in your spreadsheet while testing your work.
           The function takes no arguments, but you need the
           parentheses.

HLookup

Syntax: HLookup(*lookup-value,compare-range,index-number*)

Purpose: The HLookup function searches horizontally across the
           first row of *compare-range* for the *lookup-value* in a
           table. HLookup then moves down the column by *index-
           number* and returns the value found. (Spreadsheets
           only.)

Example: =HLookup(3000,A1:C3,2) searches the first row in the
           range A1:C3 for the value 3000. When 3000 is found, the
           search moves down that row 2 cells and places the value
           found there in the cell containing the function.

Index

Syntax: Index(*range,row,column*)

Purpose: The Index function returns the value where a column and
           row intersect in a range. (Spreadsheets only.)

Example: =Index(A1:C3,2,3) starts at the upper left corner of the
           range A1:C3 and moves down 2 rows and right 3 col-
           umns, returning the value in cell C2.

Lookup

Syntax: Lookup(*lookup-value,compare-range,result-range*)

Purpose: The Lookup function searches the *compare-range* for the
           largest value equal to or less than *lookup-value.* Lookup
           returns the corresponding entry in *result-range* to the cell
           containing the function. The two ranges must be either
           rows or columns of the same length. The *compare-range*
           values must be in ascending order. (Spreadsheets only.)

Example: If cells A1:C2 contain the following values,

A1   7

B1   11

C1   13

A2   50

B2   45

C2   20

then the function =Lookup(12,A1:C1,A2:C2) returns the value 45 to the cell containing the function.

Match

Syntax: Match(*lookup-value,compare-range,type*)

Purpose: The Match function looks in the *compare-range* and returns a number indicating the position of any items matching *lookup-value*. The type of match desired is indicated by choice of the *match-type*. Comparison proceeds left to right across rows in the range. (Spreadsheets only.)

The three match-*types* are the following:

1   Finds the largest value less than or equal to *lookup-value*. Comparison values must be in ascending order.

-1   Finds the smallest value greater than or equal to *lookup-value*. Comparison values must be in descending order.

0   Finds the first value equal to the *lookup-value*.

Example: If cells A1:C3 contain the following values,

5   12   16

4   3   10

3   55   18

then the formula =Match(3,A1:C3,0) returns the value 5.

NA

Syntax: NA( )

Purpose: The NA function is primarily a testing function that places a N/A (Not Available) value in the cell the function occupies.

Type

Syntax: Type(*value*)

Purpose: The Type function returns a number based on the contents of the cell:

If the cell contains a number, the function returns a 1.

If the cell contains text or is blank, the function returns a 2.

If the cell contains N/A, the function returns an 8.

If the cell contains *Error*, the function returns a 16.

VLookup

Syntax: VLookup(*lookup-value,compare-range,index-number*)

Purpose: The VLookup function searches vertically down the first column of *compare-range* for the largest value equal to or less than *lookup-value*. VLookup then moves across that row by *index-number* and returns the value found. *Compare-range* values must be in ascending order. (Spreadsheets only.)

Example: =VLookup(3000,A1:C3,2) searches the first column in the range A1:C3 for the largest value less than or equal to 3000. When the value is found, the search moves across that row 2 cells and returns the value found to the cell containing the function.

Chapter Summary

T his chapter provided an organized listing of the 64 functions in Works. Although you may only use a few of them, time spent familiarizing yourself with the purpose of the various functions can result in increased accuracy and saved time in any spreadsheet or database where you can put a function to work.

Working with Charts

S preadsheets are powerful tools, but spreadsheets are often difficult to interpret. You could pore over columns of figures on multiple pages and still not grasp the significance of results that may have taken many hours to compile. Charts present spreadsheet information that viewers can understand easily.

Works provides a charting resource on the Spreadsheet menu. The Chart command lets you produce effective charts ranging from quick, virtually automatic presentations to charts enhanced with varied fonts, patterns, and colors. You can choose among six chart types to find the one best suited to your purpose. You can add custom touches to emphasize specific features. Charts are linked to a spreadsheet, so changing your data changes the chart. You even can attach multiple charts to a single spreadsheet so that you can examine the same data from different viewpoints.

Understanding Chart Types in Works

One key to successfully communicating your spreadsheet message is choosing the proper chart type. The six types available in Works provide a choice for any situation. This section briefly describes each chart type and suggests when you may want to choose a particular type.

Data Series

The basis of any chart is a *data series*. A single chart element such as a bar, a line, or a pie wedge represents a series. You specify a series when the chart is created by highlighting spreadsheet ranges or typing in a range of cells you want to chart. A Works chart can represent from 1 to 4 series. Each series is comprised of one or more *data points*. A data point is a cell entry used to create a chart element. A Works chart can include up to 400 separate data points.

Bar and Line Charts

These two types of charts are grouped together because they have a number of similar features. Both use horizontal and vertical axes as their basic structure. The horizontal axis of the chart is referred to as the *x-axis*. This axis is used to display the data series. *Legends*, labels along the horizontal axis, identify each series. The vertical axis of the chart, often referred to as the *y-axis*, is typically used as a measure of quantity, such as dollars or numbers (see fig. 9.1).

Fig. 9.1
A typical bar chart.

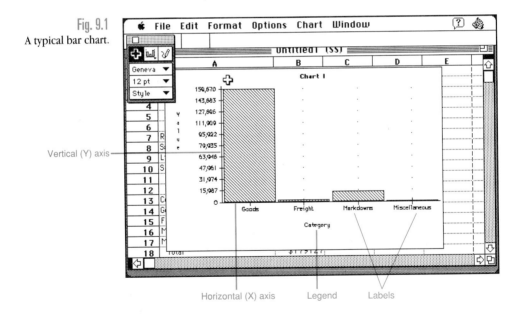

Vertical (Y) axis

Horizontal (X) axis   Legend   Labels

Bar and line charts are useful for showing trends over time and the relationships between two series of data (see fig. 9.2).

Fig. 9.2
A typical line chart based on the same information as the bar chart.

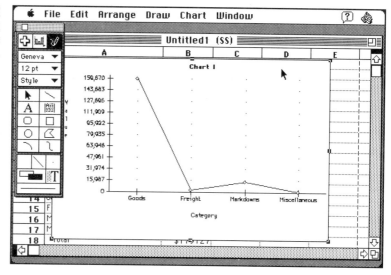

Stack and Pie Charts

Stack and pie charts also share features (see fig. 9.3 and fig. 9.4). They are both effective in showing data as part of a whole. In the section of this chapter called "Formatting a Chart," you will learn how to alter the color or pattern of chart segments to emphasize particular points. You also can pull a wedge away from a pie chart to emphasize a particular segment.

Combination Charts

The combination chart combines a bar chart of one data series with a line chart of another. The two series are combined on a single chart background (see fig. 9.5). This chart type is useful for comparing the trend of one series against another. The two series are easy to distinguish visually. The series presented as bars is emphasized.

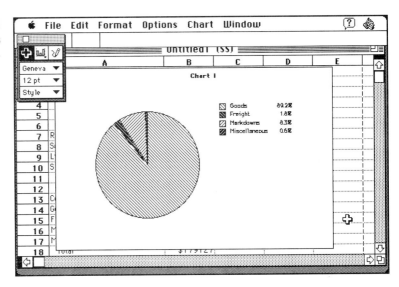

Fig. 9.3

A pie chart emphasizes portions of the whole.

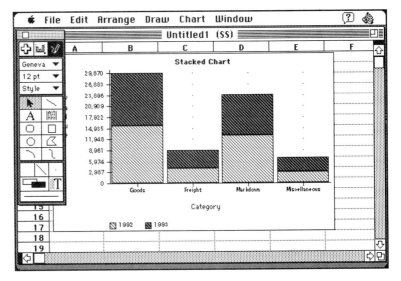

Fig. 9.4

A stack chart shows two years' results.

Hi-Lo-Close Charts

This chart type is a specialized variation of the combination chart typically used to show the high, low, and closing prices of a stock or bond (see fig. 9.6). The range for each series is shown as a vertical bar running from the high to low value. A small horizontal line crosses the chart at the closing price.

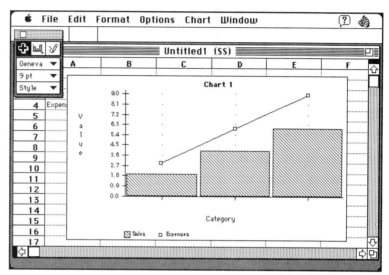

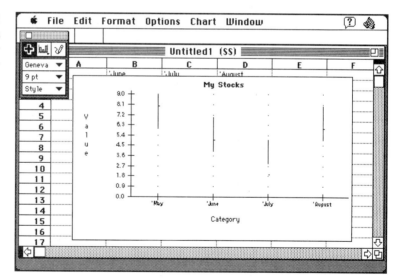

Chapter 9

Working with Charts

Setting the Default Chart Type

Although the frequently used bar chart is the default setting, you can change the type of chart that opens when you choose New Chart from the Chart menu. Use these steps:

1. Open the Edit menu and choose Preferences.

2. In the Preferences dialog box, choose the Spreadsheet icon.

3. Click anywhere in the Default Chart Type box (see fig. 9.7); then drag in the list that appears to select the type of chart you want when you choose New Chart.

4. Click OK to complete the change and close the Spreadsheet Preferences dialog box.

Fig. 9.7
Change the default chart type from this dialog box.

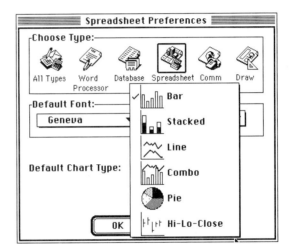

Understanding Chart Concepts

Charts are a specialized type of Draw object. When you create or edit a chart, the process and tools are similar to those used when you create a drawing. The chart appears on a Draw layer, which is created on top of the spreadsheet. The familiar Draw tools are available along with some specially tailored for charting purposes. If you are not familiar with the Works Draw module, you may want to review Chapter 5, "Creating Drawings," before modifying your charts.

Selecting Information To Chart

The only difficult part of charting is learning to select the proper information. In this section, the process is explained by demonstrating basic charting techniques. The paragraphs that follow show several completed charts. You will learn how to create similar charts in the section called "Quick Charting." For now, just observe the examples and study the principles demonstrated.

Figure 9.8 is about as basic as a chart can get. Cell A1 contains the word *Sales*, and cell B1 contains the number 10. Selecting A1 and B1, and then choosing New Chart from the Chart menu produces the chart. Although the chart looks as if it contains a rectangle, this chart is actually a bar chart with a single large bar. The vertical scale (y-axis) measures the bar's magnitude, which is 10. Notice the legend, a box labeled Sales, toward the bottom of the chart. Works derived this legend from the label in cell A1 of the spreadsheet. In addition, Works automatically added the label Category along the horizontal axis and Value along the vertical axis.

Fig. 9.8
A simple chart with only one value.

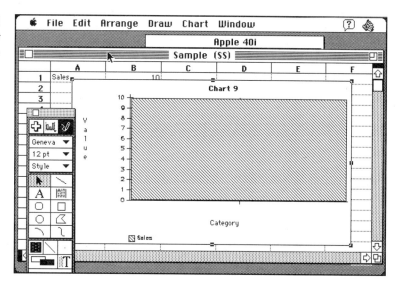

TIP

You can click the Chart button on the tool palette as a shortcut for choosing the New Chart command.

Next, a second value is added. The number 20 is put in cell C1; then cells A1 through C1 are selected, and New Chart is chosen from the Chart menu. The result is shown in figure 9.9. Now there are two bars, with values 10 and 20, on the chart. Even though you now have two cells with data, you still have only one *series* of data—a series called Sales.

Chapter 9

Working with Charts

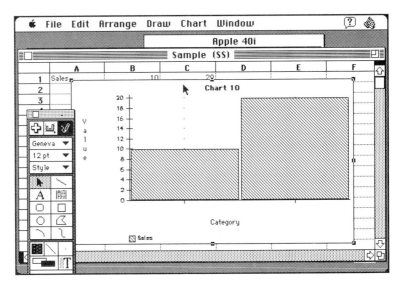

Fig. 9.9
A second value creates a
second bar.

In figure 9.10, a second series has been introduced. The Expense
numbers, on row 2, have been selected along with the original Sales
numbers. Notice that a new legend called Expense has been added. The
cells containing labels must be selected as part of the range to be
charted, or no legends will be generated.

Fig. 9.10
A new series creates new
bars and a new
legend item.

New legend

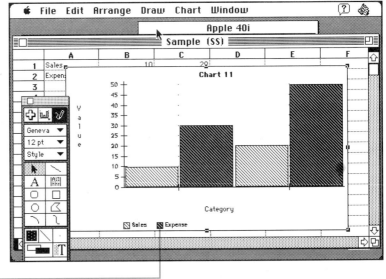

Part IV

Using Spreadsheets

The final point in this short demonstration is made by figure 9.11. Examine the spreadsheet behind this chart and notice two important changes. First, the Sales and Expense series now run vertically, down columns B and C. Second, a new set of labels has been added in column A, which defines elements of the series. Works has added labels just below the bars based on the labels in Column A. The vertical reorientation of the series has not changed the presentation.

Fig. 9.11
Labels have been added in column A.

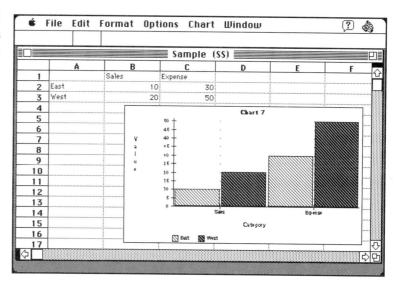

As you are learning to chart with Works, the easiest approach is to construct a simple model of your intended project, such as those in this section, before proceeding with complex data entry. Later in this chapter, you will learn how to control every aspect of a chart, but understanding the rules of automatic charting helps you use this handy feature with confidence and accuracy.

Understanding the Chart Tool Palette

The tool palette used in Chart is similar to those found in other modules (see fig. 9.13 in the section "Moving and Resizing a Chart"). You open the palette by clicking the Draw tool on the tool palette, or by choosing Draw On from the Window menu. In the spreadsheet module, the three tools at the top of the list are different from other modules. The Spreadsheet tool is identified by a plus sign. The Chart tool shows a small bar chart, and the Draw tool shows a pencil drawing a line.

Chapter 9

Working with Charts

The Spreadsheet Tool

A chart exists on a Draw layer on top of the spreadsheet to which the chart is attached. When the Draw layer is active, you must click the Spreadsheet tool to switch to the spreadsheet layer and edit the spreadsheet. When you switch to the spreadsheet layer, the drawing tools disappear from the tool palette, and you can make spreadsheet entries.

The Chart Tool

The Chart tool has a specialized purpose. When this tool is selected, the mouse pointer turns into a cross hair. You can drag the cross hair to specify the size and location of a new chart. The process is similar to drawing a rectangle in Draw. When you release the mouse button after drawing, an automatic chart appears in the rectangle you drew.

The Draw Tool

Choosing the Draw tool adds icons for the drawing tools to the tool palette and switches you to the Draw layer that contains the chart. You then can change the chart's appearance using the Draw tools.

Quick Charting

Works provides a speedy method for creating a chart. After you select the data you want to chart, choosing New Chart from the Chart menu or dragging the Chart tool immediately creates a chart of the default type built from the selected data.

You can create a chart quickly using either the tool palette or the New Chart command. Both approaches produce identical results, except that when you use the tool palette, you can control the size and placement of the initial chart. The selected cells in your spreadsheet are evaluated and charted, using the rules explained in the preceding section, "Understanding Chart Concepts."

To produce a chart quickly using the tool palette, follow these steps:

1. Create a spreadsheet containing the information you want to chart.

2. Select the information you want to chart.

NOTE

If Works cannot interpret the information you have selected, the Define Chart dialog box opens. See the following section of this chapter called "Defining a Chart" for instructions.

3. Click the Chart tool in the tool palette. The pointer changes to a cross hair.

4. Drag the cross hair to draw a rectangle to contain your chart.

5. Release the mouse button. Works draws the chart.

Defining a Chart

If the automatic charting feature does not meet your need, you can control nearly every aspect of a chart through the Define Chart dialog box. In this section, you learn techniques for specifying elements of a chart using the Define Chart command, as well as how to change chart types, move, and resize charts.

Figure 9.12 shows the dialog box that opens when you choose the command Define Chart from the Chart menu with a chart selected. Only when Works cannot interpret information you have selected will the Define Chart dialog box open without a chart on the screen. The following parts of this section explain the components of the dialog box and their functions.

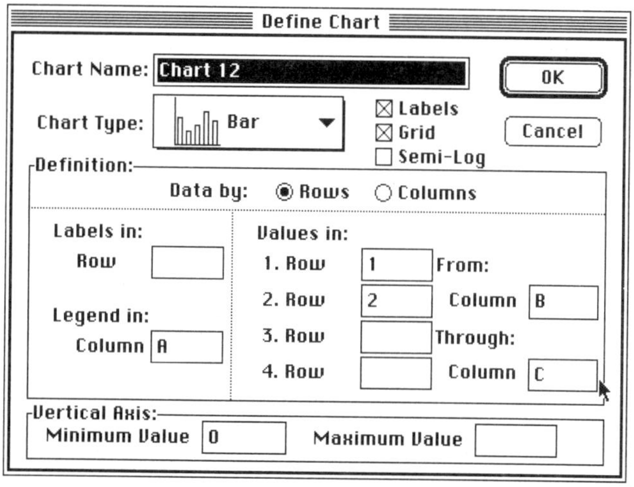

Fig. 9.12
The Define Chart
dialog box.

Naming a Chart

Works opens new charts with the generic names Chart 1, Chart 2, and so forth. To name a chart, type a name in the text box labeled Chart Name. This name appears at the top of the chart page when it is printed.

Changing Chart Type

Earlier, you learned to set the default chart type using the Preferences command from the Edit menu. You also can change chart type in the Define Chart dialog box, although the change is only for the active chart. Open a pop-up menu of chart types by clicking anywhere in the Chart Type box. Click the type of chart you want, and Works redraws the selected information in the new format.

Controlling Labels and Grids

Three check boxes, to the right of the Chart Type box, control the presence of labels and the type of measurement grid. Deselecting the Labels box prevents the display of data labels along the horizontal axis.

The *grid* is the series of horizontal lines that run across the data area. Turn the grid on or off by selecting or deselecting the Grid check box. The normal grid is comprised of evenly spaced horizontal lines. The Semi-Log option, available only when the Grid box is checked, causes the distance between each value unit along the vertical axis to decrease as you go up the scale. This scale is appropriate for showing the relative change of large variations in data because it compresses large variations within a series.

Changing Data Definitions

TIP

To quickly edit an existing chart, select the Draw tool (pencil). The mouse pointer turns into an arrow pointer. Double-click the chart. The Define Chart dialog box opens.

When you open the Define Chart dialog box with a chart selected, you see the data definitions filled. If you want to alter the definitions or select new data, you can enter new values.

By choosing one of the buttons in the Definition section, you can tell Works to read data series either by rows or by columns. In the Labels and Legends group box, you can direct Works to specific rows and columns for its label or legend information.

Depending on whether your data series are in rows or columns, you can specify their location in the Values in area. Works can chart up to four different data series, so you can specify either four rows or four columns as the source of your data.

The default vertical scale on a chart runs from zero to the largest value charted. However, you may want to alter the maximum and minimum scale markings. In the bottom box in the Define Chart dialog box, you can specify the minimum and maximum value on the vertical (value) axis. Works automatically divides your range of values by 10 to determine the values for the markings on the vertical scale.

Changing Chart Values

As you change the spreadsheet values that define a chart, the chart is automatically redrawn to reflect the new values. The steps are simple:

1. Make the spreadsheet active by choosing the Spreadsheet tool, and then clicking anywhere on the spreadsheet.

   You also can choose Draw Off from the Window menu.

2. Change values or labels in the spreadsheet.

3. Switch back to the chart by choosing the Draw tool from the tool palette and clicking the chart.

   You also can choose the chart name from the Chart menu.

Moving and Resizing a Chart

Charts can be moved to different areas of the screen and resized so that you can see both chart and chart data, or multiple charts, at the same time. Both activities require an understanding of *handles*, the small squares that appear at the edges of a chart object when it is selected (see fig. 9.13).

The presence of handles is a useful way of verifying that an object has been selected. To resize a chart, drag the handle. Dragging a middle handle resizes the chart only horizontally or vertically; dragging a corner handle resizes the chart proportionally, maintaining the ratio of height to width.

When you want to move a chart, don't drag it by the handle. If you try to move a chart by dragging a handle, you only resize the chart.

Fig. 9.13

Fig. 9.13
A chart object shows
handles when it is
selected.

Tool palette

Handles

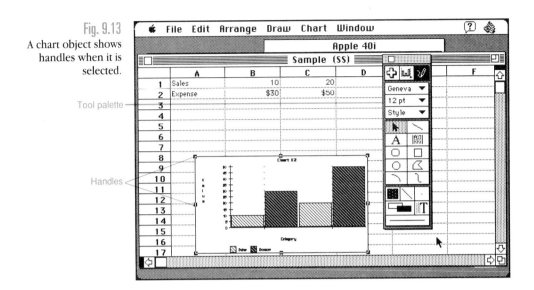

To move a chart, use these steps:

1. In the tool palette, select the Draw tool.

2. Click the chart to select it. Handles appear around the edge of the chart.

3. Place the pointer on the chart (anywhere except a handle), and drag to a new position.

To resize a chart, use these steps:

1. In the tool palette, select the Draw tool.

2. Click the chart to select it. Handles appear around the edge of the chart.

3. Drag any corner handle to resize the chart proportionally. Works maintains the ratio of height to width.

Formatting a Chart

Formatting tools help you to change the appearance of the elements in a chart. Works enables you to change chart patterns, colors, line widths, fonts, font sizes, and styles. You also can move chart elements and modify labels and legends. Used in combination, these formatting tools enable you to enhance dramatically the impact of your charts.

Changing Fill Patterns

The default patterns assigned to chart elements by Works are adequate for most purposes, but sometimes you may want to add special emphasis or correct an ineffective combination. Patterns are controlled by the Pattern tool from the Draw tool palette. You can change the pattern that fills a bar or pie wedge, or you can apply a pattern to the line that surrounds either one. When changing bars, you must change all the bars in a data series at the same time. Use these steps to alter chart patterns:

1. Click the Draw tool on the tool palette to select the chart.

   You also can choose Draw On from the Window menu.

2. Open the Chart menu and choose the Touch Up command.

   You also can hold down the Option key and click the chart.

3. Click the chart object you want to change. Handles appear on the selected object.

4. Point to the Fill Pattern tool and hold down the mouse button. The Fill Pattern palette opens (see fig. 9.14).

5. Move the pointer to the pattern you want to select, and release the mouse button. Works applies the selected pattern to the chart object.

Fig. 9.14
The Fill Pattern palette.

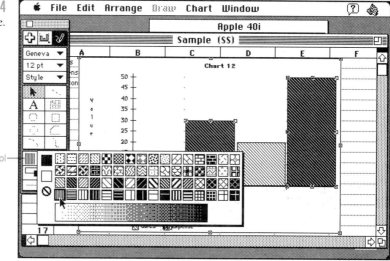

Fill tool

Chapter 9
Working with Charts

Changing Line Patterns

To alter the pattern of a line, follow the preceding steps, but use the Line Pattern tool, found just to the right of the Fill Pattern tool. To see the effect, you may need to widen the line. See the section "Changing Line Widths" that follows.

Changing Line Widths

Changing the line widths surrounding objects is another way to change the formatting emphasis of a chart (see fig. 9.15). The steps are similar to those used for changing patterns:

1. Click the Draw tool on the tool palette to select the chart.

    You also can choose Draw On from the Window menu.

2. Open the Chart menu and choose the Touch Up command.

    You also can hold down the Option key and click the chart.

3. Click the chart object you want to change. Handles appear on the selected object.

4. Point to the Line Width tool and hold down the mouse button. The Line Width menu opens.

5. Move the pointer to the width you want to select and release the mouse button. Works applies the selected width to the chart object.

Changing Fonts, Font Size, and Style

You also can change the text elements of a chart. You can change the font used, the font size, and font style (see fig. 9.16). Use these steps:

1. Click the Draw tool on the tool palette to select the chart.

    You also can choose Draw On from the Window menu.

2. Open the Chart menu and choose the Touch Up command.

    You also can hold down the Option key and click the chart.

3. Click the text object you want to change. Handles appear around the text.

4. In the tool palette, choose the tool to change font, font size, or style.

5. Hold down the mouse button to open a pop-up menu of choices.

6. Drag the pointer to your choice and release the button. The text is reformatted with your choice.

Fig. 9.15
Line widths around a set of bars modified with the Line Width tool.

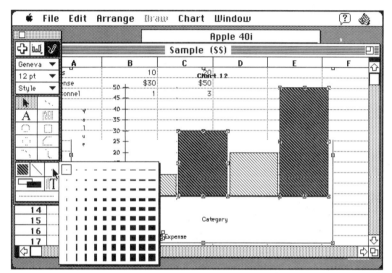

Fig. 9.16
The chart name font has been changed and enlarged.

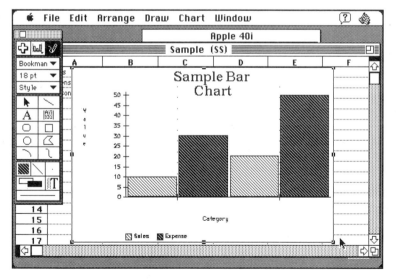

Moving Chart Elements

You can move the text that comprises a chart's name, legends, or axis labels, and you also can move wedges in a pie chart (see fig. 9.17). By unlinking the chart from its spreadsheet, you can make more extensive changes. This process is explained in the section of this chapter called "Unlinking a Chart and Spreadsheet." To move elements of linked charts, use these steps:

1. Click the Draw tool on the tool palette to select the chart.

   You also can choose Draw On from the Window menu.

2. Open the Chart menu and choose the Touch Up command.

   You also can hold down the Option key and click the chart.

3. Click the text object you want to move. Handles appear around the text.

4. Drag the text object to a new position.

   To move a pie chart wedge, apply the previous steps to a pie chart wedge instead of a text object.

Fig. 9.17
You can move a pie chart wedge.

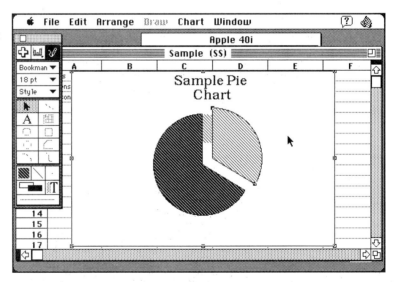

Hiding Chart Elements

For a special effect, you can hide elements of a chart. This technique is useful when you want to focus on a limited number of chart elements. The effect is accomplished by turning the chart element the same color as the chart background. Follow these steps:

1. Click the Draw tool on the tool palette to select the chart.

   You also can choose Draw On from the Window menu.

2. Open the Chart menu and choose the Touch Up command.

   You also can hold down the Option key and click the chart.

3. Click the element you want to hide. Handles appear around the element.

4. Using the Color tool from the tool palette, choose a foreground and background color for the object that matches the chart background.

Unlinking a Chart and Spreadsheet

You can unlink a chart from its underlying spreadsheet. When you unlink a chart, all chart elements, including the bars, wedges, or lines that represent data, become independent Draw objects that can be modified and enhanced using the complete range of Draw tools.

Remember that you can distort data by resizing or moving unlinked data elements. Use care to preserve a correct definition of the data, because you cannot relink an unlinked chart to its original spreadsheet. Use the following steps to unlink a chart:

1. Open the Chart menu and choose the name of the chart you want to unlink.

2. Open the Arrange menu and choose the command Ungroup. All chart elements become independent Draw objects.

Copying, Saving, and Printing a Chart

After your chart has been created and refined, copying, saving, and printing it are the final steps in preparing the chart for use. You can copy charts easily into other Works modules. You also can incorporate charts into documents from the word processor, spreadsheet, and database. Saving a chart preserves your work, and printing a chart lets you share the chart with the audience for whom it was prepared.

Copying a Chart

The process of copying a chart to another module is simple. Note that the links between the chart and its spreadsheet are broken when a copy is made. If the spreadsheet figures that generated the chart are later changed, the copied chart does not change. Use these steps to copy a chart:

1. Open the document that will receive the copy.

    This document is usually in a different module.

2. Switch to the spreadsheet module.

3. Open the Chart menu and choose the name of the chart to copy. Names of charts appear at the bottom of the Chart menu.

4. Open the Edit menu and choose the Copy command. Works copies the chart to the Clipboard.

5. Switch to the document to receive the chart copy.

6. Open the Edit menu in the receiving document and choose Paste. Works pastes the copied chart into the document.

Saving a Chart

Works saves charts as part of the spreadsheet from which they were generated. As many as 16 charts can be saved with a single spreadsheet. The names of saved charts appear at the bottom of the Chart menu when the associated spreadsheet is open.

Choose Save As from the File menu to save your chart with a name and a file format. After that initial save, you can use the Save command or ⌘-S to quickly save your chart. You also can save a workspace with the Save Workspace command from the File menu. For more information about saving, see Chapter 2, "Understanding Works Basics."

Printing a Chart

Charts are printed in conjunction with the spreadsheet with which they are associated. See the tip to learn how to print a chart by itself.

TIP

You can print a chart by itself if you drag it to an unused area of the spreadsheet. Choose the Spreadsheet tool and drag a highlight that includes the cells surrounding the chart; then open the File menu and choose Print.

Three commands on the File menu control printing choices: Print Preview, Print, and Print One. You can preview a chart before printing to see how it will look on paper. When you print, you can select print quality and the pages you want to print, or you can choose the Print One command to bypass the dialog box and print quickly with the current settings. For more information about printing with Works, refer to Chapter 2.

Setting Page Size and Orientation

To print the entire active area of your spreadsheet, including charts, print with a single cell highlighted. If you want to print part of your spreadsheet, select the part by highlighting cells. When you print, only the highlighted cells are included.

Because specifying correct document size and orientation is critical for printing, the Page Setup command, found on the File menu, links both printer and page information. When you choose Page Setup, a dialog box for the printer you have selected appears. The dialog box contains radio buttons used to select paper size and check boxes to choose printer-specific effects such as image reduction. Two buttons under the heading Orientation choose vertical (often called *portrait*) or horizontal (*landscape*) printing.

Setting Margins and Page Numbers

The Document button at the bottom of the Page Setup dialog box opens the secondary dialog box, shown in figure 9.18. This box contains Margins and Page Numbering sections used by the word processor as well as grayed out sections used by other Works modules. To change document margins, type new measurements in inches. Starting numbers for pages and footnotes are entered here. This feature lets you start at a page other than 1 if, for example, you need consecutive page numbering for multiple documents. If the Title Page check box is selected, a page number is not printed on the first page. Numbering begins with 2 printed on the second page.

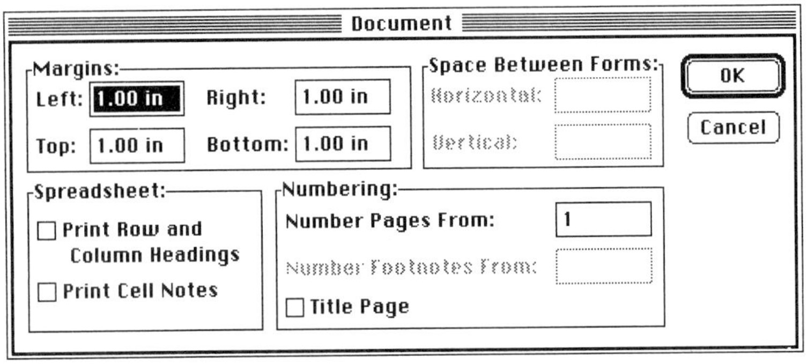

Fig. 9.18
The Document dialog box.

Adding Manual Page Breaks

As you create a spreadsheet, Works keeps track of its size and, when a page is filled, a page break is automatically inserted. In spreadsheets, you can have vertical as well as horizontal page breaks You can see how your spreadsheet has been paginated by choosing the Page Preview command from the File menu. Although you cannot remove automatic page breaks, you can add your own, which interact with automatic breaks to help correct awkward breaks.

To insert a manual page break, follow these steps:

1. Click the cell you want to appear in the upper left corner of a new page.

2. Open the Format menu and choose Set Page Break.

3. Vertical and horizontal dashed lines appear to indicate the boundaries of the new page. The previous automatic page breaks are reset to reflect the new manual page break.

To set only a vertical break, select an entire column and choose Set Page Break from the Format menu. A new break is placed to the left of the selected column. To set only a horizontal break, select an entire row and choose Set Page Break from the Format menu. A new break is placed above the selected row.

Previewing a Spreadsheet

You can save substantial amounts of time and paper by using the Print Preview command. Choosing this command from the File menu opens a display similar to the one shown in figure 9.19. Although you cannot make out individual words and numbers (unless you use large type), you can get a sense of the spreadsheet layout and page breaks. If you have more than one page, use the Previous and Next buttons to flip through the spreadsheet.

To see an enlarged view of the spreadsheet, move the cursor over the page (the cursor changes to the shape of a magnifying glass) and click an area you want to magnify. You can drag the magnified document with the cursor, which now looks like a hand. To return to the full-screen preview, double-click anywhere. If you are satisfied with the spreadsheet, click the Print button, and the Print dialog box opens. To make revisions, choose Cancel to return to the spreadsheet.

Fig. 9.19
The Print Preview window shows layout and page breaks.

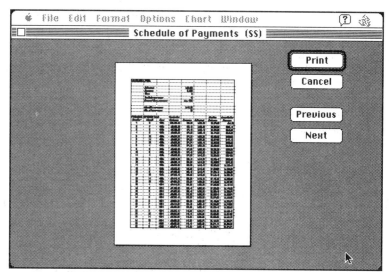

Chapter Summary

In this chapter, you learned the chart types available in Works, how to select information for charting, and how to use charting tools. The quick charting process was described as well as the more detailed method using the Define Chart dialog box.

The last part of the chapter showed you how to enhance charts by formatting both text and chart elements. The process of unlinking a chart from a spreadsheet and moving the chart to another module was described, and the steps necessary to copy, save, and print charts were detailed.

Chapter 9
Working with Charts

PART V

Using the Database

Includes

USING
MICROSOFT
WORKS

Creating Databases

he word *database* is a computer-age creation that manages to sound far more complex than it actually is. A database is simply a collection of information. A telephone book is a database, as is a recipe file or a list of birthdays. Some databases are simple enough that pencil and paper are all you need to maintain them. But when the complexity rises, particularly when you want to sort and extract specific information from a large database, the computer is an unsurpassed assistant. The Works database is a distant relative of the massive database programs that manage your credit card billings or airline reservations. Even though these databases are worlds apart in complexity, they are built upon the same concepts.

Works contains a powerful database module that can store and analyze thousands of pieces of information, organizing and retrieving parts you want. You can create customized reports that list and categorize large amounts of information, or you can print forms that contain only the information you specify. A few new terms and concepts need to be mastered, but after that is done, you will find numerous uses for Works databases.

USING
MICROSOFT
WORKS

Understanding Database Concepts

This section introduces important terms and database concepts. A framework of database concepts will help you as you create your own database.

Database Terms

To learn more about databases, you need to talk a bit of database "language." The following terms are fundamental to the topic:

Record. All the information about one item. A database is a collection of records. For example, each record in a phone book usually contains an individual's name, address, and phone number.

Field. The part of a record that holds a particular type of information. In the phone book example, each record contains a name field, an address field, and a number field.

Field entry. The data contained in a field.

Form. A database document containing an arrangement of fields used for entering or viewing records.

View. A way to organize database information on-screen and in printed reports. The Works database has four views, used for different purposes. For example, the data view shows fields in a customized arrangement, whereas the list view shows each record as a spreadsheet-like row of fields.

Filter. A set of instructions for extracting specific information from the database. For example, if a field containing city names exists, you can create a filter to extract all the people in a database who live in a specific city.

The Database Menus

Six menus contain the commands used in the database. The following list provides a brief overview of the menus. Appendix A contains a complete command reference.

File menu. Contains commands that enable you to manage files, control document layout, print, and quit the program. If you use Microsoft Mail, you activate it from this menu.

Edit menu. Contains commands that change documents; you can move, delete, or revise selected material using these commands.

Form menu. Contains commands that enable you to change views, create and edit forms and fields, and switch between forms.

Data menu. Contains commands for record selection and management (see fig. 10.1).

Report menu. Contains commands for creating and editing reports. (Covered in Chapter 11, "Preparing Database Reports.")

Window menu. Contains commands that enable you to access Draw, the tool palette, and other active database documents.

Fig. 10.1
The Data menu.

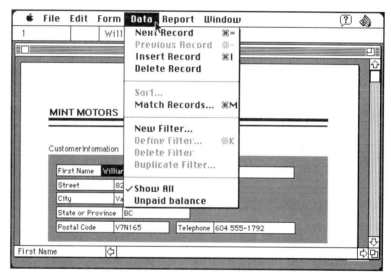

Database Views

Works provides two fundamentally different ways of looking at your data: *list* views and *form* views.

List Views

A *list* view shows information in a spreadsheet-like arrangement of columns and rows (see fig. 10.2). This type of view is useful for looking at several records at once and for adding and editing information in a number of records at the same time.

Chapter 10
Creating Databases

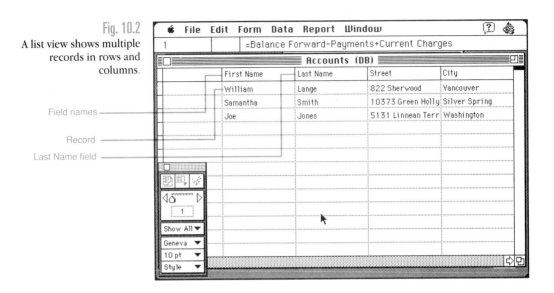

Fig. 10.2
A list view shows multiple records in rows and columns.

Field names

Record

Last Name field

A variation of a list view is a *report* view (see fig. 10.3). You use report views to print information in a tabular format and to calculate data totals and subtotals for use in reports. You cannot change information in report view. Reports are discussed fully in Chapter 11, "Preparing Database Reports."

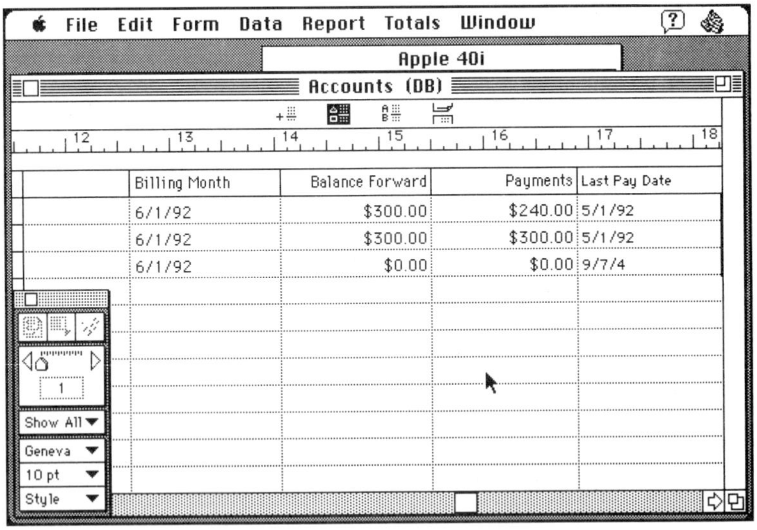

Fig. 10.3
The report view enables calculation of totals and subtotals.

Part V

Using the Database

Form Views

A *form* view enables you to see information for a single record in an arrangement resembling a paper form. The advantage of these views is that you can customize the placement and selection of fields in the view. You can choose to see only certain fields and then arrange them in any order desired. You also can enhance form views using the drawing tools.

The *data* view is one of two form views (see fig. 10.4). You use this view to add information to a single record, somewhat like filling out an electronic form on-screen.

Fig. 10.4
The data view can be filled out like an electronic form.

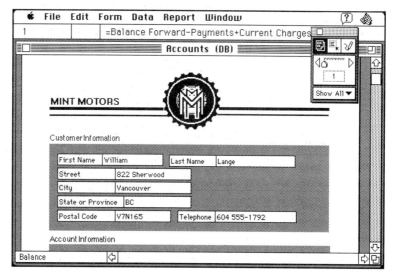

The second form view is the *design* view (see fig. 10.5). As its name suggests, this view is for creating forms. You can add, delete, move, and resize fields in the design view, but you cannot enter data. Drawing tools, which enable you to enhance your design, are also available.

Lists vs. Forms

Lists and forms provide different ways of viewing the same database information. The list view contains all the fields defined in a database. This view always reflects the total number of fields and records in your database. A form view contains only those fields specified when you design the form. With Works, you have the flexibility to add and remove fields from both list and form views, but the results are different.

Chapter 10
Creating Databases

Fig. 10.5
The design view is used to
create forms.

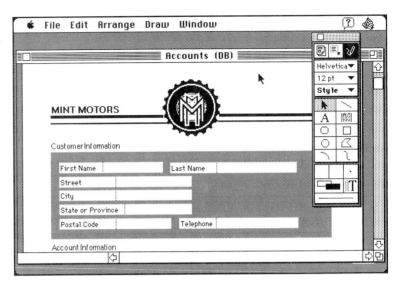

When you add a field to a list view, the program does not add the field to form views of the same database. You can manually add the new field to a form if you want. When you delete a field from a list view, however, you also remove it from any form view using the field.

On the other hand, if you add a new field to a form view, Works also adds the field to the list view if it is not already in that view. When you delete a field from a form view, however, the program does not remove it from the list view because the field may have uses in other views.

To summarize, the list view reflects the overall structure of the database. When you add or remove fields, the changes are always evident in the list view. The form view reflects only a single record. Your changes may or may not affect the form view because the fields it contains depend on your specifications.

The Database Tool Palette

Because of the importance of views in the database, the tool palette is useful. In the database, the palette contains icons that enable you to switch quickly between views and includes a button for selecting filters as well as record selection tools that extract information. The appearance of the tool palette depends on the view you are using. Figure 10.6 shows the palette as it appears in design view.

Fig. 10.6
The palette seen in
design view.

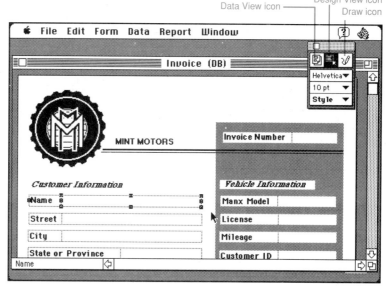

The font, size, and style buttons and the Draw icon appear in the palette in other modules. The icon at the top left switches to data view, and the icon at the top center switches to design view. Clicking the Draw icon adds drawing tools to the palette and places a Draw layer on your database form where you can add graphic enhancements.

When you switch to data view, the font buttons disappear and a navigation tool appears (see fig. 10.7). This tool has a slider, a bit like a scroll bar, you can drag to move through the database. You can click the arrows at either end to move one record forward or backward. A window below the slider shows the number of the current record. Below the navigation tool is a button marked Show All, which you use to apply and remove database filters.

Designing Your Database

The choices you make when designing the structure of your database critically influence its effectiveness. The key decision involves which fields to include. For example, if you put first and last names in a single field, you cannot sort them separately. If you do not include a field for the cities in which customers live, you have no way to extract the names of customers by city.

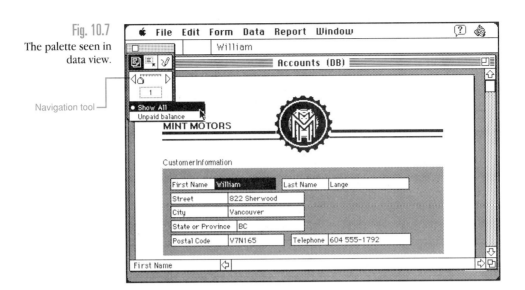

Fig. 10.7
The palette seen in
data view.

Navigation tool

Including too much information is no answer either. An overloaded
database is slow to work with and cumbersome to manage. Before
starting a new database in Works, spend time with pencil and paper
deciding what information you want your database to provide and what
fields are necessary to capture that information.

Opening a New Database

You open the Works database module from the Open dialog box that
appears when you start Works (see fig. 10.8). To open the database
module and create a new database, use these steps:

1. Click the Database icon in the Open dialog box.

   The icon looks like two Rolodex cards with a sheet of paper
   behind.

2. Click the New button.

   An empty database window opens with the New Field dialog box
   presented.

Distinguishing between the database and the views that enable you to
see its contents is important. Steps 1 and 2 create a new database, the
basic document that contains your data. As you continue to develop your
database, you do so by creating forms or using automatic views that give

you different ways of seeing your database information. You can have as many as 16 different forms in a single database, each one providing a different way to view all or part of the same underlying information.

If you have spent time planning your database, you already have an idea of which fields you need. If not, stop for a time to plan and name your fields. Revisions are easier on scratch paper than on the screen.

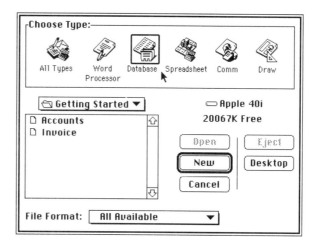

Fig. 10.8
The Open dialog box.

Creating Forms

After you have created a database file using the steps in the previous section, you have a blank document, literally and conceptually *without form*. You need to specify fields for your database and arrange them in sequences that are convenient and useful to you. Creating a new database opens the New Field dialog box (see fig. 10.9). When you see this box, proceed with the steps that follow:

1. Type a field name in the text box marked Name.

   The name must begin with a letter, not a number.

2. Click OK to add the field to your database.

   The dialog box stays open for the next field.

3. Continue entering fields in the order desired.

4. When you are finished, click Done. The dialog box closes.

Chapter 10
Creating Databases

Fig. 10.9
The New Field dialog box.

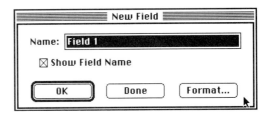

Your database is a basic one. If you open a list view of the database, it consists of columns for the fields you have entered with rows for the records to come (see fig. 10.10). For a simple database you work with in list view, this form may be all you need, but to enter or view your data in more flexible ways, you will want to create additional forms.

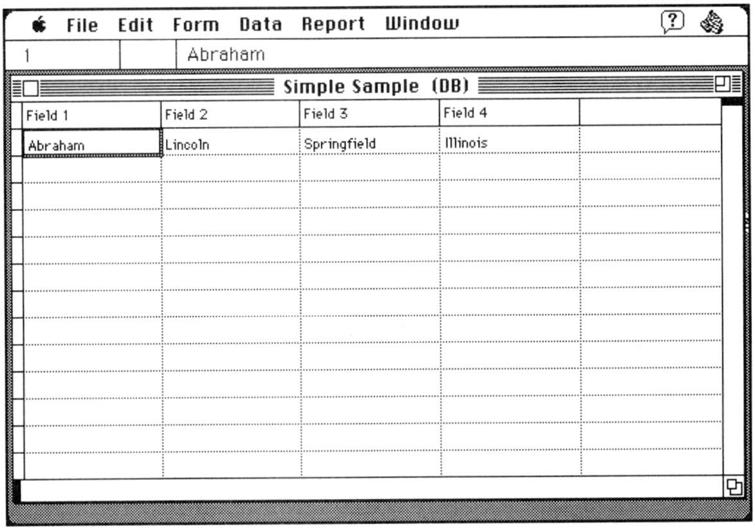

Fig. 10.10
A simple database
in list view.

Creating a New Form

Switching to the design view of the simple database created previously shows the fields in the upper left corner of a form (see fig. 10.11). You can click a field and drag it to a new location to make a data entry form that resembles a paper form. You can open the tool palette, switch to Draw, and add enhancements to your form.

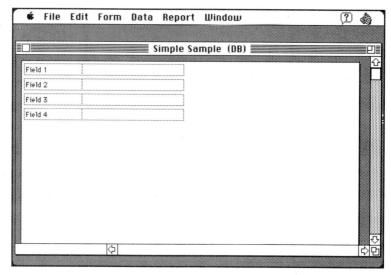

Fig. 10.11
The design view of
a simple database.

In list view, you see each record in the database on a separate row. In form view, Works displays the fields for only a single record. In the simple database example shown here, the same fields are on the form and in the list. You can create as many as 16 different forms for a single database and specify the fields and their arrangement. This process enables you to view or enter data for selected fields without having to deal with all the other fields in the database.

To create a new form, follow these steps:

1. Open the database for which you want to create a form.

2. Open the Form menu and choose the Design View command.

3. Open the Form menu and choose the New Form command. The New/Set Up Form dialog box opens (see fig. 10.12).

4. Enter a name for the form.

5. Click a radio button for one of the standard sizes or click the Custom Size button, and then enter the dimensions you want.

6. To select fields for a new form, click the Fields button. The Auto Place Fields dialog box opens (see fig. 10.13).

Chapter 10
Creating Databases

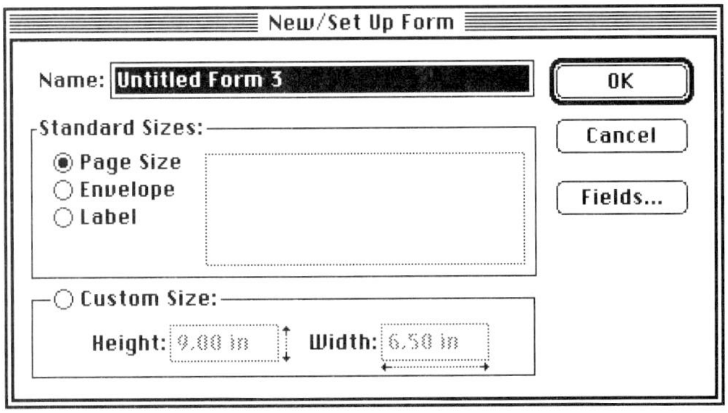

Fig. 10.12
The New/Set Up Form
dialog box.

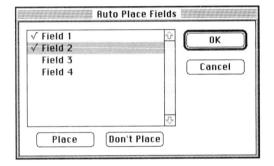

Fig. 10.12
The New/Set Up Form
dialog box.

Fig. 10.13
Select fields for the new
form in the Auto Place
Fields dialog box.

The Auto Place Fields dialog box enables you to quickly select existing fields you want to place on your new form. When the selection is complete, Works places the fields. To use the Auto Place Fields box to select the fields you want to place on your new form, follow these steps:

1. In the Auto Place Fields dialog box, click each field you want on your form and click Place to put a check mark next to the field name.

2. To remove a check marked field from the list, select the field again and click the Don't Place button.

3. When your list is complete, click OK to close the Auto Place Fields box.

4. Click OK in the New/Set Up Form dialog box. Your new form appears, and Works places the selected fields (see fig. 10.14).

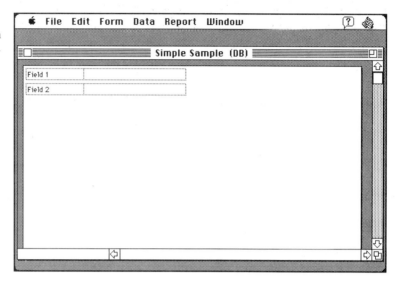

Fig. 10.14
The new form with
fields in place.

Works lists the new form at the bottom of the Form menu. You can switch between forms by selecting the form name from the menu.

Duplicating and Deleting Forms

The Duplicate Form command on the Form menu copies the active form. The Duplicate Form dialog box enables you to rename the copy of the form. You then can modify the copy using the tools described in this section and the following section, "Editing Fields."

To delete a form, make it the active form by choosing its name from the bottom of the Form menu. Then choose the Delete Form command from the Form menu. A warning message gives you a chance to change your mind. Clicking OK eliminates the form.

After a form is created, you can enhance it by editing and arranging the fields it contains. The following section introduces the necessary tools and techniques.

Editing Fields

After you have created the fields needed for your database, you will undoubtedly find reasons to change their properties or arrangement. This section explains how to select and move fields and other ways of adding, deleting, or changing fields.

Selecting Fields

Selecting fields and their contents is the same in the database module as it is in other Works modules: you highlight the field or text to be modified. The procedure is slightly different for form and list views.

To select a field or field entry in a form view (design view or data view), click anywhere in the field. In design view, where the field is an object, handles appear on a selected field, allowing you to move or resize it (see fig. 10.15). If you are not familiar with resizing and moving objects with handles, see the section called "Creating Text Objects" in Chapter 6, "Enhancing Documents with Draw." You can select multiple fields in design view by holding down the Shift key while clicking additional fields. Clicking in a field in data view highlights the whole field, anything you type replaces the selected text.

Fig. 10.15
The field selected in design view can be moved and resized.

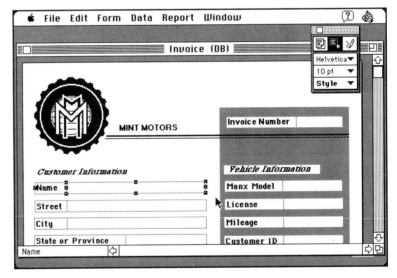

Field selection in list view is similar to the selection process in a spreadsheet. Clicking the field name at the top of a column selects the entire column. To select an entire record, click the empty box to the left of the record. You can select a group of entries by dragging the mouse across them (see fig. 10.16). To select a single entry, click the rectangle the entry occupies. (In report view, you can select only a single field at a time.) You also can select the entire database by opening the Edit menu and choosing Select All or by clicking the box to the left of the field names. With any selection, clicking outside the selected area removes the highlight.

Fig. 10.16

In list view, a group of entries selected by dragging the mouse across the record.

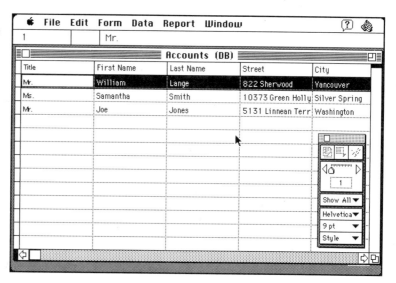

Renaming a Field

You can rename a field in either list view or design view, but you cannot rename a field in data view. To rename a field, follow these steps:

1. Click to select the field to rename.

2. Open the Form menu and choose the Field Name command. The Field Name dialog box opens (see fig. 10.17).

Fig. 10.17
Rename a field in the Field
Name dialog box.

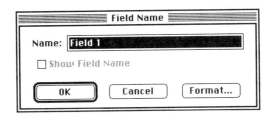

3. Type a new name in the text box; then click OK.

If the field names appear next to the data on the form, you can open the Field Name dialog box by double-clicking the field name (not the field data). Type a new field name and click OK.

Moving a Field

You can move a field anywhere space permits in design view. To move a field, follow these steps:

1. Switch to design view or list view. See the tip at the end of these steps.

2. Click the field you want to move. The field displays handles on its border.

3. Drag the field to a new location. Do not drag by the handle or you will only resize the field.

You can only move fields left or right in the grid of the list view. Point to the name of the field you want to move; then drag right or left to a new location.

TIP

To switch quickly from design view to list view, double-click anywhere in the gray background of the form. To switch quickly from list view to design view, double-click the small rectangle to the left of any record.

Resizing a Field

Works enables you to resize fields in design view or list view. In design view, you can resize a selected field by dragging the handles that appear on its border (see fig. 10.18). Dragging a corner handle diagonally changes both height and width. Dragging a side handle at a right angle to the side changes height or width alone.

Fig. 10.18
In design view, the Last Name field resized by dragging a side handle.

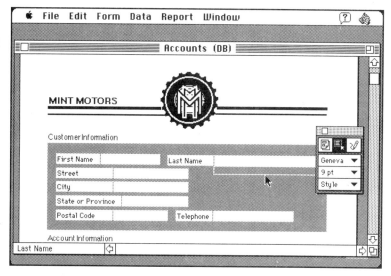

The handle at the left end of a field controls the width of the area used to display the field name. You can hide the field name completely by dragging the left handle toward the right until the name disappears. You also can hide field names by removing the X from the Show Field Name box in the New Field or Field Name dialog boxes.

In list view, you can widen a field by placing the mouse pointer on the border between two field names and dragging the border. When properly positioned, the pointer changes to a vertical line with an arrow on each side. You cannot change height in list view.

Adding a New Field

You can approach adding a new field to your database in two ways. You can add a field in the list view, or you can add a new field to a form. The effects of each type of addition are different. When you add a new field to a list view, the field becomes part of your database, but the field does not automatically appear on any form view. You establish the fields a form contains when you design the form. If you want to use the new field from the list view in a form, you have to add the new field to the form. However, when you add a new field to a form, the field is automatically added to the list view because the list view has to contain all the fields in the database.

Add a New Field in List View

To add a new field to the list view, follow these steps:

1. Select the column to the right of where you want the new field column. Click the column name to select the entire column.

2. Open the Form menu and choose the command New Field. The New Field dialog box opens.

3. Type the field name in the New Field dialog box and click OK. Works inserts the new field to the left of the selected field.

Add an Existing List View Field to a Form

To add an existing list view field to a form, follow these steps:

1. Switch to design view. Choose Design View from the Form menu.

2. Open the Form menu and choose the Place Field command. The Place Field dialog box opens.

3. Select the field to add from the list box.

4. Click the Place button to put the field on the form.

Works places the field in the upper left corner of the form. If the field is covered by another field, drag the fields apart with the mouse pointer and position them properly.

Add a New Field to a Form

To add a new field to a form, follow these steps:

1. Switch to design view. Choose Design View from the Form menu.

2. Open the Form menu and choose the New Field command. The New Field dialog box opens.

3. Type a field name in the New Field dialog box and click OK. Works places a new field on the form.

Control the Location of a New Field on a Form

The Place Field command appears when you are in design view. You can use this command to draw a field in the place you want. To position a new field, follow these steps:

1. Switch to design view. Choose Design View from the Form menu.

2. Open the Form menu and choose the Place Field command. The Place Field dialog box opens.

3. Click the Place button. The dialog box disappears.

4. Move the mouse pointer where you want the new field to begin.

5. Hold down the mouse button and drag to the width of the new field. A dotted line follows the mouse pointer.

6. Release the mouse button. The Place Field dialog box reappears.

7. Click the New button in the Place Field dialog box. The New Field dialog box opens.

8. Type a name for the new field, and then click OK. The new field appears where you outlined it on your form.

Removing a Field

The differences between actions in the list and form views also apply when a field is removed. When you remove a field from the list view, the field disappears entirely from the database. When you remove a field from a form, it does not affect the entire database, but only that form.

To remove a field from list view—and the entire database—follow these steps:

1. Open the Form menu and choose List View.

2. Click the field name in the column containing the field you want to delete.

3. Open the Form menu and choose Delete Field.

4. Choose OK in the dialog box to confirm your deletion.

   Works removes the field and all the information it contains from the database. Be certain you want to delete a field permanently before taking this action.

Removing a field from a form is simple. Follow these steps:

1. Open the Form menu and choose Design View.

2. Click the field you want to remove.

   Handles should appear on the field perimeter.

3. Open the Form menu and choose Delete Field.

You also can press Delete.

Works removes the field only from the form. The data remains in the database and displays in list views.

Saving Your Work

The first time you save a database, use these steps:

1. From the File menu, choose Save As.

2. In the dialog box that opens, type a name for the database.

3. Use the list box and or the pop-up menu to locate the folder where you want to save the file.

4. Click Save to save the database.

After you have named and saved the database for the first time, choose Save—or press ⌘-S—to save your work quickly.

Applying Field Formats

A field can contain formatting information that affects the appearance of any field entry. At any time, you can apply field formats to properly display dates, times, numbers, and text. You also can insert fixed values or formulas into every instance of a specific field. Formatting fields is similar to formatting cells in the Works spreadsheet.

A format is a property of the field, not the field entry. If you put a number in a field formatted for time of day, the field tries to present the number as a time. If you put a number in a field formatted for text, Works treats the number as text and does not use it in calculations.

TIP

To apply a format quickly, double-click a cell if you are in list view or double-click a field if you are in design view.

You apply formats by using the Format Field command and its dialog box (see fig. 10.19). You also can open the Format Field dialog box by clicking the Format button that is present in the New Field and Rename Field dialog boxes. To set or change a format, you must be in design view and have the relevant field or fields selected. Changes apply only to the highlighted field.

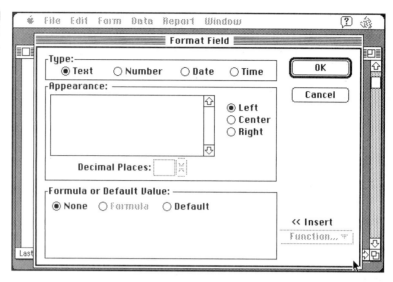

Fig. 10.19
The Format Field
dialog box.

Choosing Format Types

The Type box in the Format Field dialog box contains radio buttons for selecting four different format types. Works does not use the contents of any field designated Text in numeric calculations. Choosing Number enables you to format numbers like the specimens that appear in the dialog box's scrolling list. You also can specify the number of decimal points to be displayed (see fig. 10.20).

Choosing Date or Time fields also produces scrolling lists of format examples. To choose a format, click the example in the scrolling list. You may want to make other selections, such as alignment, that are described in the following paragraphs. When you have completed your choices, click OK to apply them to the selected field.

You can align all four format types to the left, right, or center of the fields they occupy by clicking the appropriate radio button at the right in the Appearance group box.

At the bottom of the Format Field dialog box is a group box labeled Formula or Default Value. You have three choices for defining the number, date, or time field entry for selected fields. The usual choice is None. Fields with this format are empty. If you choose the Formula button, you can enter a formula that appears in all cells affected by your formatting (see fig. 10.21). This procedure is described in detail in the section called "Using Calculated Fields."

Fig. 10.20

Number format choices are
shown in the Format Field
dialog box.

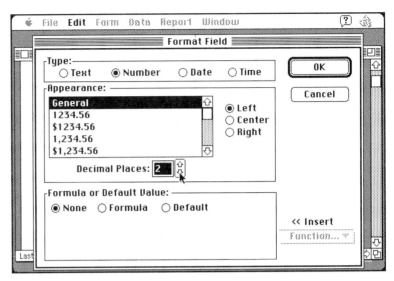

Fig. 10.20

Number format choices are
shown in the Format Field
dialog box.

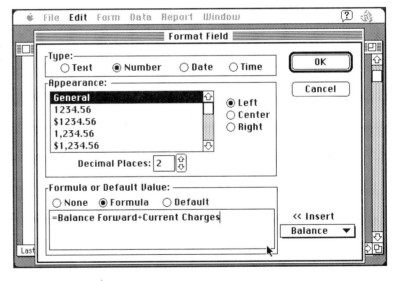

Fig. 10.21

A Formula for Number
fields entered at the
bottom of the Format Field
dialog box.

If you choose the radio button labeled Default, an insertion point
appears in the box below the selections, enabling you to type text or a
value you want to appear in every field carrying the format. This option
is useful for filling records with initial values. For example, you can place
a 0 (zero) in a specific field of every record. Later, you can change the

value on a field-by-field, as-needed basis; or, if you want to reset all the values in a field, you can specify a new default value.

Performing Other Field Formatting

You can change the font, font size, and style of the contents of any field using the tool palette, or the Format Character command found on the Form menu. The tool palette contains buttons that open pop-up menus containing font, font size, and style choices. The Format Character dialog box offers the same choices, as well as an option for selecting a text color. Figure 10.22 shows the dialog box displaying a sample of selected text.

Fig. 10.22
Italicized, 18-point,
Helvetica font selected in
the Format Character
dialog box.

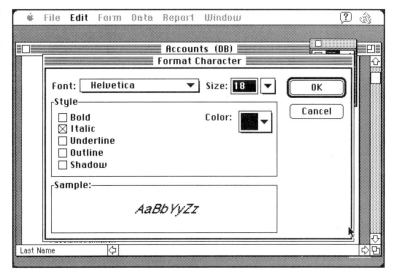

By default, a grid divides field records and columns in a list view. Open the Form menu and choose the command Show Grid. Choosing this command again removes the X indicating the command is active. To restore the grid, choose the command again.

Using Calculated Fields

Works can increase the power of your database by using the contents of fields to perform calculations. For example, if you have a field that records hours worked and one that specifies hourly wages, you can create a formula to multiply hours by wages and place the result in the field containing the formula. The creation and use of formulas in the database follow the same general rules as they do in the spreadsheet. You also can use Works functions in database formulas.

Entering Database Formulas

You type formulas in a box at the bottom of the Format Field dialog box. Several steps are necessary to prepare for formula entry:

1. Select the field to contain the formula.

    If necessary, insert a new field.

2. Open the Form menu and choose Format Field. You also can double-click the field to open the dialog box.

3. Choose an appropriate field type.

    You cannot enter formulas in text fields.

4. Click the Formula button at the bottom of the dialog box.

    An equal sign (=) appears in the box below the button.

5. Type the formula immediately after the equal sign.

6. Click OK to enter the formula in the field.

Creating Database Formulas

NOTE

You can use numbers in a database formula when needed. For example, **=hours*5** is a valid entry. This section emphasizes field names because the use of field names varies from what you may have previously learned about spreadsheet formulas.

A database formula consists of a combination of data—often field names—and mathematical operators that describe what to do to the data. In the formula =2+2, the twos are the data and the plus sign is an operator. The result of the formula, 4, is the outcome of the interaction between the operators and the data.

In a database, you can designate data by entering field names in the formula. In other words, if a Wages field and an Hours field both contain the number 2, you create a formula to multiply the contents of the cells by typing **wages*hours** in the box at the bottom of the Format Field dialog box. Works places the result, 4, in the field that contains the formula. Notice the equal sign (=) is already in the box to indicate the start of a formula.

Works does not recognize misspelled field names in a formula. To avoid this problem, you can paste field names into formulas using the Insert pop-up menu (see fig. 10.23). Clicking the down arrow below the name << Insert opens a list containing the name of every field in the database. To paste a field name, drag down the list to highlight the name you want, and then release the mouse button to paste the name.

Fig. 10.23

Balance Forward, Payments, and Current Charges selected from the Insert pop-up and pasted in the Formula box.

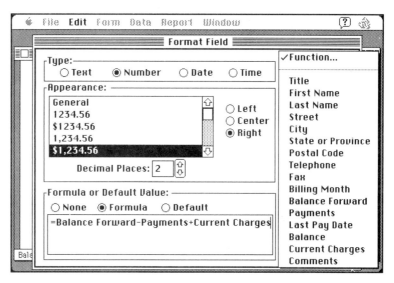

You also can paste functions into your database formula. Click the down arrow below the name << Insert and drag to highlight the choice labeled Function.... When you release the mouse button, the Paste Function dialog box opens (see fig. 10.24). Choose a function and click OK to paste it into your formula. Chapter 8, "Applying Spreadsheet Functions," explains the structure and application of all 64 Works functions, 57 of which you can use with the database.

Performing Data Entry Operations

After you have established the fields and perfected the forms, your database is ready to receive data. This section explains techniques for entering data and for adding, deleting, editing, and saving records.

Chapter 10

Creating Databases

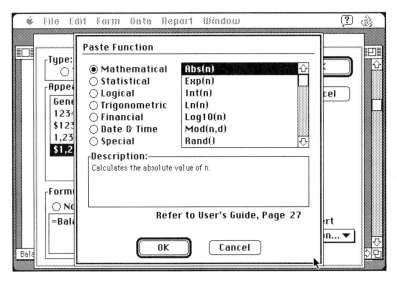

Fig. 10.24
The Paste Function
dialog box.

Choosing a Data Entry View

You can enter information in data view or list view. Data view presents a form containing the fields inserted during form design (see fig. 10.25). List view presents rows of records containing all the fields (see fig. 10.26).

Data view is appropriate for entering information in several fields of a single record. You can move from field to field entering different information in each. In list view, working with several records is convenient because the records are presented as compactly arranged rows.

Switching Views

Several menu commands enable you to switch views rapidly. The Form menu contains commands for switching between data, list, and design views. The tool palette contains tools for switching between data view and design view (see fig. 10.27).

Fig. 10.25
Data view presents a form
for each record.

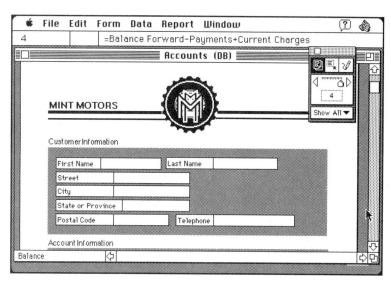

Fig. 10.26
List view shows all fields in
rows of records.

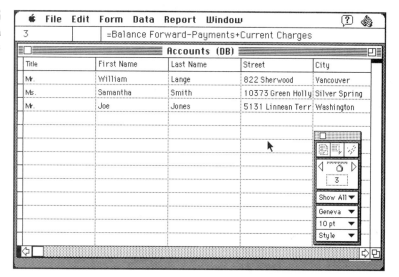

Chapter 10

Creating Databases

Fig. 10.27
The Data View tool and
Design View tool.

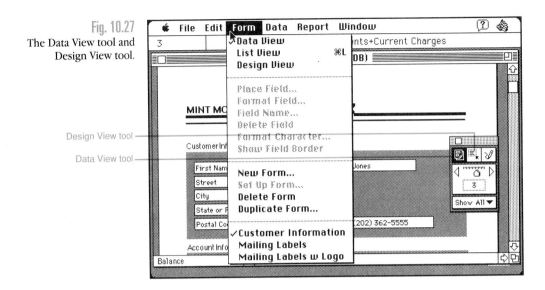

Fig. 10.27
The Data View tool and
Design View tool.

Design View tool

Data View tool

Two shortcuts for switching between views also are quite useful. Double-clicking a form view, away from any fields or objects, switches you to list view. Double-clicking the empty box to the left of a record switches you from list view to the form view for that record that is currently selected on the Form menu.

Entering Data

To begin entering data, click a field and type your information. You have several ways of entering that data in the field. Your choice depends on where you want the highlight to move after you finish entering the data. Table 10.1 shows the keys to press to enter data and then move the highlight in different directions.

Table 10.1
Data Entry Keys

View	Key	Highlight movement
Data or List	Enter	No movement
Data or List	Tab	To next field in same record
Data or List	Shift-Tab	To preceding field in same record
Data	Return	To next field in same record, or in last field, to next record
Data	Shift-Return	To preceding field in same record, or in first field, to preceding record

Part V

Using the Database

View	Key	Highlight movement
List	Return	Down to same field in next record
List	Shift-Return	Up to same field in preceding record

Editing Data

When you type data in a field or select a field by clicking it, the contents of the field appear on the entry bar just below the menus. You edit field contents on the entry bar (see fig. 10.28). Use the Delete key to remove characters to the left of the insertion point, or highlight the information and type replacement text. You also can use the Cut, Copy, and Paste commands from the Edit menu.

Fig. 10.28
Entry bar with the contents (Mr.) of the selected field.

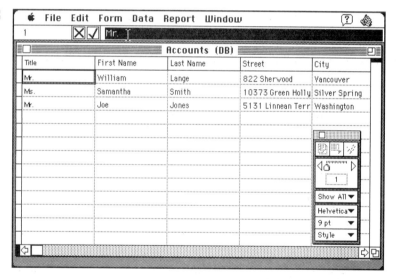

Inserting and Deleting Records

While entering data, you frequently will need to add a new record. In list view, highlight the row below the location where you want the new record. Open the Data menu and choose Insert Record. Works inserts a new, blank record above the highlighted record (see fig. 10.29).

Chapter 10
Creating Databases

Fig. 10.29
The new, blank record is
inserted above the
highlighted record.

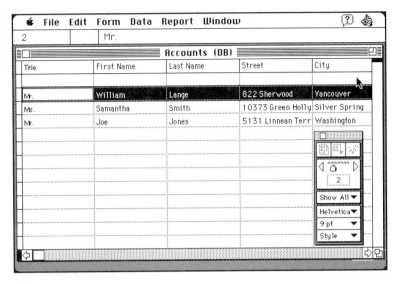

Adding a record in data view can be confusing. When, with a data view record on the screen, you choose Insert Record from the Data menu, Works adds the record before the current record, just as it does in list view. To see the new form, you have to move backward in your records.

Imagine you have only two records: Record 1 and Record 2. You are in data view, with Record 2 on the screen. When you choose Insert Record from the Data menu, you notice that the record number at the left end of the entry bar changes to 3. Using the Previous Record command from the Data menu, you move back one record and find a new record which is now Record 2.

The best way to avoid this confusion is to add records in list view. You can see several records at once and visualize the position of new records. On the other hand, if you have no problem with the concept of new forms appearing before the current form, you can use either method.

To delete a record, select the record by highlighting it in list view or scrolling to it in data view. Then open the Data menu and choose Delete Record. If you delete the wrong information, immediately open the Edit menu and choose Undo to reverse the deletion.

Retrieving Data

The only purpose for compiling a database is to retrieve information from it later. The searching and filtering capabilities of the Works database enable you to analyze your databases in several ways. In this section, you will learn ways of sorting and searching a database and how to construct filters, which enable you to retrieve data that meets specific tests.

Sorting the Database

Sorting enables you to change the order of your records based on sorting criteria you specify. You can sort alphabetic or numeric information, in ascending or descending order. With a little planning, you also can conduct multilevel sorts.

To sort your database, follow these steps:

1. Open the Data menu and choose Sort.

   The Sort Criteria dialog box opens (see fig. 10.30).

2. Click the down arrow in the Sort on Field box.

   A list of all fields drops down.

3. Drag down the list to highlight the sort field.

4. Release the mouse button to select the highlighted field.

5. If you want to sort in descending (Z–A) order, click the Descending box.

   Ascending is the sort default setting.

6. Click Sort to complete the sort.

Multilevel sorting enables you to sort by multiple criteria. Imagine you want to sort a database of names so that first names and last names are in alphabetical order. The rule to remember is to sort the least significant field first. In sorting names, the first name is usually less significant because most lists of names are arranged by last name.

To conduct the multilevel sort, follow these steps:

1. Open the Data menu and choose Sort.

2. Specify the first name field as the first sort criterion.

3. Click the Sort button to arrange the list by first names.

4. Choose the Sort command again, and this time specify the last name field as the sort criterion.

5. Click the Sort button to arrange the database by last name.

The arrangement of the final sorted list is alphabetical and in ascending (A–Z) order, by both first and last names. Works retains the order of the first sort as it makes the second sort.

Fig. 10.30
The Sort Criteria dialog box.

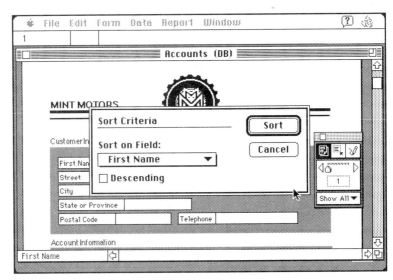

Searching for Specific Information

Two quick methods are available for locating specific data. The first method finds the next field containing specified data, and the second shows all records matching the specified data.

To search for the next field containing specified data, use these steps:

1. Open the Edit menu and choose Find.

The dialog box shown in figure 10.31 opens.

2. Type the search information in the text box.

To include numeric information, uncheck the box marked Search Text Fields Only.

3. Click the Find Next button.

   Works searches every field, until it finds and highlights the first match.

4. To continue the search, choose the Find command again. Or you can use the ⌘-F keyboard shortcut.

Fig. 10.31
The Find Next Field
dialog box.

The second type of quick search finds and displays all records containing the specified data. The database displays only matching records; the program filters others out. This process is a quick application of the type of filter discussed in the following section called "Creating Conditional Filters."

To find matching records, follow these steps:

1. Open the Data menu and choose Match Records.

   The Match Records dialog box opens (see fig. 10.32).

2. Type the search information in the text box.

   To include numeric information, uncheck the box marked Search Text Fields Only.

3. Click the Match button.

   Works displays all records matching the search information.

Fig. 10.32
The Match Records
dialog box.

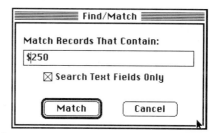

Chapter 10

Creating Databases

When you are through with the filtered display, open the Data menu and choose Match Records to remove the check mark from the command. Works removes the filter and displays all records in the database again.

Creating Conditional Filters

Filters enable you to select records from your database according to conditions you establish. With this powerful database feature, you can extract specific records from your database for analysis and reporting. In moments, you can electronically extract information that otherwise takes hours of hand sorting. Filters also enable you to rearrange temporarily your database to highlight specific features. You then can undo the changes or filter the records in another way.

Understanding Filter Concepts

You describe the records you want your filter to find by creating a record-selection rule—a formula-like description of your desired criteria. You can have as many as six record-selection rules per filter. A record-selection rule has three required parts:

- A field name
- A comparison phrase
- Data to compare to field contents

In a database containing a salary field, for example, you can create a record-selection rule to find salaries greater than $10,000. The rule would resemble the following phrase:

> Salary greater than $10,000

"Salary" is the comparison field name, "greater than" is the comparison phrase, and "$10,000" is the data to compare to field contents.

Using Comparison Phrases

Table 10.2 lists the specific phrases Works allows in record-selection rules.

Table 10.2
Record Selection Phrases

begins with	does not begin with
ends with	does not end with
contains	does not contain
equal	not equal
greater than	greater than or equal
is blank	is not blank
less than	less than or equal
(none)	

Using And and Or Links

You also can create multiple selection rules and link them with *And* and *Or* connectors. When rules are linked with And, Works finds only those records that satisfy all the rules. For example, the rule "Salary equals $15,000 and city equals Seattle" selects only those employees in Seattle whose salary equaled $15,000. The rule "Salary equals $15,000 or city equals Seattle" selects all employees who live in Seattle as well as all whose salary equals $15,000, regardless of where they live.

In summary, the And link is cumulative, selecting only records that meet all rules. The Or link requires that only one of the linked rules be met.

Creating a Filter

Figure 10.33 shows the New/Define Filter dialog box that opens when you choose the New Filter command from the Data menu. You can enter as many as six selection rules for each filter, although using more than two or three rules is unusual.

To list all fields and eliminate spelling errors, Field, Comparison, and rule connector (And/Or) boxes contain pop-up lists of valid choices. Use the following steps to create and save your filter:

1. Open the Data menu and choose New Filter.

   The New/Define Filter dialog box opens.

2. In the Filter Name box, type a name for the filter.

3. In the first Field box, click the down arrow. A list of fields opens.

4. Drag to the first field you want to search on and release the mouse button to select that field.

5. In the first Comparison box, click the down arrow. A list of valid comparison phrases opens.

6. Drag to the comparison phrase and release the mouse button to select that phrase.

7. In the Compare to box, type the text or value against which to compare the fields.

8. If you want a second rule, choose a field and then a connector (And/Or) from the boxes at the left.

9. Continue creating and connecting rules using steps 3 through 8.

10. When you are finished, click OK to save and apply the filter.

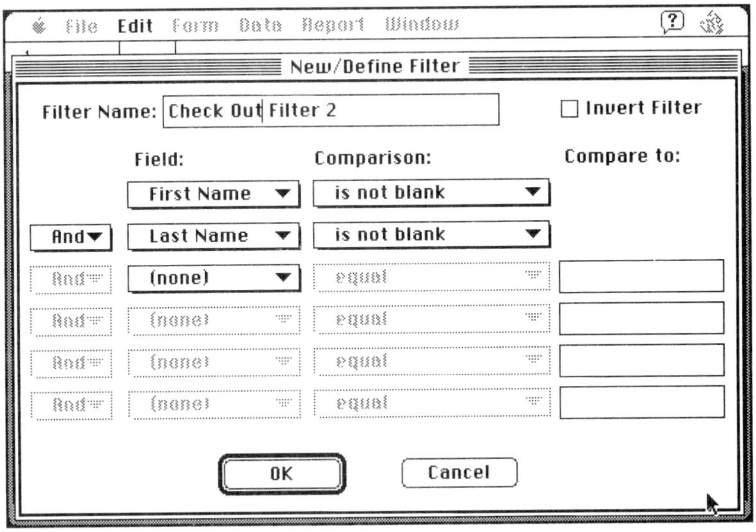

Fig. 10.33
The New/Define Filter
dialog box.

Inverting Filter Logic

A check box, labeled Invert Filter, at the top right of the New/Define Filter dialog box enables you to invert the logic of the filter. When this box is checked, Works presents only those records that do not match the filter selection rules. By creating an identical pair of filters and then inverting one, you can switch between both parts of a filtered database.

See the section of this chapter called "Duplicating a Filter" for a quick way to create a filter copy that you then can invert.

Inactivating Selection Rules

Notice that unused Field and Comparison boxes contain the value (none). This entry inactivates a selection rule. To inactivate an existing rule, enter (**none**) in any Field box for the rule. Works moves the inactive rule to the end of the list, and that rule no longer affects the filter (see fig. 10.34).

Fig. 10.34
A selection rule has been inactivated by entering (**none**).

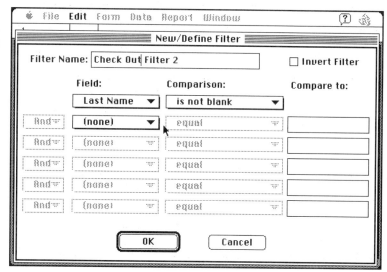

Using Existing Filters

A list of existing filters appears at the bottom of the Data menu. Choosing a filter name applies that filter to the current database. You also can open the filter list by clicking the button at the bottom of the Filter tool found on the tool palette (see fig. 10.35).

Duplicating a Filter

Duplicating an existing filter provides a head start on the construction of a new one.

To duplicate a filter, follow these steps:

1. Choose a filter to serve as a model.

2. Open the Data menu and choose Duplicate Filter.

   A dialog box opens.

3. Type a name for the new filter (see fig. 10.36).

4. Click OK to save and display the new filter.

   You now can modify the new filter.

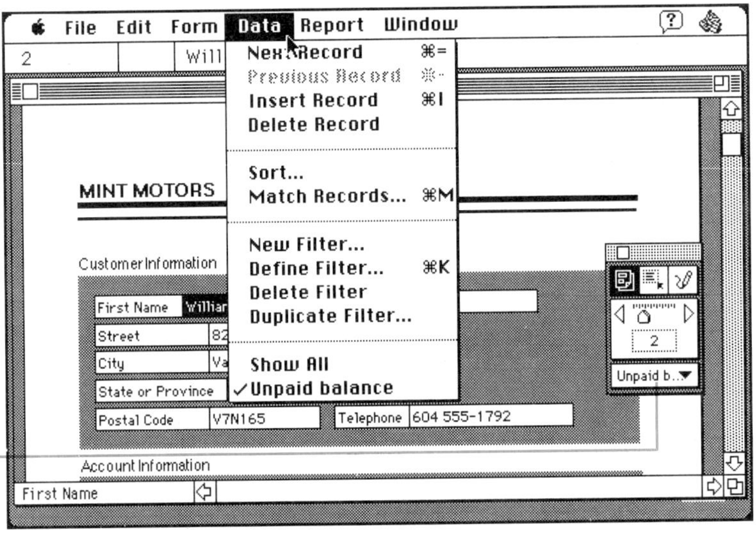

Fig. 10.35
The Filter tool button lists existing filters.

Deleting a Filter

To remove a filter, select it from the Filter tool or Data menu. Then choose the Delete Filter command from the Data menu and click OK.

Using Draw with the Database

As in other Works modules, you can add a Draw layer on top of any form in design or data view. In the database, Draw enables you to add annotations and decorations to forms. To activate Draw, click the Draw icon on the tool palette, or choose Draw On from the Window menu. You then can use the full range of Draw tools as explained in Chapter 5, "Creating Drawings."

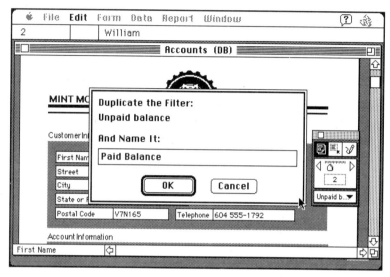

Fig. 10.36
The And Name It box
containing a new filter
name.

Transferring Data to Other Modules

Using the database's moving or copying steps, you can move or copy
database information to the spreadsheet, word processor, or Draw
modules. In the word processor and Draw, computed fields become
inactive, so results that depend on that information are not recalculated
if the information changes. Formulas copied to the spreadsheet remain
"live" and can be recalculated.

Works places each record moved to the word processor in a row, with
fields separated by a tab. If the records are long, you may need to work
with font size, tab placement, and document orientation to fit the data in
a single row.

Records moved to the spreadsheet are placed one per row, with each
field in its own cell. Because data takes on the format of the cell in which
Works places it, you may need to reformat some entries.

Works places records copied to Draw one per line, separated by spaces.
Any formulas underlying numeric data are inactivated by the copy and
are no longer updated if data changes.

Using Existing Databases and Stationery

Procedures for opening existing databases and the Stationery samples furnished with Works differ from those used when opening new databases.

Use the following steps to open an existing database:

1. Open the File menu and choose Open.

2. Click the Database icon.

3. Locate the file you want, or change drives or directories to locate it.

4. Double-click the file to open it.

The procedure for opening a Stationery document is quite similar:

1. Open the File menu and choose New.

2. Click the Database icon.

3. Click the Show Stationery check box to activate it.

   The file list box shows only database stationery.

4. Select the stationery file you want, and double-click to open it.

5. When the copy opens, save it with a new name to make it an independent database.

   You then can edit the contents.

Closing and Quitting

When you are finished with a database, you may want to close it and start another, or you may want to quit Works. To close the active database, open the File menu and choose Close, or click the close box in the window's upper left corner. If you have a number of files open, use Close All to close all open files. If you want to quit Works, you can go directly to Quit. Works gives you a chance to save your files. For more information about saving and quitting, see Chapter 2.

Chapter Summary

ome computer users avoid using databases because databases are unfamiliar. As this chapter shows, however, the Works database module is a powerful yet approachable tool. In this chapter, you learned database terminology and design concepts. Chapter sections dealt with editing and formatting fields and methods of calculating with fields.

After you designed and created your database, you learned how to choose the appropriate view for data entry. After putting data in place, you learned how to sort, locate, and filter data that meet your requirements. Database reporting is covered in Chapter 11.

Preparing Database Reports

Accumulating a useful database can be a slow and costly project. Compiling the names and addresses of your customers and entering invoices can take hours of paid data entry time, but after you have captured the information, you have a tool of great potential power.

Notice the word *potential* in the last sentence. The data in a database is of little use in its raw form. When you sort, organize, and extract information, the power of a database emerges. How many customers have past due bills? How many live in a certain ZIP code area? What is Henry Smith's address? How many widgets did you sell last month? All these questions can be answered with the right question put to the right database. You can put the results on paper with a database report.

This chapter builds on the database concepts introduced in Chapter 10, "Creating Databases." If you are not familiar with Works databases, you should read Chapter 10 before proceeding with this chapter.

USING
MICROSOFT
WORKS

Designing a Report

Report design consists of creating a new report specification, choosing the fields you want to print, and defining the criteria for selecting records. In the simplest case, all records are printed. If a selection of records is to be used, a filter needs to be prepared. If totals and subtotals are needed, they must be added to the design specification.

As many as 16 report definitions can be attached to a single database. This capability enables you to define multiple ways of viewing database information. You also can use the database to automatically calculate and print totals and subtotals.

A well-planned report design helps you to easily extract and print useful information. Reports are the payoff for the work involved in creating a database. Because generating reports is the main function of a database, anyone who uses a database should have an understanding of how reports are created and used.

Using the Report View

To create a new report, open the Report menu and choose the New Report command. The Name the Report dialog box opens (see fig. 11.1). When you enter a name and click Create, a report view screen similar to the example shown in figure 11.2 appears.

The report view screen is a row and column display much like list view, but additional tools are present to assist with report design. A ruler is present to help set the width of the printed area. Icons are available on the ruler to assist in placing totals and subtotals. The functions of these icons are explained in the section called "Computing Totals and Subtotals."

Designating Fields for Reports

You design a report by placing the fields you want, in the order you want them, in a printable area. The report view shows every field in the current database. If the fields all fit between the triangular margin markers on the ruler, they all appear in your report. Fields that don't fit between the margins don't print. Fields that are cut off by the ruler margins are truncated on the report.

Fig. 11.1
A report name can contain
up to 31 characters.

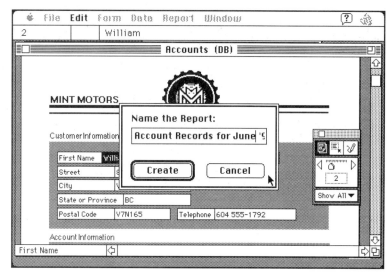

Fig. 11.2
A report view screen can be
identified by the presence
of a ruler.

Triangular margin markers

Designating fields for a report includes arranging the fields you want to
print so that they fit the space available on your paper. You have three
principal tools to work with: field width, document width, and field
position. By adjusting these three factors, you can get a surprising
amount of information on a printed page.

Chapter 11

Preparing Database Reports

You can widen or narrow a field in report view by dragging the field's column borders. Point to the right edge of the box at the top of a column that holds the column name. When the pointer turns into a vertical line with arrows pointing left and right, drag the border to the desired position (see fig. 11.3). Adjacent columns adjust to compensate for the change.

Fig. 11.3
You can drag column boundaries to change width.

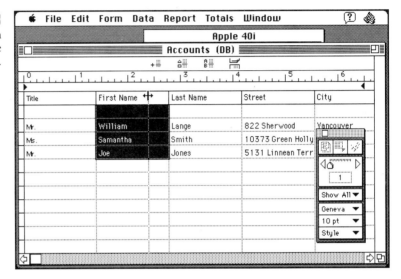

If the entry in a field is too wide to allow narrowing the field, use the steps below to reduce the width of the field entry for all records containing the field:

1. Highlight the column by clicking its field name.

2. Open the Form menu and choose the Format Character command.

   You also can use the font buttons on the tool palette.

3. In the Format Character dialog box, use the buttons and text boxes provided to choose a smaller or narrower (condensed) font.

4. Click OK to reduce the width occupied by the entry and exit the dialog box. Works returns you to the report view screen.

5. Drag the column boundaries to narrow the column.

When you have exhausted your options for narrowing fields or field contents, you can, in effect, widen the paper by changing the printer orientation from vertical to horizontal. Depending on your printer, you can use most of the 11-inch dimension of your paper for printing additional information. If your printer has the capability, you also can specify horizontal printing on legal-size paper (8 1/2" x 14") by clicking the button labeled US Legal in the Page Setup dialog box. Use these steps to change paper orientation:

1. Open the File menu and choose the Page Setup command. The Page Setup dialog box opens.

2. Click the icon that represents horizontal page orientation.

3. Click OK to put the settings in place and return to report view.

Approximately seven inches of report view width shows on a small Macintosh screen. If you change to a horizontal page orientation or choose a larger paper size, a scroll bar appears at the bottom of the screen, and you can scroll right to see fields that are out of view. You can only scroll to the right edge of the field farthest right, regardless of the paper width. The right margin marker appears at the 9-inch mark on the ruler (you have to scroll right to see it). If you are printing horizontally, often called *landscape* orientation, on legal-size paper, you can move the right margin marker even further to the right.

Sometimes you may want to omit fields for clarity or because you don't have room to print them all. You can specify certain fields for printing in several ways. If, for example, you wanted only two fields to print in a report, you could widen those fields so that other fields wouldn't have enough room to appear in the print area between the margin markers on the ruler. You also could narrow the margins so that only those two fields would print.

Margin changes are an important way of controlling what is displayed in reports. You can narrow the right margin to exclude fields you do not want to print, by dragging the right margin triangle on the ruler to new settings. To alter the left margin, choose Page Setup from the File menu and then click the Document button. The Document dialog box has a section for setting all margins. Use the Print Preview command on the File menu to check your results.

Moving Fields

In order to be able to use effectively the techniques described in the previous section, you need to know how to move fields into the sequence you want. To move a field, click the field name at the top of the field column, hold down the mouse button, and drag the field to a new position. Notice that the mouse pointer changes into a hand while you drag the column. Other fields are rearranged to accommodate the change (see fig. 11.4).

Fig. 11.4
You can drag fields to new positions.

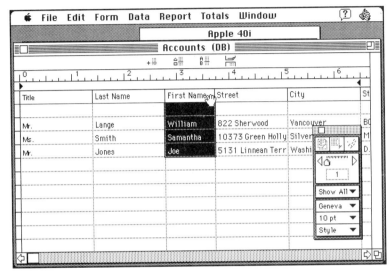

Suppose you have a database containing four fields, but you want to show only two in a report. Move the two fields you want to print so that they are the first two fields on the left. Next, widen the field columns until they push the other fields out of the printing area, or drag the right margin marker to the left until the unwanted fields are excluded.

Selecting Records for a Report

If no filter is used, every record in a database is printed in a report. If a filter is used, only the records selected by the filter are printed or used in computing totals and subtotals. The creation and application of filters is explained in the section of Chapter 10 called "Creating Conditional Filters."

Formatting Reports

A report reflects the formatting of the list view from which it is derived. Tools to change formatting are available in the report view. But remember that any changes (except for column width) made to the format of field entries in report view, affect the list view and any other reports that use the list view.

Formatting Text and Numbers

The tools used to format field entries in reports are the same ones used for formatting in other database views. Use these steps:

1. Select the field you want to format by clicking the field name at the top of the column.
2. If the tool palette is not displayed, open the Window menu and choose Show Tools.
3. Use the font, size, and style buttons to make changes.

   You also can choose Format Character from the Form menu.

NOTE

Draw tools are not available in report view. However, you can add Draw enhancements, including small images, to report headers and footers.

Performing Other Report Formatting

You can turn off the grid that separates field entries to provide a cleaner look to printed reports. To turn off the grid, open the Form menu and choose the Show Grid command. Works removes the check mark next to the command, and the grid disappears (see fig. 11.5).

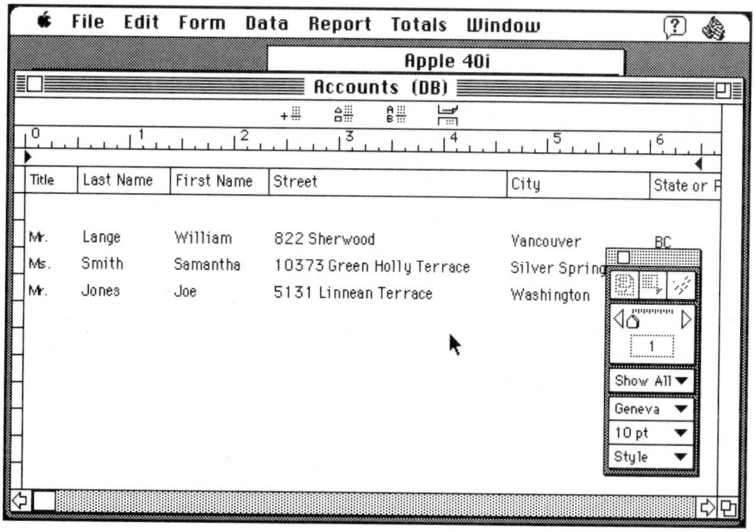

Fig. 11.5
Removing the grid can simplify a report layout.

Headers and footers are lines that appear automatically at the top (header) or bottom (footer) of each page. They can be used to automatically add page numbers and the time and date of printing along with other information you may add (see fig. 11.6). In multipage reports, automatic page numbering can be very helpful. Headers and footers are created in special windows reached by choosing Show Header or Show Footer from the Window menu. You can find complete instructions for using headers and footers in the section of Chapter 4 called "Working with Specialized Features."

Fig. 11.6
You can see headers or footers with Print Preview.

Header

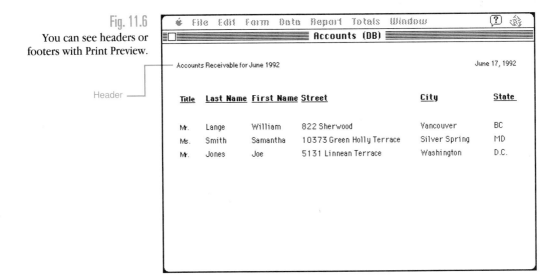

Computing Totals and Subtotals

The capability to compute totals and subtotals and embed them in reports is built into the report view. When you switch to report view, a new menu named Totals appears. Four icons, equivalent to commands on the Totals menu, appear on the report view ruler (see fig. 11.7). Using these commands and icons, you can total and subtotal the information in your database and print the totals in clearly formatted reports.

Works lets you total any field. You can subtotal a field under two circumstances: the content of a field changes, or the first character in a field changes. For example, you can total a field called *Salary* to find the total salary paid to all employees. You can cause a subtotal of salaries to print when the Department field changes from Manufacturing to Accounting, and you can print a subtotal when a product number changes from 20 to 30. When you plan a report that makes effective use of filters, totals, and subtotals, you create a powerful tool for interpreting and understanding your data.

Fig. 11.7

Report view ruler buttons control totals, subtotals, and page breaks.

Sum This Field button

Subtotal When Contents Change button

Subtotal When 1st Char Changes button

New Page After Subtotal button

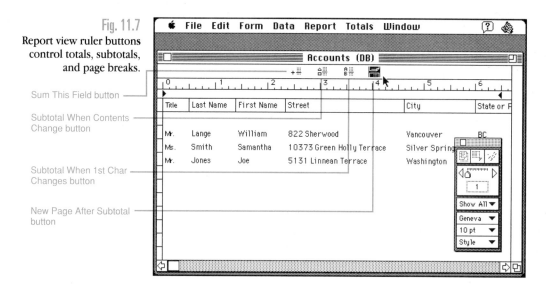

Computing Totals

Totalling a field involves selecting it and applying the Sum This Field command. Use these steps:

1. Choose Report View from the Report menu.

2. Click the field name of the field you want to total.

3. Open the Totals menu.

    The grayed-out name of the selected field appears at the top of the Totals menu.

4. Choose the Sum This Field command.

    A check mark appears next to the command.

    You also can click the Sum This Field button on the ruler.

The total does not appear in the report view although the total is printed in the report. The following list illustrates two ways to view the total before printing the report:

- Choose Print Preview from the File menu. The total appears in the preview. To enlarge the total, place the pointer over it and click.

- Choose Copy Totals from the Edit menu. Then choose View Clipboard from the Window menu. A window opens containing the total (see fig. 11.8).

Fig. 11.8
Totals can be viewed on the Clipboard.

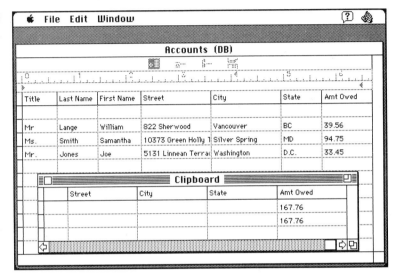

Calculating Subtotals

Two fields are involved in the subtotal process. One field serves as the key field that triggers the subtotal when the field changes. The other field is the field you want subtotalled. For example, you may want to create a subtotal in the Salary field each time the Department field changes value—from Purchasing to Manufacturing, for instance.

The steps used to create subtotals are simple, but an understanding of the theory behind subtotals can help you design a more powerful database. When planning a database, one design consideration should be the choice of fields that provide useful keys for grouping information in reports.

For example, by including a Department field in a database of salary information, you can sort salaries by department and print reports that subtotal salaries by department. The Department field becomes a key field in extracting and analyzing information. A Part Number field in a parts database enables you to sort the database by part number and create reports that subtotal information such as cost and quantity for each part number.

Two approaches to subtotals exist. The first lets you create a subtotal each time the contents of a field change; the second creates a subtotal when the first character in a field changes. Generally, the Subtotal When a Field Changes command works well with text fields. For example, when the content of a field changes from Seattle to San Francisco, a subtotal is generated for another field.

Although the command can be used with text or numbers, Subtotal When 1st Character Changes works particularly well with numbers. For example, it can be used to generate a total of parts when a part number changes from 200 to 300, and so on. You can use the subtotal when the first character changes in a text field, but notice that it wouldn't work with Seattle and San Francisco, because both names begin with the same character. You need some ingenuity to use subtotal fields effectively. The best approach is a bit of planning, both when the database is developed and when a report is created.

To insert a subtotal when the field contents change, use these steps:

1. Switch to the report view.

2. Click the name of the field you want to subtotal.

3. Open the Totals menu and choose the Sum This Field command.

   You also can click the Sum This Field button on the ruler.

4. Click the name of the key field that triggers the subtotal when the field changes.

5. Open the Totals menu and choose the command Subtotal When Contents Change.

   You also can click the Subtotal When Contents Change button on the ruler.

The steps for subtotalling when the first character of a field changes are similar to those used for subtotalling changed fields:

1. Switch to the report view.

2. Click the name of the field you want to subtotal.

3. Open the Totals menu and choose the Sum This Field command.

   You also can click the Sum This Field button on the ruler.

Chapter 11
Preparing Database Reports

4. Click the name of the key field that triggers the subtotal when the field's first character changes.

5. Open the Totals menu and choose the command Subtotal When 1st Char Changes.

You also can click the Subtotal When 1st Char Changes button on the ruler.

Printing a New Page after a Subtotal

You can add to the clarity of a report by placing subtotalled information on separate pages. Works provides the New Page After Subtotal command and ruler button for this purpose. Applying this command causes page breaks to appear after any subtotal. Follow these steps:

1. Switch to report view if necessary.

2. Open the Totals menu and choose the New Page After Subtotal command.

You also can click the New Page after Subtotal button on the ruler.

Saving and Modifying Reports

Because a report can take some time to design and create, knowing how to save your work is important. Because each database can have as many as 16 reports saved with it, you also benefit when you learn how to duplicate reports, which enables you to build new reports based on existing ones.

Reports are automatically saved when you save the database with which they are associated. When you switch to report view and open the Report menu, a list of all saved reports appears at the bottom of the menu (see fig. 11.9). To use a particular report form, click its name to select it and apply it to the database.

By duplicating a report, you easily can create a variation on it by changing only a few sections rather than starting over. Use these steps:

1. In report view, open the Report menu and choose the report you want to duplicate.

2. Open the Report menu again and choose the command Duplicate Report. The Duplicate the Report dialog box opens (fig. 11.10).

3. Enter a new name for the report and click OK. Works creates a copy of the report with a new name. The new report becomes the current report.

4. Edit the new report to meet your requirements, and then save it.

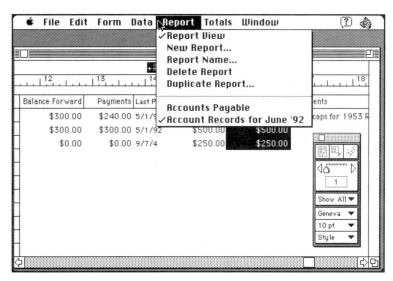

Fig. 11.9
All reports associated with a database appear at the bottom of the Report menu.

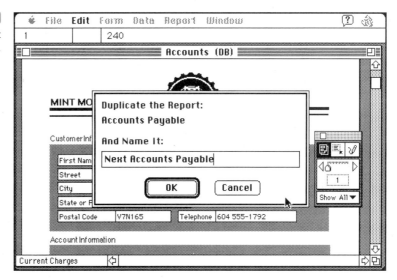

Fig. 11.10
The Duplicate the Report dialog box.

You can use the Report Name command to clarify or rename existing reports. For instance, because reports are listed alphabetically, you can bring a frequently used report to the top of the menu list by renaming the report so that it starts with one of the first letters in the alphabet.

To rename a report, choose it to make it the current report, and then open the Report menu and choose the Report Name command. In the dialog box that appears, type a new name for the report. Click OK to complete the renaming (see fig. 11.11).

Fig. 11.11
You can rename a report to reposition it in the menu list.

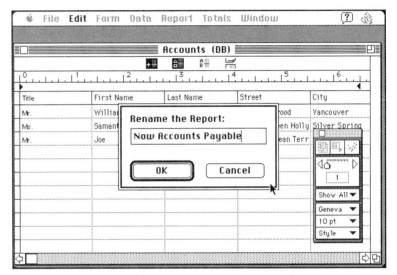

Caution is in order when deleting a report. To delete a report, follow these steps:

1. Switch to report view.

2. Make the report you want to delete active by choosing it from the Report menu.

3. Open the Report menu again and choose the command Delete Report. A dialog box opens asking you to confirm your deletion (see fig. 11.12).

4. Click OK to remove the report.

   If you make a mistake, immediately open the Edit menu and choose Undo to reverse your last action.

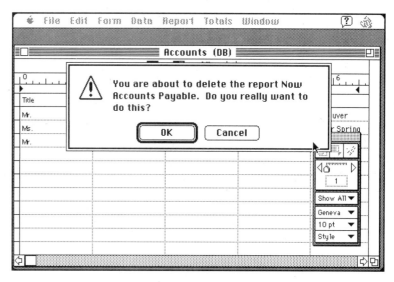

Fig. 11.12
Confirm your intention to
delete a report.

Printing from the Database

By the time you have completed designing a report, several printing issues have already been decided. Your choice and positioning of fields determines which fields print. Field formatting affects the appearance of the text. Page orientation and margins affect the number of fields that fit the page. If you chose to use subtotals and place page breaks after them, pagination has been decided. These issues have been discussed in previous sections of this chapter. This section discusses the final adjustments and printing procedures.

Printing Reports

Opening the File menu and choosing Print Preview enables you to see the appearance of your finished report (see fig. 11.13). You can evaluate the positioning of fields, totals, subtotals, and page breaks. You then can print using the current settings by clicking the Print button in the Print Preview window.

If you need to make corrections before printing the report, switch back to report view and make the changes. Then, when you are ready to print, use these steps:

1. Select the report and filter you want to use.

2. Open the File menu and choose Print. The Print dialog box for the selected printer opens.

3. Make selections for the printing options you want.

4. Click the Print button to begin printing.

Fig. 11.13
Print Preview lets you evaluate the printed document.

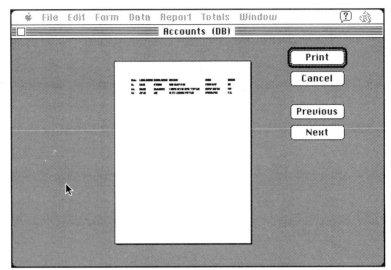

Printing Forms

The default standard form uses an 8 1/2-by-11-inch sheet. The fields you place on the form can use part or all of the available space, but when you print a single default form, it always uses an entire sheet. If, when you created the form, you specified a custom form size, Works attempts to print as many forms as possible on a single output sheet (see fig. 11.14).

The final appearance of your printed form also can be affected by margin and form-spacing settings. You can check these settings by choosing Page Setup from the File menu and then clicking the Document button (see fig. 11.15). You can check the effect of your work by choosing the Page Preview command from the File menu.

Fig. 11.14
You can print multiple custom-sized forms on a single sheet.

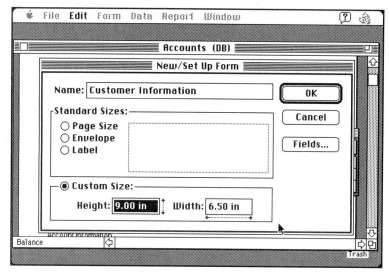

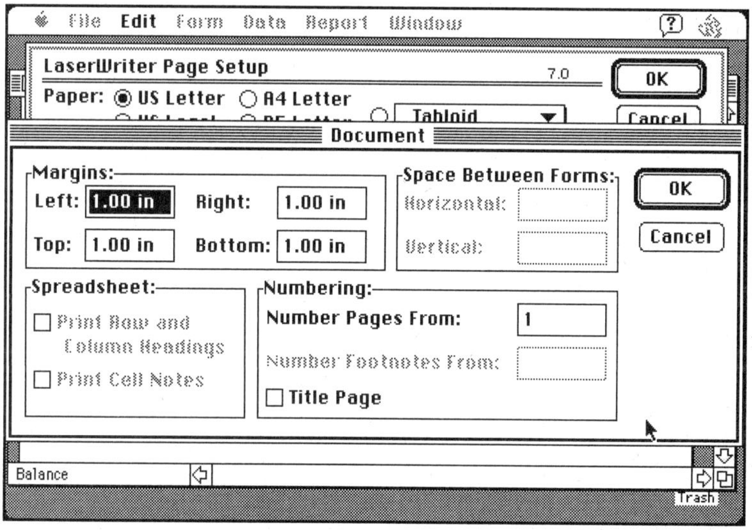

Fig. 11.15
You can control margins and record-spacing from the Document dialog box.

Use these steps to print one or more forms:

1. Open the Form menu and select the form to print by clicking its name.

2. Open the File menu and choose Print. Select any printing options desired.

3. Click the Print button to print the forms.

Creating Labels and Envelopes

Labels and envelopes are created using prepared database forms furnished with Works. Form letters, hybrid documents that use features of both the word processing and database modules, are discussed in Chapter 13, "Integrating Works Applications."

Preparing Label and Envelope Forms

Labels and envelopes are created using specialized database forms. The setup in Works has already been done for common envelope and label sizes. If the label or envelope size you need is not furnished, you can create a custom form with the correct dimensions.

Labels and envelopes are created in the same way. Use these steps:

1. Open the database that furnishes the information for the labels and/or envelopes.

2. Open the Form menu and choose the command New Form. The New/Set Up Form dialog box appears (see fig. 11.16).

3. Type a name for the form.

4. Click either the Envelope or Label button. A list of sizes appears in the Standard Sizes box.

5. Select the size you want. Scroll the list if necessary to locate the size.

6. Click the Fields button. The Auto Place Fields dialog box opens (see fig. 11.17).

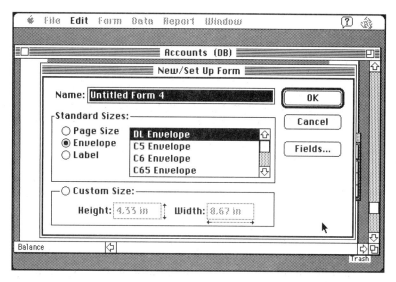

Fig. 11.16
The New/Set Up Form
dialog box.

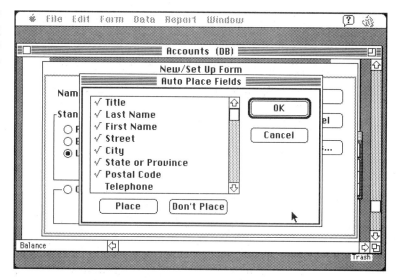

Fig. 11.17
Choose envelope and label
fields in the Auto Place
Fields dialog box.

7. Select a field for the envelope or label and click Place. A check
    mark appears next to the field.

    Repeat this step until all the fields you want have check marks.

Chapter 11

Preparing Database Reports

8. To remove a field from the list, select a checkmarked field name and click Don't Place.

9. Click OK to finish placing fields.

   Works returns you to the New/Set Up Form dialog box.

10. Click OK in the New/Set Up Form dialog box to complete your design.

    Works shows you the design view of your document.

Arrange the fields by dragging them into position on the form. If you want to change the appearance of the field contents, select the field, and choose the Format Character command from the Form menu.

Printing Labels and Envelopes

Printers vary widely in how they feed labels and envelopes. If you have not printed them before, consult your printer documentation for recommendations and cautions involved in envelope and label handling.

The Works database views envelopes and labels as forms. To print from form view, choose Print from the File menu, specify the number of copies and any other settings desired in the Print dialog box, and then click OK.

Some printers feed envelopes lengthwise. In this situation, when you begin to design your envelope form, open the File menu and choose the Page Setup command. In the Page Setup dialog box, select a horizontal (sometimes called *landscape* orientation) page arrangement. Depending on whether your printer feeds from right or left, you may have to move the fields to match. Use the Print Preview command to check your work, and then print with scrap paper to check the alignment in the printer. After you have created an accurately positioned form, you can duplicate the form with the Duplicate Form command from the Form menu.

> **TIP**
>
> To include information that prints identically on every form, with the form in design view, choose Draw On from the Window menu. Choose the Draw Text tool (it looks like the letter A), and click where you want the permanent information to appear. Type the constant information and format it as desired.

Chapter Summary

Chapter 11 is a companion to Chapter 10, "Creating Databases." Chapter 10 covered general database concepts. This chapter explained using Works' report-creation features to extract and format information from your databases. You learned about report features that total and subtotal fields, and about strategies for designing your database to provide the reports you need. You also learned to print reports and forms, and to create and print labels and envelopes.

The next chapter, "Using Works Communications," provides a practical introduction to telecommunications and the Works communications module.

PART

VI

Using
Advanced Features

Includes

USING
MICROSOFT
WORKS

Using Works Communications

12

omputer communications has a reputation as one of the most complex areas of personal computing. And with concepts such as baud rates, protocols, and stop bits, that reputation is easy to understand. Truthfully, *telecommunications*, as the activity is often called, is not the easiest computing activity to master, but the rewards are remarkable. You can swap files with a friend across town or be part of a live round table with participants from Europe and Asia. Telecommunications can bring news flashes, stock quotes, and computer tips to your desktop. True, the telephone bill may rise, but what hobby doesn't have some related expenses?

Communications is not impossible to master; it just takes a bit more attention and technical know-how than some other computer activities require. The communications module in Works is an excellent place to begin learning about computer communications. This module is a capable program that shares Works' easy-to-use features. If you have the necessary equipment, this chapter should help you use the module effectively. You also may want to look into some of the books devoted entirely to the subject, however, because so much additional information about computer communications is available.

USING
MICROSOFT
WORKS

Understanding Communications Concepts

This section gives a general overview of telecommunications and introduces some of the terms necessary to understand the process of communicating using Works. This information provides a framework to help you understand the elements of telecommunications. The information also clarifies the reasons for some of the procedures you follow while using the communications module.

A Typical Communications Session

To give you an overview of the process, here is a walk-through of a typical computer-to-computer communications session:

1. Before starting, you get the necessary communications settings from the person at the other end. Computers don't have to use the same software package on both ends, but computers do need to have the same settings for transfer speed and other signals you will learn about as you proceed in this chapter.

2. You start the communications module next and adjust settings to match those of the remote computer with which you want to connect. You dial the remote computer, which by prearrangement is waiting to answer your call.

3. If the two computers' settings agree, you see a series of messages confirming the connection. At that point, you can use your keyboard to conduct a live conversation with the person at the other end. You also can send a file (*upload*) or receive a file (*download*).

4. If you want to download a file, you obtain the file name and tell Works to begin the downloading process using its error-checking protocol. The two computers transfer the file, exchanging signals to keep track of the process. The program notifies you when the process is finished, at which point you can resume live communications, exchange more files, or sign off.

5. When you end your communications session, you can break the telephone connection and review the files you received without accumulating further phone charges. Many strategies in communications are designed to reduce expensive on-line time. For example, Works enables you to prepare a message before you go on-line. After you store the message as a file, you can upload it

much more rapidly than you can type it. In a similar vein, you can store downloaded messages in a storage area called a *buffer* so that you can scroll back and read the messages after you have disconnected.

Information Services

One reason increasing numbers of computer users are using telecommunications is the growth of on-line information services. An information service is a commercial venture that creates and manages an information and communications network you can access from your computer. Many of them have local phone numbers in the larger metropolitan areas of the U.S. Within such areas, you avoid long-distance tolls, although the service charges you for your minutes on-line. Some of the best-known services are CompuServe, GEnie, Prodigy, and America Online.

Cross-Platform Communications

Another benefit of telecommunications is that it enables you to share information and files with users of other types of computers. If you have the same communications settings on both ends, a Macintosh user can talk live with a remote PC user, or a VAX or UNIX mainframe. Conceptually, all your computer needs to know are the rules that govern the structure and flow of signals over a telephone line. In reality, linking different types of computers is challenging, but it can be done. One of the reasons that the Works communications module has so many options is the need to synchronize your computer with a wide variety of remote computers. You may never use this full potential, but if you become a communications enthusiast, you should know the possibilities.

Communications Equipment

Computer signals cannot travel over phone wires without modification. The device used to change computer signals to phone signals is called a *modem* (pronounced "moe' duhm"). If you have ever picked up a phone with a modem on the line, you have heard the distinctive high-pitched squeal information makes when moving over the phone lines. To use the communications module, you need a modem and the cable that connects it to your Macintosh. You do not need an additional phone line, because every modem has a jack where you can plug in your telephone.

Modems are rated by transmission speed. The unit of measurement is the baud. Think of the baud as a measurement of the number of information characters transmitted in a second. In other words, a 1200-baud modem can transmit or receive 1200 characters per second. The faster you can move information, the less on-line time you pay for. Currently, the most popular modem speed is 2400 baud. You can buy economy models at 1200 baud or high-speed screamers that run at 9600 baud or more. Remember, however, that you can't communicate any faster than the system on the other end.

You can use an Apple-brand modem or any other that responds to the command set created by the Hayes company. When provided with the proper cable and software, a Hayes-compatible modem works on a Macintosh or PC. The Works communications module works with a variety of modems.

Your Macintosh talks to the modem through a *serial port*, the plug marked with an icon of a telephone handset on the back of the computer. You need a cable that matches the ports on your computer and modem. The connections are standardized, but check your documentation to be sure.

Understanding the Communications Screen

The Works communications screen resembles screens from other modules, but the concept behind it is somewhat different (see fig. 12.1). Although the window does serve as an electronic scratch pad recording text you type and receive, the primary purpose of the communications document that appears in the window is to save the settings necessary to communicate with a remote computer. When you save the document, it preserves settings for phone, ports, file transfer, and terminal emulation so that you do not have to re-create them when you next want to call.

Starting Communications

To start Works and create a new communications document, click the Communications icon in the Open dialog box, and then click the New button to create a blank document. Having created the document, you can proceed to establish the necessary settings. The major portion of this chapter, the section called "Establishing Communications Settings," is devoted to a description of the purpose and establishment of the necessary settings.

Fig. 12.1
The Works communications screen.

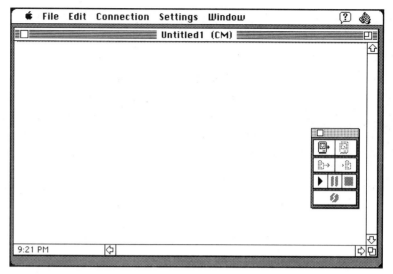

After settings are correct, open the Connection menu and choose Open Connection to begin the process of communication. After exchanging text and files, choose Close Connection to disconnect. When you save your communications document, Works preserves the settings for the next time you want to call. You can create several communications documents, each containing the settings needed to contact a specific remote computer.

The Communications Menus

The following list gives a general description of the five communications menus (see fig. 12.2). Appendix A contains detailed command references.

File menu. Contains the commands used to open, close, and save document files. Commands for page setup and printing also are in this menu. If you are on a network using Microsoft Mail, the Open Mail and Send Mail commands at the bottom of the menu become active. You also quit Works from this menu.

Edit menu. Contains the commands that cut, copy, and move material within and between documents. The Clear Overflow Area command empties the memory area that holds text that has scrolled off the screen.

The Preferences command enables you to determine the overflow area's size and to set defaults for capturing text and notification of closing connections.

Connection menu. Contains the commands that control communications sessions. These commands enable you to open or close communications, download files to disk, and monitor the status and duration of your session.

Settings menu. Contains the commands for establishing the communications rules between your Macintosh and a remote computer. If you save settings in a communications document, you have to set up the configuration only once for each remote computer.

Window menu. Contains the commands that control the display of open documents. Commands controlling the Clipboard display, tool palette, and drawing tools are in this menu. You also enter the Works macro utility here.

Fig. 12.2
The communications menus.

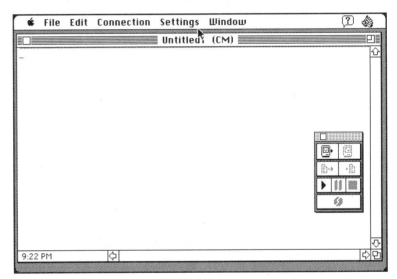

The Communications Tool Palette

Icons on the tool palette provide a point-and-click method of using important commands also found on the menus (see fig. 12.3). Using these icons, you can open and close communications, send or receive a file, and control the capturing of on-screen text.

Fig. 12.3
The tool palette.

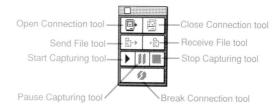

Open Connection tool — Close Connection tool
Send File tool — Receive File tool
Start Capturing tool — Stop Capturing tool

Pause Capturing tool — Break Connection tool

Choose Show Tools or Hide Tools from the Window menu to show or hide the tool palette. You can move the palette on-screen by dragging the title bar, and close the tool palette by clicking the small close box on the title bar.

Performing Quick Communications

If you want to start using Works' communications capabilities immediately, you can use Stationery documents furnished with Works, which enable you to communicate with several popular on-line communications services. You have to find the proper phone numbers and open an account, but the settings are already established.

Using On-line Services

An on-line information service is a company that sells telecommunications services to its subscribers. More than half a dozen active services provide support for both Macintosh and PC systems. The largest, CompuServe, has more than 500,000 subscribers.

On-line services furnish an amazing array of services. You can get computing problems solved quickly in support forums, trade tips with hobbyists in many fields, play interactive games, obtain free or low-cost software, or just chat with other telecommunicators. Because communications software is similar for both Macintosh and PC, you can connect to virtually every facet of an on-line service. Downloadable software and certain types of graphics are machine-specific, but you can converse with anyone.

The cost of these services ranges between $5 and $12.50 per hour of connection time. The larger services have local numbers in metropolitan areas across the country, so you can connect without paying long-distance charges. Most services furnish low or no-cost software to simplify and speed access. You can find advertisements for many services in computer magazines and newspapers. Free or low-cost initial membership offers are often packaged with software from the companies that maintain support forums on one of the services.

Going On-line with Communications Stationery

Works comes with communications stationery—communications documents with settings already established for popular on-line services. Using stationery is a quick way to get on-line because the hard work of establishing settings is already done.

Before beginning communications, you need to obtain a phone number and account number from the information service you plan to use. Some services have special numbers and temporary accounts that enable you to sign up on-line.

When you are ready to proceed with a communications session, follow these steps:

1. Start Works by double-clicking the Works icon.

2. When the Open dialog box appears, click the Communications icon.

3. Open the Stationery folder, and then open the CM Templates folder (see fig. 12.4).

Fig. 12.4
Communications stationery in the CM Templates folder.

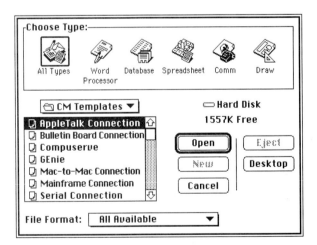

4. Double-click the document for the on-line service you want to use.

   A communications document window opens.

5. From the Connection menu, choose Open Connection.

   Works asks you to enter a phone number for the service.

6. Enter the phone number.

   You need to enter the number only the first time you use the document.

   Works continues and makes the connection.

7. Follow any additional on-screen instructions to complete the connection.

   After the connection has been made, the on-line service controls the procedures for navigating through the service. Consult the documentation furnished by the service, or use on-line help provided by the service.

8. When you have completed your communications, log off the service.

   Several services use *bye*, *off*, or *quit* to disconnect.

9. Open the Connection menu and choose Close Connection to break the telephone connection.

10. To end your session, open the File menu and choose Close, or click the close box.

    Your communications document closes.

If you cannot connect with the on-line service, you probably have a problem with the settings in your communications Stationery document. To understand and modify the settings, read the next section of this chapter called "Establishing Communications Settings."

Establishing Communications Settings

Settings are the most complex part of telecommunications because of the great variety of remote computers with which you can connect. You can talk to other Macintosh machines, to PCs, and to mainframe systems. In each case, communications settings need to be adjusted so that both ends of the connection are speaking the same language. After you have discovered the proper settings and saved them in a communications document, communications becomes a simple matter of opening the saved document and choosing Open Connection.

Until you gain some experience with communications, expect a bit of frustration. Remain patient and work methodically to modify settings until they are correct. Seeing the first words from a remote computer appear on your screen is a thrill well worth the frustration.

The communications document is the key to creating and preserving settings. Open a new document for each group of settings you want to create and save. Using the commands described in this section, establish the settings you need, save them, and give the document a name that reflects its use, such as CompuServe or America Online. Settings are grouped by their three purposes: connection settings, file transfer settings, and terminal settings.

Choosing Connection Settings

When you open the Settings menu and choose the Connection command, the Connection Settings dialog box opens (see fig. 12.5). Your first choice should be the method of connection. Clicking the arrow at the right end of the box labeled Method displays three tools: Apple Modem Tool, AppleTalk ADSP Tool, and Serial Tool (see fig. 12.6). This section focuses on the Apple Modem tool.

Fig. 12.5
The Connection Settings dialog box for phone, port, and modem settings.

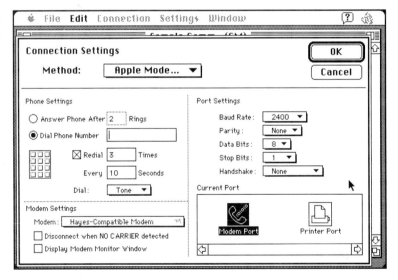

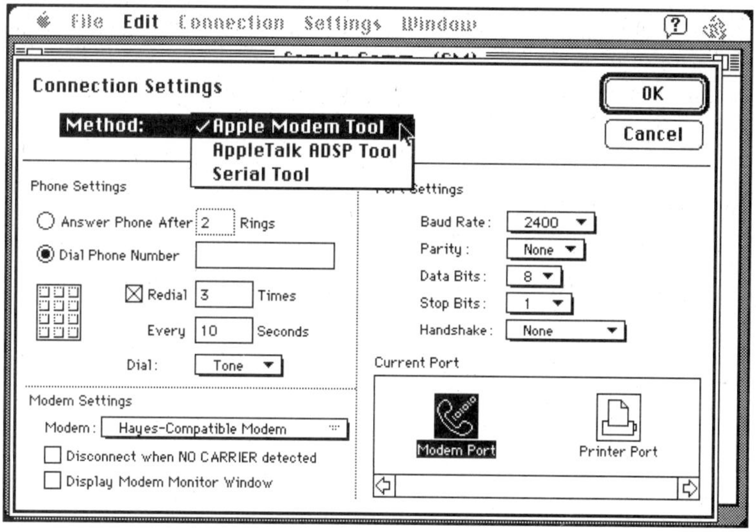

Fig. 12.6
The three connection
methods.

Choosing Phone Settings

Phone settings control when your modem answers incoming calls, the number for your modem to dial, the dialing method (tone or pulse), and redialing instructions. You can automate subsequent dialing after properly establishing these settings.

Answer Phone after (xx) Rings

Use the rings setting when you want to wait for an incoming call. When you click the radio button to activate the command, the other phone settings are grayed out and an icon of a ringing phone appears (see fig. 12.7). This setting enables you to establish the number of rings allowed before your modem answers. Enter a number that is convenient for you. If the number gets too high, however, some modems trying to call your system may give up and report No Answer to their users.

Dial Phone Number

Enter all necessary digits, including access codes (9, for instance), area code, and number. You can use hyphens or parentheses for clarity, but they are not required. Sometimes, you need a delay between parts of the number. For example, you may need to dial 9 and then wait for an outside line. To insert a short delay, type a comma in the string of numbers.

Ringing phone ——

Redial

You can instruct the modem to redial when it doesn't make a connection initially. Enter the number of times to redial and the interval, in seconds, between dialing attempts. If you do not want the modem to redial, uncheck the Redial check box (see fig. 12.8).

Dial

You can specify tone, pulse, or mixed tone and pulse dialing. If you have a mixed dialing type, put a **P** before the digits to be dialed with a pulse and a **T** before those dialed using a tone.

Fig. 12.8

A checked redial box and specifications for redial attempts and their frequency.

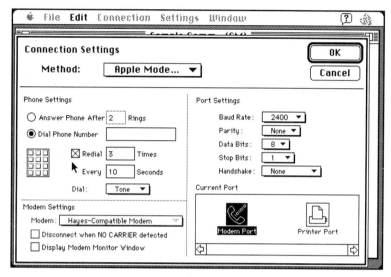

Choosing Modem Settings

The Apple Modem Tool enables you to select a number of popular modem brands by opening the Modem drop-down list. Notice that the list scrolls to show more choices. Although all modems work in the same general way, you can select a modem brand with features and capabilities specific to your needs. Consult your modem literature for a listing of nonstandard features. If your modem is not on the drop-down list but is described as Hayes compatible in your modem literature, choose Hayes-Compatible Modem from the list.

Choosing Port Settings

Port settings are critically important to the success of a communications session. Both computers must be using the same settings, or one computer will not understand the other. A typical sign of improper setting is the appearance of textual "garbage" on the screen during an attempt to communicate. Commercial services and bulletin boards typically publish their communications settings. You may read in a magazine that the specifications for a bulletin board are "2400, N, 8, 1." Those specifications mean you should set your port settings so you communicate at 2400 baud with no parity, 8 data bits, and 1 stop bit. You don't need to understand the effect of these settings to use them, but the abbreviated definitions that follow should help you build your communications knowledge.

Baud Rate

Baud rate is the speed at which your modem sends and receives information. This rate is roughly equivalent to the number of characters per second that a modem can transmit or receive. The speeds available depend on your modem. The best combination of price and speed at present is a 2400-baud modem, although prices are falling for the faster 9600-baud variety. Works has capabilities for a wide range of rates—from 110 to 57,600 baud. Remember, however, that you can transmit or receive only as fast as the computer on the other end.

Parity

Parity checking is a relatively primitive way of ensuring the accuracy of a transmission. When precision is critical, a communication protocol, discussed in the section called "Establishing File Transfer Settings," usually supplants parity. Depending on the remote computer, you can choose parity settings of None, Even, or Odd.

Data Bits

The setting for data bits establishes the number of binary digits (bits) used to send a single character. Works offers a choice of four settings, ranging from 5 to 8 bits.

Stop Bits

The Stop Bits setting specifies the number of bits to attach to the end of each character to indicate that the entire character has been transmitted. Works provides a selection of 1, 1.5, or 2.

Handshake

At times, hardware handling a communications transfer may need to stop the communications flow briefly to catch up with information on hand. The process used by communicating computers to start and stop the data flow is called *handshaking*.

When using a modem, choose between the XON/XOFF and None settings. Unless you encounter data loss in complex transmissions, the None setting is appropriate because the XMODEM and KERMIT file transfer protocols are not compatible with XON/XOFF. The DTR and CTS options are used only with direct connections involving hardware handshaking.

Current Port

The Current Port setting indicates the port to which your modem cable is attached. Click the appropriate icon for this setting.

Establishing File Transfer Settings

NOTE

Don't let the technical complexity of protocols discourage you. The great majority of file transfers proceed correctly with the default settings. Understanding the alternative settings and their purpose helps when you encounter problems, but you will probably not use alternative settings with any frequency.

When important information needs to move from computer to computer, the transmission must be accurate. With text, you can work around an occasional missing character or word, but in a program file transmission, a single missing character can cause the program to fail.

File transfer protocols are sets of rules that ensure correct file transfers regardless of the type of hardware or software being used. These protocols incorporate rules for such things as error detection and correction, as well as the amount of data sent in a single block. Works offers three protocols: Text, XMODEM, and Kermit. You access these protocols by opening the Settings menu and choosing File Transfer (see fig. 12.9).

This section describes the reasons for choosing specific protocols and the settings associated with them. The section of this chapter called "Sending and Receiving Data" covers the process of using a protocol to send or receive a file.

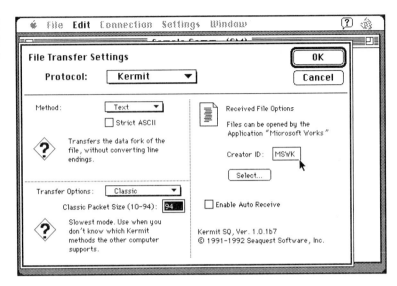

Fig. 12.9

The File Transfer Settings
dialog box.

Text File Transfers

For transferring ordinary text files, like word processing files, use the text file transfer tool. This tool is fast and simple to use, although more prone to error than the Kermit or XMODEM protocols. Phone line disturbances can cause words or characters to be lost or garbled. On the other hand, when a less than perfect copy is acceptable, the transfer tool's speed and simplicity recommend it.

To access the text file transfer tool, open the File Transfer Settings dialog box by choosing File Transfer from the Settings menu. Then choose Text Tool from the pop-up menu of protocols. A dialog box for protocol settings opens (see fig. 12.10). The Text Tool protocol has only two settings: Timing and Line Endings.

Timing

If the remote computer cannot receive information as fast as Works can send it, and one computer cannot tell the other to pause sending (see *handshaking* in a preceding section), you can insert delays after the transmission of each character or each line. You need to use this technique only when words or lines of text are consistently missing from your transmission. To set the delay, type a value in 60ths of a second.

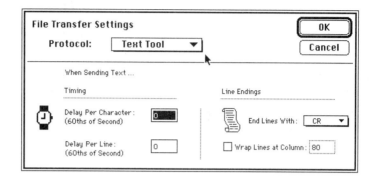

Fig. 12.10
The Text Tool dialog box.

Line Endings

Many communications programs differentiate between a carriage return instruction and a line feed instruction. When a carriage return is received, the cursor moves back to the left end of the current line. A line feed instruction moves the cursor down one line. You or the user of the remote computer can observe the way the cursor behaves, and add or remove line feeds and carriage returns by using the drop-down list labeled End Lines With.

The XMODEM Protocol

In the late 1970s, XMODEM was introduced as one of the first error-checking protocols for personal computers. This protocol comes in several "flavors," some adapted specifically to the Macintosh, others in use by all types of computers. Today, although some newer protocols are faster, XMODEM remains the most widely used method.

To establish XMODEM settings for a file transfer, open the Settings menu and choose File Transfer. In the File Transfer Settings dialog box, selecting the XMODEM Tool from the pop-up menu of protocols opens the dialog box shown in figure 12.11. The sections that follow explain the settings available for XMODEM: Method, Timing Options, Transfer Options, and Received File Options.

Method

Works supports four XMODEM protocol variations adapted for different purposes. Select an option by opening the drop-down list labeled Method and highlighting one of the following protocol variations:

Fig. 12.11
The XMODEM Tool
dialog box.

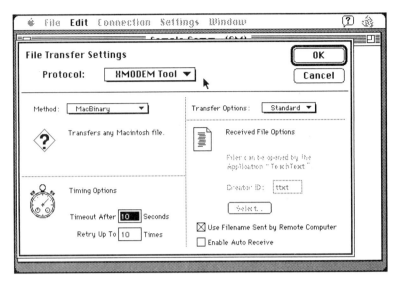

MacBinary. Because of the two-part structure of a Macintosh file (consisting of a *data fork* and a re*source fork*), this default method works well for Mac-to-Mac transfers. MacBinary transfers the file resource fork with the file.

MacTerminal 1.1. This method also preserves the distinctive Macintosh file structure for Mac-to-Mac transfers. In addition, it handles file reception automatically.

Straight XMODEM. You might choose this option to transfer a complex file to a non-Macintosh user. This method transfers only the data fork of a Macintosh file.

XMODEM Text. This method is appropriate for exchanging text with a non-Macintosh system. It modifies line endings to match the needs of the receiving system, retaining line and paragraph spacing.

Timing Options

The transfer protocol attempts to resend a packet of information when an error is made. The Retry specification tells the program how many times to resend before giving up on the transmission. If transmission is interrupted, the Timeout specification tells the program how long to wait before abandoning the file transfer.

Transfer Options

Alternative transfer options can speed your transmission, but you need to be certain the remote computer is using the same options. You can establish communications using the Standard setting and then ask the other operator whether the remote system supports one of the following alternatives:

Standard. This option uses 128K blocks and basic error checking.

CRC-16. This option uses 128K blocks with improved error checking.

1K Blocks. This option is faster than CRC-16, but uses the same error checking.

CleanLink. This is the fastest option, but requires an error-free serial connection, such as cable. Phone lines are not usually clean enough.

Received File Options

With MacBinary or MacTerminal 1.1 XMODEM protocols, you can save a file with the file name used by the remote computer when you check the first box at the bottom of the Received File Options box. By checking the second box, you can enable a MacBinary protocol transfer to proceed automatically if the transmitting program supports the option.

With Straight XMODEM or XMODEM Text protocols, a series of choices in the Received File Options box becomes available. Each Macintosh file normally includes a Creator ID which identifies the file's program, although non-Macintosh transfers do not include this information.

By default, Works adds TeachText as the creator application for received files. If you want to change this designation, click the Select button to display the names of applications to open received files (see fig. 12.12). When you select an application, Works attaches the Creator ID to incoming files. Then, opening the transferred file launches the designated program.

The Kermit Protocol

Kermit is another widely used file transfer protocol. Whereas XMODEM requires 8 data bits per byte for correct transfer, some computer systems cannot handle the 8th bit. Kermit can use 7 or 8 data bits. The sliding windows Kermit method enables the program to send a continuous stream of data while receiving responses at the same time, thus speeding transmission.

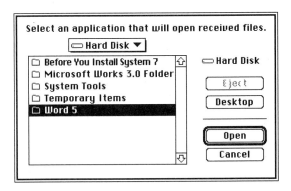

Fig. 12.12
The Creator ID dialog box.

To establish Kermit settings for a file transfer, open the Settings menu and choose File Transfer. In the File Transfer Settings dialog box, selecting the Kermit Tool from the drop-down list of protocols opens the dialog box shown in figure 12.13. The sections that follow explain the settings available for Kermit: Method, Transfer Options, and Received File Options.

Fig. 12.13
The Kermit dialog box.

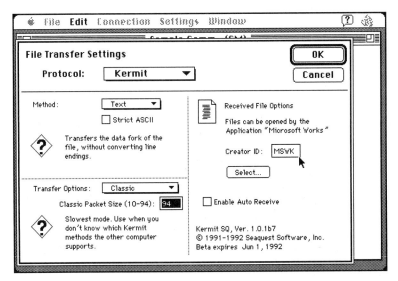

Method

Works supports three Kermit protocol variations adapted for different purposes. Select an option by opening the pop-up menu labeled Method and highlighting one of the following options:

Text. Choose the Text method to transfer text files to a non-Macintosh system because this method retains line and paragraph spacing. By choosing the Strict ASCII check box associated with this method, you can transfer only alphanumeric characters, omitting control codes and extended characters that some systems may not recognize.

MacBinary. This method is appropriate for Mac-to-Mac exchanges. It transfers both the data and resource forks of a file.

Binary. Use Binary for transfer of complex files to non-Macintosh systems. This method transfers only the data fork of a Macintosh file.

Transfer Options

Alternative transfer options can speed your transmission, but you need to be certain that the remote computer is using the same options. You can establish communications using the Classic setting and then ask the other operator whether the remote system supports one of these alternatives:

Classic. This option is the slowest, but most universal mode.

Long Packet. Using larger packets to speed transmission, Long Packet is the fastest option. You type a packet size—256 or greater—in the text box. Both computers must use the same setting.

Sliding Windows. This option is faster than standard. Both computers must specify the same number of windows. Type the number in the text box.

Received File Options

When using the Text, MacBinary, or Binary Kermit protocols, you can mark the check box at the bottom of the Received File Options box, enabling a protocol transfer to proceed automatically if the transmitting program supports the option.

With Text or Binary Kermit protocols, a series of choices in the Received File Options box becomes available. Each Macintosh file normally includes a Creator ID that identifies the file's program, although non-Macintosh transfers do not include this information.

By default, Works adds Microsoft Works (MSWK) as the creator application for received files. If you want to change this designation, click the Select button and use the pop-up menu to find the application for opening received files. When you select an application, Works attaches the Creator ID to incoming files. Then, opening the transferred file launches the designated program.

Chapter 12

Using Works Communications

Terminal Emulation

In the context of communications, a *terminal* is the type of keyboard and monitor a specific computer uses. To communicate successfully with a different computer, your computer must be able to imitate the behavior of the remote terminal. Works provides the capability to imitate—often called *emulate*—three popular terminal types: TTY, VT102, and VT320.

Before using terminal emulation, be sure that the remote computer expects or is set to the emulation you plan to use. If the remote system is not using the same emulation, you cannot connect successfully. To choose a terminal emulation, open the Settings menu and choose the Terminal command. The dialog box shown in figure 12.14 opens. The following list explains terminal settings.

Fig. 12.14
The Terminal Settings dialog box.

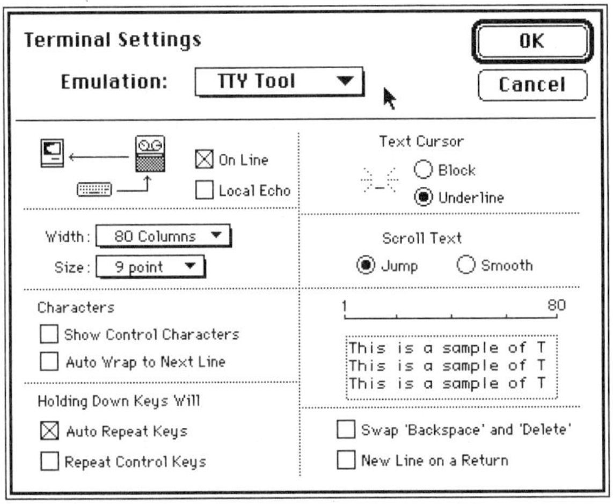

NOTE

You do not need an actual terminal type to use that type of terminal emulation. When two computers are using the same emulation, both understand the meaning of keystrokes in the same way. In other words, you might get a Macintosh and a PC talking the same language by having both emulate a VT102 terminal.

TTY. TTY is an abbreviation for Teletypewriter. It is the simplest emulation; each keystroke generates a character code that is sent to the receiving machine. Use TTY when you do not know what emulation the remote computer expects or when other emulations do not work.

VT102. The VT102 is a popular terminal made by Digital Equipment Company (DEC). Many mainframe and minicomputers use DEC terminals. The VT102 emulation provides keyboard functionality similar to the basic features of a Macintosh or PC keyboard.

VT320. The VT320 is another DEC terminal widely used in business and widely emulated in communications software. In general, the VT102 and the VT320 behave somewhat like a Macintosh or PC, responding to tab, backspace, and cursor-movement keys as you would expect.

A full listing of settings and keyboard codes for the VT102 and VT320 emulations is beyond the scope of this book, but some general observations may be helpful if you regularly use these emulations.

The emulation settings fall into four groups: general, screen, keyboard, and character set. When you open the dialog box for VT102 or VT320 emulation, icons down the left side of the window enable you to display settings for the four groups.

Understanding two settings should help you get started using the emulations. In the middle of the Terminal Settings dialog box is a diagram of a Macintosh, a keyboard, and a mainframe computer connected by arrows. Next to the diagram are check boxes for two important emulation settings: On Line and Local Echo (see fig. 12.15).

Fig. 12.15

The Terminal Settings dialog box with the On Line box marked.

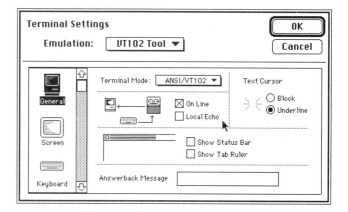

Normally, the On Line box is selected, and you can communicate with the remote computer. If you need to go off-line temporarily, to change a setting for instance, uncheck this box and click OK. You keep the connection, but do not transmit any activity from your computer to the remote location. Be sure to restore the On Line check mark when you are through with off-line changes. Notice that the directions of the arrows change.

In most communications, the remote computer receives what you type and then echoes it back to your screen. This feedback provides one way of judging the accuracy of the transmission. In cases when the remote computer does not echo your typing, you need to turn on a local echo by choosing the Local Echo check box. You easily can judge the correct setting by watching your screen. If the screen is blank when you type, turn on Local Echo. If you see double characters, lliikkee tthhiiss, turn off Local Echo.

If you make frequent use of one of the VT terminal emulations, contact the user of the remote computer to get a listing of the keyboard functions. Fully exploring terminal emulation, however, is beyond the scope of this book.

Direct Connection and Networks

The Connection Settings pop-up menu of methods includes an AppleTalk ADSP Tool. This tool facilitates connections and file transfer on an AppleTalk network. Consult your network manager for information about settings and the use of this tool.

Sending and Receiving Data

After specifying the correct settings and saving a communications document for the remote computer you want to reach, you are ready for the actual communications process. Prepare your transmission, connect to the remote computer, type or transmit a file, and sign off when you are done. In this section, you learn the procedures for keyboard-to-keyboard communication, simple text transfers, and transfers of complex files with the use of error-correcting protocols.

This section assumes that you have created a communications document containing settings and the phone number for the remote computer to which you want to connect. If you are not familiar with these procedures, please review the previous sections of this chapter.

Connecting with a Remote Computer

Assuming that your communications document is complete and correct and your modem is set up and turned on, follow these steps to go on-line:

1. Open the File menu and choose Open.

   You also can click the Communications icon.

   Works displays a list of communication documents.

2. Double-click the communications document you want to open.

   Works opens the document.

3. Open the Connection menu and choose Open Connection.

   You also can click the Open Connection tool on the tool palette.

4. Watch the modem status window to follow the status of the call.

5. After you have connected, begin typing to converse with the remote computer.

6. To end the call, open the Connection menu and choose Close Connection.

   You also can click the Close Connection tool on the tool palette.

TIP

You can tell Works to dial automatically when you open a communications document. Open the document, and then open the Settings menu and choose Options. In the dialog box that opens, choose the check box labeled Open Connection Automatically (see fig. 12.16), and then choose OK. The next time you open the document, the program dials automatically.

Fig. 12.16
The Open Connection Automatically check box is selected.

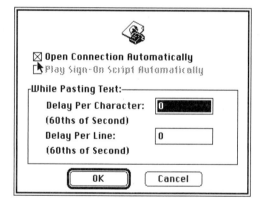

Capturing Text

You can save the information that scrolls across your screen while you are communicating with another user or an information service. Works temporarily saves on-screen text in a capture buffer in memory. Using a file capture protocol, you can specify that the program also copy the text you enter to a capture file on your disk.

Although you also can capture text files sent to the screen by a remote computer, you do not have the benefits of error correction or flow control because you cannot use a file capture protocol with those files.

To capture text from the screen, follow these steps:

1. Open the Connection menu and choose Start Capture.

   The File to Capture Text To dialog box opens (see fig. 12.17).

Fig. 12.17
The File To Capture Text
To dialog box.

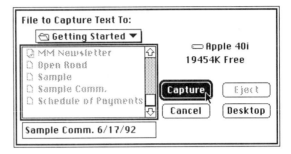

2. Choose a folder and name the file to receive communications.

3. Click the Capture button to start the capture process.

You can control capturing by choosing the commands Pause Capture, Resume Capture, and Stop Capture from the Connection menu; but for greater convenience, open the tool palette and use the three icons shown in figure 12.18. You can drag the tool palette to a convenient corner of the menu and use it throughout your communications session.

Fig. 12.18
Tool palette icons
for controlling
communi-
cations.

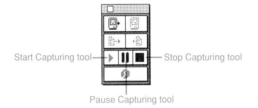

Controlling the Overflow Area

Text that scrolls off the screen goes into an overflow area in memory that holds the text temporarily. In communications, this type of storage area is often called a *buffer*. You can control the size of the overflow area from the Communications Preferences window, which you activate by opening the Edit menu and choosing Preferences (see fig. 12.19).

Fig. 12.19
Overflow Area Size
dialog box.

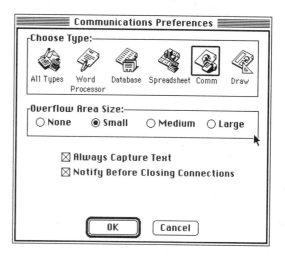

Increasing the size of the overflow area decreases the amount of free memory available to Works. If you have limited memory resources, you may want to restrict the size of the overflow area. If the overflow area fills, the program discards the first material stored to fit in new material. You can permanently preserve all screen text by creating a capture file using the instructions in the section of this chapter called "Capturing Text."

To discard the contents of the overflow area, open the Edit menu and choose the command Clear Overflow Area.

Transmitting and Receiving Files

The best way to transmit and receive complex files is with an error-correcting protocol. You can use XMODEM or Kermit, depending on the requirements of the remote computer. Use of error-correcting protocols ensures accurate transmissions.

If you have not read the section of this chapter called "Establishing Communications Settings," you may want to read it before continuing. The current section assumes that you are familiar with the protocol choices and settings described previously.

The procedure for receiving a file involves the following steps:

1. Before beginning, try to determine the protocol for both computers to use.

2. Open a communications document containing settings to contact the remote computer.

3. Choose File Transfer from the Settings menu, and then select a protocol to govern the file transfer.

   Alter other settings at this time if necessary.

4. Choose Open Connection from the Connection menu.

5. Tell the remote computer operator to begin sending the file.

   You can make this command by remote menu selection or keyboard message.

6. Open the Connection menu and choose Receive File.

   You also can click the Receive File tool on the tool palette.

7. Monitor the transfer periodically.

   You can switch to other Works modules while the transfer proceeds.

8. When the transfer is complete, sign off if required.

   Some information services require a sign-off procedure.

9. To end the session, open the Connection menu and choose Close Connection.

To send a file, follow the same procedure used for receiving a file, except for steps 5 and 6. Instead of those steps, choose Send File from the Connection menu, or use the Send tool on the tool palette.

Waiting for a Call

If the remote computer originates your communications session, you need to set your Macintosh to answer. Follow these steps:

1. Open the proper communication document and turn on your modem.

2. Open the Communications menu and choose Listen For Connection.

   Works waits for the call and connects when it arrives.

To change the number of rings before answering, open the Settings menu and choose Connection. Choose the connection method used in the current communications document and locate the option labeled Answer Phone After *xx* Rings. Type the desired number of rings.

Automating Sign-On

With some remote computers, you go through a series of steps to sign on. Works can record and play back the steps to automate your connection. To automate a sign-on, follow these steps:

1. Open a communications document for the service you want.

2. Open the Settings menu and choose Record Sign-On.

3. Open the Connection menu and choose Open Connection.

   Works records your subsequent actions.

4. Go through the steps necessary to sign on to the remote computer.

5. When the sign-on is complete, open the Settings menu and choose Stop Recording Sign-On.

   Works stores your sign-on actions with the communications document. If you use a password, the program sends it whenever you use the document.

To use a recorded sign-on sequence, follow these steps:

1. Open the communications document containing the sign-on information.

2. Open the Connection menu and choose Open Connection.

3. Open the Settings menu and choose Play Sign-On.

To fully automate the sign-on, open the Settings menu and choose Options. Choose the check box labeled Play Sign-On Script Automatically, and click OK. The next time you use the communications document, the sign-on script should run when you make the connection.

Tracking Costs and Time

The first bills for communications costs can come as a shock. In the excitement of live telecommunications, you can easily forget that the meter is running, adding up costs by the minute. Works provides an excellent array of reminders that keep track of connection time and costs. With these features activated, you can track costs while communications are underway and review a screen that accumulates session costs and totals.

When you activate a group of commands located on the Connection menu, Works can place cost and time information on the status bar at the bottom of your screen. To control the status bar display, follow these steps:

1. Open the Connection menu and choose Status Bar.

   A cascade menu appears (see fig. 12.20).

2. Drag the mouse down the cascade menu to choose the desired option.

   Table 12.1 describes the options.

3. Release the mouse button to place the selected option on the status bar.

Fig. 12.20
The Status Bar
cascade menu.

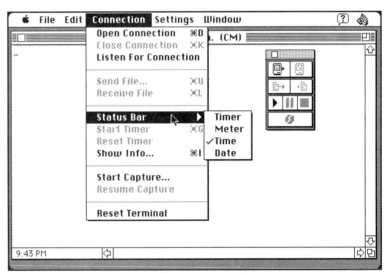

Table 12.1
Status Bar Options

Option	Result
Timer	Counts elapsed time from the start of a connection
Meter	Counts dollars spent from the start of a connection
Time	Displays the current time
Date	Displays the current date

Works keeps session totals and cumulative totals in the Show Info dialog box, which you can reach by choosing Show Info from Connection menu (see fig. 12.21). You control the charge rate used by the program by entering a cost in the Estimated Cost box and choosing a unit of measurement from the drop down list below the box. The program then computes charges by multiplying the estimated cost by the elapsed connection time. Although only estimates, these tallies can help you keep in touch with the cost of communicating.

To clear all totals and the estimated cost figure, choose the Reset All button in the dialog box.

Fig. 12.21
The Show Info dialog box.

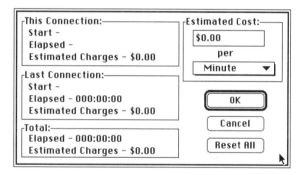

Chapter Summary

orks provides excellent tools that enable you to enter the world of on-line communications. In this chapter, you learned communications concepts, quick communications methods using communications stationery, and ways to understand and control the settings required to match your communications with that of a remote computer. The chapter described techniques for capturing the flow of on-screen activity and explains methods of sending and receiving files. In Chapter 13, you will learn how to move information among the different Works modules.

Integrating Works Applications

ndividually, each Works module is quite useful. Combined, they provide a synergy that makes the whole of Works more powerful than the sum of its parts. With multiple modules, you can produce results beyond the capability of any one module. You can enhance word processing documents with drawings, incorporate spreadsheets into letters, and paste files into the flow of on-line communications.

Moving information between modules has been discussed in the chapters about individual modules. Those concepts and procedures have been gathered in this chapter to make them easy to locate and to encourage you to experiment with the power of integrated documents.

Understanding Integration Concepts

The ability to integrate information from multiple modules is made possible by a combination of Macintosh features and Works programming. The Macintosh Clipboard stores the data you are moving from one module, and the Works program design ensures that the other modules can manage that data. You can apply a Draw layer to enhance several modules. The skill with which your Macintosh manages multiple windows enables you to flip from document to document as you would on a real desktop, moving and combining pieces as you go.

Clipboard and Scrapbook

The Clipboard and Scrapbook are features of the Macintosh operating system. The Clipboard is the area in memory where the system stores information you cut or copy from the screen while you move the information to another location. The Scrapbook provides permanent storage of material you copy or cut from the screen.

The Clipboard has the unusual property of storing one item, no matter how large or small, until you turn off the computer or replace the item with another one. If you copy an entire document to the Clipboard, for example, and then copy a period from the page, the period displaces the document. If you do not replace an item with something new, you can use the item over and over.

The amount of memory in your computer controls the capacity of the Clipboard. The operating system, the Works program, and open documents use substantial amounts of memory. You can view the current contents of the Clipboard by opening the Window menu and choosing the View Clipboard command. A window opens to display the contents (see fig. 13.1).

A desk accessory located on the Apple menu, the Scrapbook enables you to paste material from the screen into a file you can reuse in the future (see fig. 13.2). Unlike the Clipboard, when you shut off your Macintosh, material in the Scrapbook does not disappear.

Fig. 13.1
The View Clipboard
command shows the
contents of the Clipboard.

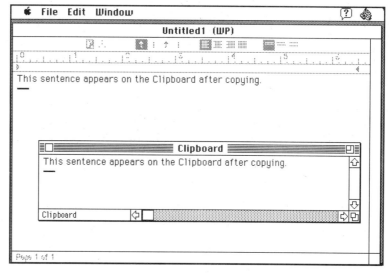

Fig. 13.2
You can reuse Scrapbook
contents.

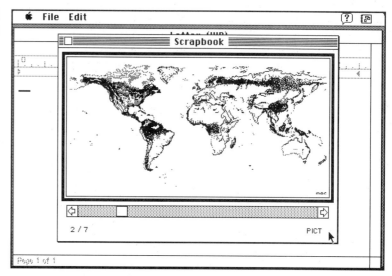

Follow these steps to place an item into the Scrapbook:

1. Copy the item you want to place in the Scrapbook. The item now resides in the Clipboard.

Chapter 13

Integrating Works Applications

2. From the Apple menu, select Scrapbook. The Scrapbook opens, displaying its first entry. New items are pasted in front of this first entry.

3. With the Scrapbook open, paste your copy. Note that the Scrapbook numbers the copy 1 / 1 to assist you in later finding the data, and tells you the format and originating application of the copy.

4. To retrieve an item from the Scrapbook, open it from the Apple menu and use the Copy or Cut procedures to place the data into the Clipboard. Return to your application document by clicking the mouse anywhere in the document window. Use the Paste procedure to place the data from the Clipboard into your application.

5. To exit the Scrapbook, click the close box in the upper left corner of the title bar.

Memory Requirements

As operating systems and programs become more complex, the need for Macintosh memory grows. System 7 alone requires nearly two megabytes of memory. If you are using MultiFinder, you need at least one megabyte of memory reserved for its operation. Works also requires at least two megabytes of memory to function.

You may run out of memory if you have multiple Works documents open and then cut or copy a large document. If you do run out of memory, you can close windows or reduce the size of what you put in memory, but if you plan to make use of Works' integration capabilities, you should consider purchasing additional memory for your Macintosh.

In System 7, the Finder is always running to manage disks, files, memory allocation, and access to documents. You can open as many other programs and desk accessories as you have memory space. The number of programs you can have open is restricted by the amount of RAM available. You only can open a new program if there is sufficient free memory.

Be aware of your RAM situation. To avoid fragmenting your system, first load the program you use most often and rarely quit, then load the next useful, and the next, and so forth, until you have finished opening programs.

You can keep opening applications until you run out of RAM. The Macintosh will tell you when this occurs with a message box (see fig. 13.3) telling you to close some applications before opening any more programs.

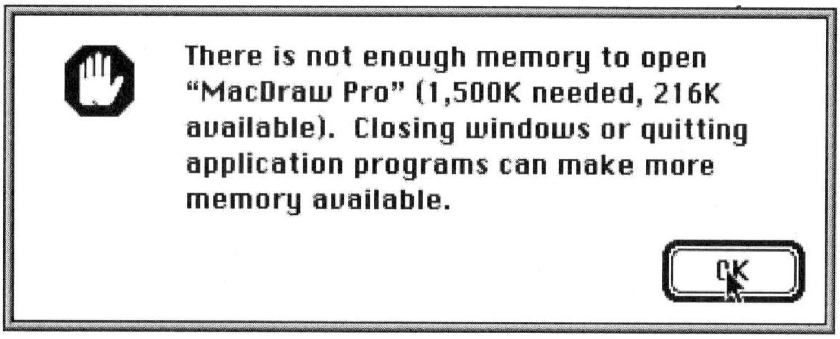

Fig. 13.3
This is the warning
message if you have run
out of RAM.

There is not enough memory to open
"MacDraw Pro" (1,500K needed, 216K
available). Closing windows or quitting
application programs can make more
memory available.

OK

Added memory is a good investment, both for improved performance
and the capability to create larger documents, use more applications
concurrently, and use the full power of System 7.

Workspaces

To move material among Works documents, having several documents
open on-screen at once is helpful. If you use a group of files together,
instead of repeatedly opening and closing them, you can open the
documents you need and then save them all as a workspace file. A
workspace file keeps your common files organized and accessible.

A workspace file saves the structure and content of the screen as it
appears when the file is created. When you open the workspace file,
Works reproduces the window sizes and locations and reopens the
modules that were running when you created the workspace file. Use
the following steps to create a workspace file:

1. Open the files you want to include in your workspace file.

2. Place the windows in the arrangement in which you want them
   saved.

3. Open the File menu and choose Save Workspace. The dialog box
   shown in figure 13.4 opens.

4. Choose a folder for the workspace file and type the file name in
   the Save Workspace As dialog box.

5. Click Save to store the workspace file.

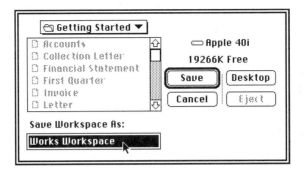

Fig. 13.4
The Save Workspace dialog
box.

NOTE

A file that is not saved will not be saved in a workspace.

When you want to use the workspace file, open the File menu and choose Open. Workspace files are listed with your other Works files. Be sure that the File Format pop-up menu displays All Available as the format.

Moving Data

The procedure for moving data is similar in all modules. In this section, the general procedure is described, and then special considerations involved in specific modules are discussed. You can move information either by copying it, which leaves the original material intact, or by cutting it, which removes material from the source document. In either event, the copy moves to the Clipboard, the memory area described in the "Scrapbook and Clipboard" section of this chapter. The general procedure for copying or cutting data includes these general steps:

1. Open the source and the target documents.

2. Select the information to be cut or copied.

3. Open the Edit menu and choose Copy or Cut, as appropriate.

4. Click the target document to make it active, or select the document from the Window menu.

5. Click in the document where you want the Clipboard contents to appear. For details, see the discussion in the following sections.

6. Open the Edit menu and choose Paste. The cut or copied material is pasted in place.

Integrating Material with the Word Processing Module

The word processor is often the logical center for integrating information. The elements of combined documents are often linked with passages of explanatory text. You might prepare a report that analyzes database information in a spreadsheet and then graphs it, but the final document probably would end up in the word processor as you arranged and explained the information.

Pasting from a Spreadsheet

Spreadsheet formulas do not survive a trip to the word processor. You can paste only the values generated by the formula. If you later edit the information in the word processor, the values affected by formulas do not change.

In the spreadsheet, select only the cells you want to copy. Including excess cells can cause problems with formatting. The contents of a spreadsheet are pasted into the word processor as rows of text or values separated by tabs. Tab widths are equivalent to spreadsheet column widths. A return is placed at the end of each row.

You can reformat the information by adjusting the tabs. Be sure to include the rows containing your column headings when you highlight the area of the spreadsheet you want to copy or cut to a word processing document. Column headings automatically follow their text into a database module unless you hold down the Option key while pasting. Figure 13.5 shows an example of spreadsheet material pasted into a word processor document.

To copy material from a spreadsheet to the word processor, use these steps:

1. Select the cells to be copied.

2. Open the File menu and choose Copy. The selected information is placed on the Clipboard.

3. Switch to the target word processor document.

4. Place the insertion point where you want the copied material to appear.

5. Open the Edit menu and choose Paste.

Fig. 13.5
Spreadsheet information appears as values separated by tabs.

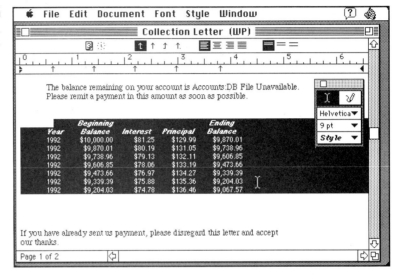

Pasting a Chart

Charts are Draw objects. When a chart is pasted into the word processor, the chart automatically activates and is pasted to a Draw layer on top of the document. Because the text does not automatically move out of the way, accommodating the chart may take some editing and moving of text.

When pasted to the Draw layer, the chart may cover text in the document. When pasted to the word processor, a chart loses its link to the spreadsheet from which the chart was created. You can resize and drag the chart using Draw commands or the tool palette. Figure 13.6 shows a chart pasted into a word processor document.

Fig. 13.6
Charts are pasted as Draw
objects.

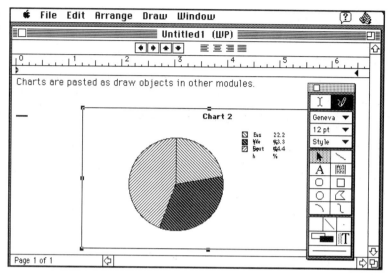

Pasting from the Database

The procedure for moving database information into a word processing document is similar to the process used to move spreadsheet information. Database information arrives as rows of information with the contents of each selected field separated from the adjacent field by a tab (see fig. 13.7). Field names are copied automatically, unless you hold down the Option key while pasting. They appear as the first line of the pasted selection. After the information is pasted, it can be edited and enhanced as normal word processing text.

You can reformat the pasted material by selecting it and then moving the tabs to control the distance between fields and using the Format Character command to change text appearance. If you copy fields that contain calculations, the calculations are inactivated and do not change if you change information they use.

Pasting Database Totals

Although you cannot copy complete database reports into a word processor document, you can copy report totals. As explained in the section of Chapter 11 called "Computing Totals," you can use the Copy Totals command to put totals from an active report onto the Clipboard. From the Clipboard, you can paste the totals into the word processor.

TIP

Don't forget the option of moving both chart and text into Draw where you can create a columnar layout. See Chapter 5, "Creating Drawings," for more information.

Chapter 13
Integrating Works Applications

Fig. 13.7
Database information is
pasted as tab-separated
fields.

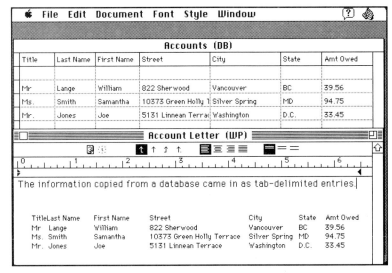

Integrating Data in a Spreadsheet

When you need to analyze numbers, the spreadsheet is the proper tool. You can transfer information to the spreadsheet from either the word processor or the database. The spreadsheet can display both text and values. A key point to remember is that the format of pasted information is controlled by the format of the receiving spreadsheet.

When pasting to a spreadsheet, be sure you have a large enough area of empty cells to receive the pasted information. If not, you can inadvertently overwrite information.

Pasting Data from the Word Processor Module

The key to moving data successfully from word processor to spreadsheet lies in the use of tabs. If you select text or values as a continuous row, everything you select is pasted into a single cell. If, in the word processor, you separate items with tabs, each item is placed in a separate cell in the spreadsheet. In figure 13.8, the top line of text was a single selection. The text and values on the row below were separated by tabs.

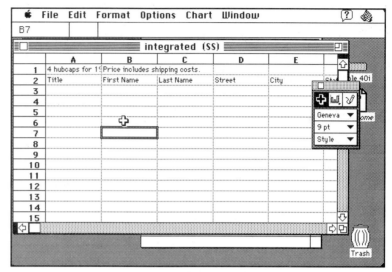

Fig. 13.8
Tabs separate items into
individual cells.

Pasting Data from the Database Module

Information moves easily from database to spreadsheet because both use
a grid system (see fig. 13.9). To move information, drag to select it in the
database list view, select Copy or Cut from the Edit menu, switch to the
spreadsheet, and paste the information. The spreadsheet treats text as
labels and values as numbers. Calculated fields cannot be recalculated
after you move them from database to spreadsheet because their
formulas are not transferred.

Pasting Data from Another Spreadsheet

When moving data between spreadsheets, formulas are retained and cell
references are adjusted to their new location. The format of the receiving
cell controls the format of the pasted information.

Integrating Data in a Database

The database module can receive information from the word processing
and spreadsheet modules. For example, you may want to add a list of
names and addresses from a letter to an address database or copy
spreadsheet financial totals to a company database. Copying is faster
than keying in the information a second time.

Fig. 13.9
Database information is
easily transferred to a
spreadsheet.

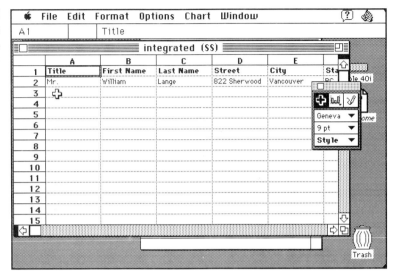

Pasting Data from a Spreadsheet

Spreadsheet rows become database records when pasted into a database
list. Each cell is placed in its own field. These simple rules call for some
care in application to avoid losing data or overwriting existing information.

In spreadsheet-to-database transfers, numbers take on the format of the
field into which they are pasted. Because the default database field type
is text, some of the numbers you paste may become text. Numbers that
are converted to text can cause problems in report totals or calculated
fields.

You can change the default database field type to number by opening
the Edit menu, choosing Preferences, and clicking the Number button.
Alternatively, be sure the fields used for numbers are properly formatted
using the Format Field command found on the database Form menu.

You can paste new records at the bottom of the database list or use the
Insert Record command from the Data menu to open up an area inside
the database. Because pasted cells become database fields, they should
match the sequence of the receiving database. If you paste dates in a
time field or vice versa, Works does not correct the problem. Be con-
scious of potential format conflicts. The format of the database cells
controls the pasted information, so you may get unexpected changes.
Formulas are not transferred when you copy their results.

Part VI

Using Advanced Features

If you select the area in which you want to paste, Works uses all the selected fields to accommodate the copied area. If this involves pasting over filled fields, Works does so without warning. You can use the Undo command to reverse the process. Also note that if you paste more cells than there are selected fields, cells that don't fit the area are discarded.

A better way to paste a block of cells is to choose only the field in the upper left corner of the destination area of the database in list view. If the pasting will overwrite unselected fields, two consecutive dialog boxes warn you (see fig. 13.10 and fig. 13.11).

Fig. 13.10
A warning that pasting will overwrite existing data.

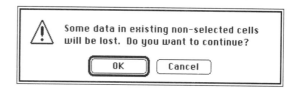

Fig. 13.11
A warning that pasting will generate incorrect totals.

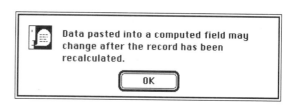

Pasting Data from a Word Processor

To prepare data in a word processor for pasting into a database, separate the items to be placed in fields with tabs. Press Return to mark the end of a record. Blank lines in the information are interpreted as blank records in the database. Choose the database list view, and then use these steps:

1. Create a table in the word processor, separating entries with tabs.

2. Select the material to be transferred and copy or cut it from the word processor.

3. Switch to the target database and select the field in the upper left corner of the area in which you will paste.

4. Open the database Edit menu and choose Paste.

   Works will warn you if you are about to overwrite existing data. Click OK to continue pasting, or click Cancel to return to list view and create additional rows to fit the amount of data you want to paste.

5. Check for correct formatting in the pasted fields.

Pasting from Another Database

To copy records from one database to another, you need to arrange the field orders so that they match properly. Your target database can have additional fields, but they must not interrupt the sequence of pasted information. Use the following steps:

1. Open list views of the source and target databases.

2. Arrange the source and target fields in the same sequence.

3. Select the source material you want to copy.

4. Open the Edit menu and choose Copy.

5. Switch to the target database.

6. Select the field in the upper left corner of the area where you will paste.

7. Open the Edit menu and choose Paste.

   Works will warn you if you are about to overwrite existing data. Click OK to continue pasting, or click Cancel to return to list view and create additional rows to fit the amount of data you want to paste.

Transferring Communications Documents

When you receive a communications document as described in Chapter 12, "Using Works Communications," the document's format is controlled by the originating computer. Works can open documents in a variety of formats. You can examine the choices by choosing Open from the File menu, selecting the All Types icon, and then clicking the down arrow to open the File Format pop-up menu.

If a file type is listed, you should be able to open it in Works by double-clicking. When opened, the contents of the file can be cut or pasted into Works modules using the same instructions given in the preceding sections of this chapter.

An efficient way to send a file, using the communications module, is to paste it to the screen. The communications document screen behaves a good deal like a word processor. You can click the mouse button and choose Paste from the Edit menu to place a document from the Clipboard on the screen. If a connection with a remote computer is active, the document is transmitted at the same time that it is pasted.

The pace of transmission can be controlled by choosing File Transfer from the Settings menu, selecting the Text Tool protocol, and changing settings for character and line delay (see fig. 13.12). See Chapter 12 for a description of these settings and options.

Understanding the Role of Draw

Works differentiates between its Draw module and the drawing tools provided in every other module. The word processing, spreadsheet, and database modules have drawing tools. Database forms can be enhanced with Draw. Chapters 5 and 6 contain complete instructions for using Draw. This section deals only with the integration of graphic material with other modules.

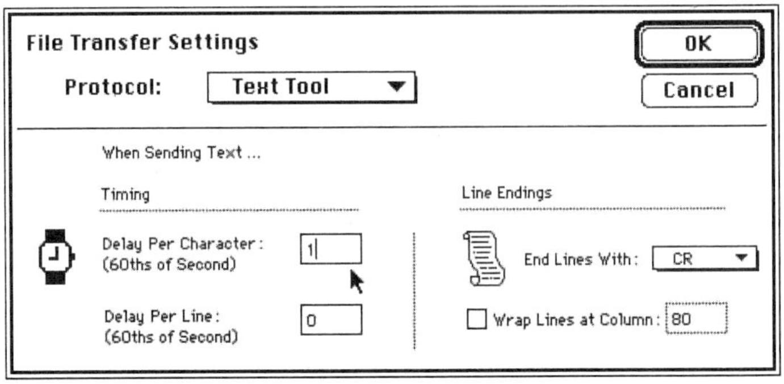

Fig. 13.12
If pasted text is sent too
rapidly, increase these
settings.

```
┌─────────────────────────────────────────────────────────────────────┐
│  File Transfer Settings                              ┌──────────┐     │
│                                                      │    OK    │     │
│     Protocol:      ┌─────────────┬───┐               └──────────┘     │
│                    │ Text Tool   │ ▼ │               ┌──────────┐     │
│                    └─────────────┴───┘               │  Cancel  │     │
│                                                      └──────────┘     │
│                                                                       │
│        When Sending Text ...                                          │
│                                                                       │
│        Timing                          Line Endings                   │
│                                                                       │
│     Delay Per Character:  ┌────┐                                      │
│     (60ths of Second)     │ 1  │       End Lines With: ┌──── ┬──┐     │
│                           └────┘                       │ CR  │▼ │     │
│                                                        └─────┴──┘     │
│     Delay Per Line:       ┌────┐                                      │
│     (60ths of Second)     │ 0  │    ☐ Wrap Lines at Column: │ 80 │    │
│                           └────┘                                      │
└─────────────────────────────────────────────────────────────────────┘
```

Understanding the Draw Layer

Think of the Draw layer as a sheet of acetate laid over a text document. Using the tools provided, you can draw on top of the underlying document. Graphic objects can cover text beneath them, but they also can be moved and resized to accommodate the layout. The Draw layer is activated when you choose the Draw On command from the Window menu or when you click the Draw icon on the tool palette. The draw layer is also activated automatically when you paste an imported graphic or a chart.

Remember that what you draw does not merge directly with your document. Your drawing resides in a separate layer you can move in front or behind your document's contents by using the commands in the Arrange menu. Therefore, your drawing can seem to overlay some of your document's contents. You must make a space for a drawing to avoid this occurrence.

Using Draw with the Spreadsheet Module

The principal use of Draw with the spreadsheet centers on charts. A chart is a Draw object, so whenever you create a chart, the Draw layer is activated. If you move a chart from one spreadsheet to another, pasting the chart into the target spreadsheet activates the Draw layer. You then can use Draw tools to enhance the chart.

Another use of Draw with spreadsheets is annotation. You can draw boxes next to your data and add explanatory text in them using your drawing tools. The boxes can be repositioned and resized with the commands on the Arrange menu. By using transparent background options, you can make the annotation appear as a line of text superimposed on the spreadsheet.

Part VI

Using Advanced Features

Using Draw with the Word Processor Module

Many imaginative ways to use Draw with the word processor exist. You can design logos, create letterheads, paste charts, and add illustrations. Works also accepts clip art, in the Macintosh PICT format, from a variety of sources including commercial vendors, on-line databases such as Shareware and Freeware, and drawing applications. All this activity takes place on the Draw layer that is activated when the Draw tools are chosen or a graphic is pasted in a word processor document.

Don't overlook the possibility of moving text into Draw. The only way to effectively create multiple columns in Works is to use the Draw module. The Draw module also provides some enhancements—such as allowing text to surround graphics—not available in the word processing module. Prepare your text in the word processor; then open a new Draw document and move your text to it. Instructions for using columns are found in the section of Chapter 6 called "Using Text in Draw."

Using Draw with the Database

Database forms can be enhanced with Draw features. For example, you may want to use Draw to create annotations. Boxes with instructions and arrows can help a user understand how to complete a form document.

Although you can't use Draw directly on a report, to add a logo for example, you can add enhancements to the headers and footers you specify for your reports. You can paste graphics into the header or footer window, so that they are reproduced when the report is printed. Keep graphics small so that they fit within the space allocated for the header or footer. Check the document with the Print Preview command to see the effect of your header or footer enhancements.

Integrating Works with Other Applications in System 7

Works does not exist alone on your Macintosh. You may have information stored in other applications that you need to perform your tasks in Works. All you have to do is open the other applications you want to use via the various ways described in Chapter 2. The Macintosh then makes it easy to access the information by enabling you to move easily between programs.

Use the Application menu to switch between applications. The Finder runs in the background at all times to manage the swapping of programs, as well as any file or folder maintenance that is required. The

Finder is also accessible from this menu. To switch to another active application or the Finder, pull down the Application menu and select the application program. You also can click the other application's window, if it is available, to go to that application.

After you have opened the applications you need, you can use the Application menu to move out of Works and into the other program. You use the same Copy and Cut commands to move the data you want onto the Clipboard. You then highlight Works on the Application menu to return to your module. When there, paste the data into your document. You can do this operation with any Macintosh program, be it a spreadsheet, word processor, project management program, or even compiler, because the Macintosh treats all text as text (sometimes loosing your formatting) and all graphics as PICT files (sometimes loosing details) when moving them into and out of the Clipboard. You also can move information from your Works documents to other applications for further massaging and then transfer the results back to Works.

Creating Form Letters

Form letters are integrated documents that use features of both the word processing and database modules. A form letter document containing field name placeholders is used to extract information from one or more databases. This section assumes you are familiar with the Works word processing and database modules. If you are not, or if you need a refresher on word processing and database procedures, refer to Chapters 3, 4, and 10.

Creating a Form Letter Document

A form letter document is prepared as a conventional word processor document except for the inclusion of field placeholders that mark where information from a database will be merged. Completing the body of the letter before inserting fields is the most efficient way to create form letters. You can use a text placeholder such as an X to mark locations where you want to insert information from database fields. When you are prepared to insert field placeholders, proceed with these steps:

1. Move to the database module and open the database(s) containing information you want to use.

2. Switch to the word processor and open the prepared merge document.

3. Place the insertion point where you want the first placeholder. If you have previously placed a marker, such as X, select it.

4. Open the Document menu and choose the command Merge Fields. The Merge Fields dialog box opens (see fig. 13.13).

Fig. 13.13
The Merge Fields dialog box.

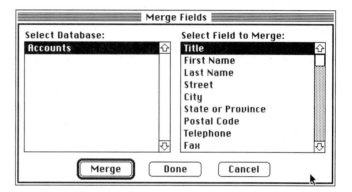

5. Select the database from which you want to extract a field by clicking its name. A list of fields appears in the Select Field to Merge box.

6. Select the field for which you want a placeholder in the document.

7. Click the Merge button to insert the placeholder.

8. Click Done to close the dialog box.

9. Repeat steps 4 through 8 to add additional placeholders.

   The inserted fields show data from the current record of the selected database. To see field placeholders, choose Show Field Names from the Document menu (see fig. 13.14).

If you have a number of fields to insert, you can click Merge after you select a field. Repeat this action until you have selected all the fields you are going to use in the form letter, and then click Done. Works inserts all the placeholders for the document in a continuous row. The string of placeholders can then be cut and pasted into their proper locations. This approach saves having to repeatedly reopen the Merge Fields dialog box.

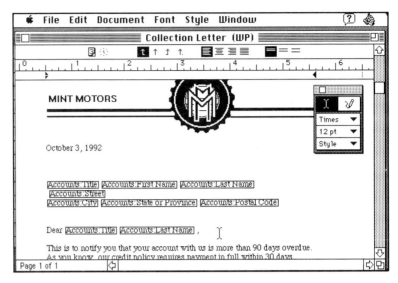

Fig. 13.14
Field names can be
displayed instead of field
contents.

Printing Form Letters

Printing requires the same arrangement of files used when creating the form letter. The database providing the information needs to be open and the merge document needs to be the active document. You can use the Print Preview command to examine the finished appearance of your document. Use these steps to print your form letters:

1. Open the database document that provides information for the fields.

   If you used more than one database in a document, all of the databases you used must be open.

2. Open the form letter.

3. Open the File menu and choose Print.

4. In the Print dialog box, check the box titled Print Merged Fields.

5. Click the Print button to proceed.

TIP

You can use a workspace file effectively in a mail-merge situation. Open the database and the merge document; then choose Save Workspace from the File menu. Name your workspace file and save it for use when you need the mail-merge configuration again. For details, see the section of this chapter called "Workspaces."

Exchanging Files

By using Works' capability to exchange files with other programs, you can broaden your access to information and share your work with others who may not use Works. The key to file exchange is file translation, the ability to create or interpret the structure of electronic files from other programs. Works can read and write files in 21 different formats, although not all file types can be saved in all formats.

General Translation Procedures

The procedures for opening documents from other applications and for saving documents for use in other applications are similar in all modules and are described in this section. The following sections discuss variations among the modules.

To open documents created by other applications, use these steps:

1. Open the File menu and choose Open.

2. Choose the icon for the Works module to which the file will be imported.

3. From the File Format pop-up menu, choose All Available (the default).

4. Locate the file to be imported in the scrolling list.

5. Click the Open button. Works converts the file.

To save Works files for use by other applications, use these steps:

NOTE

Each module has a different list in Save As, unlike the File Open list that has all formats.

1. Open the File menu and choose Save As. The dialog box shown in figure 13.15 opens.

2. Open the File Format pop-up menu.

3. Drag the mouse to highlight the desired format, and then release the mouse button.

4. If desired, choose a new destination folder for the file.

5. Type a new name for the file and choose the Save button. Works saves the file to the specified destination.

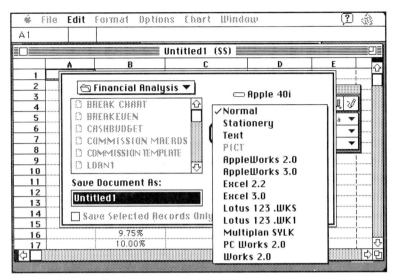

Fig. 13.15
Choose a different file
format in the Save As
dialog box.

Word Processing Translations

A majority of the translators furnished with Works are used to translate
documents to various word processing formats. Translations include
important Macintosh and PC products, such as Word and WordPerfect as
well as the word processing modules of integrated programs such as
AppleWorks or PC Works.

The Text Format

Saving a Works file in text format produces what is known as an *ASCII*
file. (ASCII stands for American Standard Code for Information Inter-
change.) An ASCII file is a universally recognized generic text format that
contains characters, spaces, punctuation, carriage returns, and sometimes tabs and end-of-file markers. An ASCII file does not carry formatting information. This type of file can be read by many programs.

Table 13.1 lists the word processing formats Works can read and write:

Table 13.1 Word Processing Formats Translated by Works
AppleWorks 2.0
AppleWorks 3.0
MacWrite 5
MacWrite II v1.1
RTF (Rich Text Format)
PC Word 5x
PC Works 2.0
Word 4
Word 5
Word for Windows 1.x
Word for Windows 2.x
WordPerfect 5.1
WordPerfect 5.0
Works 2.0

Spreadsheet Translations

Spreadsheet translation is an activity to approach with caution. Simple spreadsheets with limited formulas can be converted with little trouble, but if you attempt conversion of complex spreadsheets that use features not found in Works, changes can occur.

Works does not support some features used in full-featured spreadsheet programs. External references, cells, rows, columns, or selections that are named; styles and multiple fonts; and linked spreadsheets are not supported.

Formula error values are different in Works and Excel. Also, Works does not support intersection, concatenation, and union operators. Very large or very small numbers may produce small differences when calculated in Works or in the source spreadsheet due to the different internal representation and mathematical procedure used by Works.

The functions HLookup, Index, Lookup, Match, Type, and VLookup are implemented differently in Works than they are in Excel. The And, Or, Not, True, and False functions return the values 1 and 0 in Works and TRUE or FALSE in Excel.

You can work to correct these problems in either the original spreadsheet or in Works. If you have access to the program that generated the spreadsheet, you can use the program to modify problem areas before importing the spreadsheet into Works. Be sure to test the formulas and functions in your newly imported spreadsheet. You can have a successful import that still does not perform as intended.

Table 13.2 lists the spreadsheet formats that Works can read and write:

Table 13.2 Spreadsheet Formats Translated by Works	
	AppleWorks 2.0
	AppleWorks 3.0
	Excel 2.2
	Excel 3.0
	Lotus 1-2-3 (WKS)
	Lotus 1-2-3 (WK1)
	Multiplan (SYLK)
	PC Works 2.0
	Works 2.0

Database Translations

Although less complex than spreadsheet translation, database conversion still requires some planning. The list of specific database programs from which Works can import files is not long, but almost every database program can save material in a way Works can use. Examine the Save or Save As command in the non-Works database for options that enable you to control field and record "delimiters" such as commas and Return characters. If fields are separated by tabs and records by a Return character, the fields and records can be read into a Works database as text.

When you export a database as a text file, Works exports it with tabs and Return characters embedded. All records in the database are exported unless you choose the check box titled Save Selected Records Only. With the box checked, only records selected by the current filter are exported.

Graphics Translations

Works imports and exports graphics formatted in the generic Macintosh PICT format. Most Macintosh drawing packages can save files in PICT format. Using a Macintosh-to-PC file conversion package like MacLink Plus, you can convert PICT to the equivalent PC PCX format and thereby exchange files from one type of machine to another.

Communicating with PC's

Nearly half the file translations Works can do are translations to file types used by programs that run on IBM PC-compatible computers. The principal obstacle to exchanging this type of file is the differing disk format used by the two types of machines. Although diskettes are the same physical size, their electronic structure is different. Fortunately, there are effective solutions available.

If the Macintosh and PC are in physical proximity, you can connect a cable between them and use a utility program such as MacLink Plus to transfer the file over a cable. If both machines are connected by modem, use the communications module from Works to connect via telephone to the PC's communications program.

If your Macintosh has a SuperDrive, you can read or create 3 1/2" diskettes in PC format. The SuperDrive is one of the several ways to create a diskette that can be read by both types of machines. PC's that can create diskettes formatted for the Macintosh are rare.

A third option for cross-platform data transfer uses Works' communication module and a modem. You can connect directly to a remote PC and send the file. A PC user can receive a Macintosh file that has been formatted for a PC program. PC programs such as Works for the PC also have the capability to translate some Macintosh files, so if you know the receiving party can do the file translation, you can send using the standard Macintosh Works file format. You also can use an information service such as CompuServe. You can use the communications module and a modem to leave a file in the electronic mailbox of another subscriber where it can be picked up later.

Table 13.3 lists the PC file translations provided by Works 3.0.

Table 13.3 PC Text Formats Translated by Works	
	RTF (Rich Text Format)
	PC Word 5x
	Word for Windows 1.x
	Word for Windows 2.x
	WordPerfect 5.1

continues

Chapter 13

Integrating Works Applications

Table 13.3 Continued	
	WordPerfect 5.0
	PC Works 2.0
	Excel 2.2
	Excel 3.0
	Lotus 1-2-3 (WKS)
	Lotus 1-2-3 (WK1)
	Multiplan (SYLK)

Chapter Summary

n this chapter, you learned the techniques that increase your effectiveness by using Works modules together. Methods of moving data from module to module were described, and issues of file compatibility were explained. A second section of the chapter described how to prepare a mail-merge document that combines word processor and database information automatically. The chapter concluded with a discussion of importing and exporting Works files to other products.

Using Macros

I f you find yourself repeating an action in Works—switching windows perhaps, or using the same command again and again— you have identified a candidate for a *macro*. A series of recorded keystrokes and mouse actions played back with a keystroke shortcut, a macro automates repetitive activities.

Because macros always replay the same sequence, they can be used to minimize errors in typing formulas, phrases, or commands. Macros can automate programs for beginners by enabling them to run a complex series of commands with simple key codes. The Works macro feature is available in all Works modules. The feature works the same way in each module, although, as you will learn, macros from one module may not work in another.

What Is a Macro?

A macro is a recording of the keystrokes and mouse movements needed to accomplish a specific Works activity. Using the Macro command from the Window menu, you turn on a macro recorder that tracks keystrokes and mouse movements until you switch it off. You can assign a short keystroke combination to start the macro from the keyboard, or you can activate the macro from a dialog box. Although macros are created in memory, you can save them in special macro files to reload and reuse in future sessions.

USING
MICROSOFT
WORKS

Understanding Macro Behavior

A macro plays back in the position in the window where it is invoked. For example, if you recorded a macro that typed your name in the word processor, the macro would type your name wherever the insertion point was when you applied the macro, not in the location where the recording was originally made.

The Works macro recorder tracks mouse activity by noting the position where the button is clicked or released. The recorder cannot record positions between clicking and releasing, so some actions, such as freehand drawing, cannot be reproduced by macros. However, you can record an action such as drawing a box, which involves only clicking, dragging, and releasing the mouse button.

Macros and Windows

Macros are useful for automating repetitive work with windows. You can record actions such as zooming, resizing, or moving a window. Macros are useful for quickly establishing a specific configuration of multiple windows. You also can use macros to switch from window to window.

Although macros are specific about their starting and ending position within windows, they can work with a window that is moved. Because macros are recorded relative to the window boundary, they are not sensitive to the position of the window on the screen.

Resizing a window can cause a macro to fail if the starting or ending position of the macro falls outside the new window boundary.

Creating Macros

If you turn on the recorder with only a vague idea of the steps to take, you probably will record an error. The only way to deal with an error is to cancel the recording and begin again. Before recording, go through the macro steps slowly and write them down. When you begin recording, your written instructions ensure a smooth session.

Recording a Macro

Macro activity is controlled from a cascading menu opened by choosing the Macro command from the Window menu (see fig. 14.1). Depending on your Macintosh screen size and the position of the Window menu, the cascade menu opens to the right or left of the menu. To select a command, drag the mouse pointer sideways into the cascade menu; then drag up or down until the command you want is highlighted and release the mouse button.

Fig. 14.1
The Macro cascade menu.

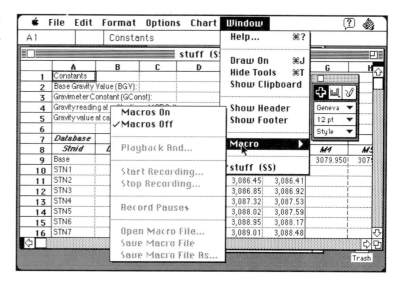

To begin recording a macro, use these steps:

1. Plan your macro on paper and practice the action on the screen.

2. Open the Window menu and choose Macro. The Macro cascade menu opens.

3. Choose Macros On to activate the macro feature.

4. In your document, position the insertion point, active cell, or active field where you want to start recording.

5. Open the Window menu and choose Macro again.

6. From the Macro cascade menu, choose Start Recording.

Chapter 14
Using Macros

Choosing a Key Code

At this point, the Start Recording dialog box opens (see fig 14.2). You are asked to enter a key and a description for the macro. The key is a letter or number that, pressed together with the Option key, runs the macro.

Fig. 14.2
Enter your key code in the Start Recording dialog box.

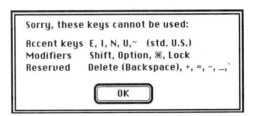

When you have assigned a key code and name, click Record to close the dialog box and begin recording your actions. If you have assigned a key code Works cannot use, you will see a warning dialog box (see fig. 14.3).

Fig. 14.3
This alert box appears if you assign the wrong key to a macro.

```
Sorry, these keys cannot be used:

Accent keys  E, I, N, U, ~  (std. U.S.)
Modifiers    Shift, Option, ⌘, Lock
Reserved     Delete (Backspace), +, =, -, _, `

                 OK
```

Pausing and Resuming During the Recording Session

While the recorder is active, your keystrokes and mouse clicks are transcribed. If needed, you can stop the macro and resume recording with these steps:

1. Open the Window menu and choose the Macro command. The Macro cascade menu appears.

2. From the Macro cascade menu, select the Stop Recording command. The Currently Recording dialog box opens (see fig. 14.4).

3. To resume recording, click Continue.

If your macro is successfully completed, click the Stop button in the Currently Recording dialog box. To delete an incomplete or incorrect macro, click Cancel in the Currently Recording dialog box.

NOTE

Some keys are reserved for other uses and cannot be used as key codes. The letters E, I, N, and U cannot be used. Nor can the Option, ⌘, Control, Shift, Caps Lock, and Delete keys. The symbols +, –, =, ' also are reserved. Works notifies you if you choose a reserved key.

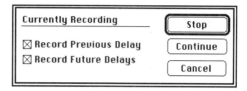

Currently Recording   Stop

⊠ Record Previous Delay   Continue
⊠ Record Future Delays   Cancel

Fig. 14.4
Change the status of your macro in the Currently Recording dialog box.

The Currently Recording dialog box contains two additional check boxes: Record Previous Delay and Record Future Delay. When these boxes are checked, Works records pauses and delays in an already active macro recording session.

Using Pauses and Delays

Speed is a major advantage of macros. They can move through menus far faster than you can. However, there are times when you need a macro to slow down so you can read a list or inspect a dialog box. Works enables you to activate a feature that records your macro in "real time," incorporating actual delays or pauses. To preset this feature before you start a macro recording session, choose one of these methods:

1. From the Macro menu, choose Record Pauses. A check mark next to the command indicates it is active.

2. In the Start Recording dialog box, click Record Pauses.

You can incorporate delays while recording is underway by choosing Stop Recording from the Macro cascade menu and clicking the check box to Record Previous Delay, which records the pause immediately before you choose the Stop Recording command, or Record Future Delays, which records the pauses that occur after you click the Continue button, in the Currently Recording dialog box. You can choose both check boxes if needed.

Saving Your Macro

Although Works automatically opens a macro file when you record a macro, your macro is stored first in memory when you create the macro. If you turn off the Macintosh without saving the macro in a file, the macro is discarded. You can save all your macros in a single file (the default) or create multiple files you open for particular purposes, such as spreadsheet macros or word processing macros.

When you are finished recording your macros, save the file using these steps:

1. Open the Window menu and choose the Macro command. The Macro cascade menu opens.

2. On the Macro cascade menu, choose the Save Macro File As command. The dialog box in figure 14.5 opens.

3. Press Return to save using the default file name, or type a new name and click Save.

Fig. 14.5
The Save Macro File As
dialog box.

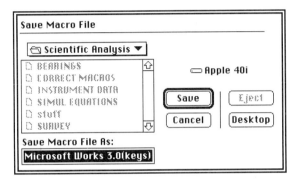

Adding to a Macro File

When you create a macro and then save it, the new macro is added to the macro file that is open at the time you create the macro. If an existing macro file is open, choosing Save Macro File from the Macro cascade menu adds the new macro.

If you have not opened a macro file but turn on the macro feature and start recording, Works records the file in memory. When you choose Save or Save As, you are given an opportunity to accept the default macro file name (a name that Works provides) and location or specify new ones.

Running Macros

Macros are usually specific to the module in which they are recorded. Because macros record specific mouse locations, they can fail when run in a window that doesn't contain objects or commands in the expected location.

You successfully can use a macro created in one module in another module when the activity accomplished by the macro is the same in each module where it is run. For example, a macro that chooses the New command from the File menu would work in all modules because the menu and its commands are always in the same position and sequence.

Opening Macro Files

Before using a macro, you must load the macro file that contains the macro you want to use. Use these steps to open an existing macro file:

1. Open the Window menu and choose the Macro command.

2. From the Macro menu, choose Macros On to activate the feature if it is not already activated.

3. Reopen the Macro menu and choose Open Macro File. The Open Macro File dialog box appears (see fig. 14.6).

4. From the Document list, choose the macro file to open and click Open. The file is read into memory for use. You also can double-click the file to open it. To find macros in other folders, use the Current Folder pop-up menu and Desktop button along with the scrolling list.

Fig. 14.6
The Open Macro File
dialog box.

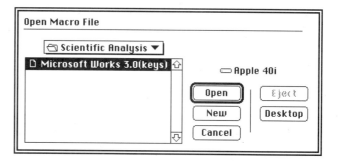

Choosing and Running Macros

Two ways to run a macro exist. You can use the key code assigned when you recorded the macro, or you can use the list found in the Playback Macro File dialog box (see fig. 14.7). To use the key code in the document where you want the macro to run, hold down the Option key, and then type the key code assigned to the macro you want to run. If you have forgotten the code or purpose of the macro, open the Playback Macro File dialog box by choosing the Playback And command from the Macro cascade menu in the Window menu. The dialog box presents a scrolling list of macros alphabetized by their descriptions. To activate a macro from this list, highlight the macro name and click Play or double-click the macro name. Macro keys are listed to the right of the description in case you forget them.

Fig. 14.7
Macros are listed in the
Playback Macro File
dialog box.

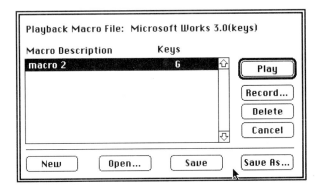

Managing Macros

Effective use of macros requires planning and organization. You may want to group macros by the type of action they take or perhaps by the type of document to which they apply. Incorrect or seldom-used macros should be removed or revised, and you may want to apply a naming plan to your macro files to find them more easily. All of these tasks can be accomplished using the dialog box opened by choosing Playback And from the Macro menu.

Using the Playback Macro File Dialog Box

The Playback Macro File dialog box is a multipurpose work center for macros. Buttons in the window enable you to record, play, delete, create, open, save, and rename macros. Except for the Play and Delete buttons, other buttons in the dialog box are duplicates of buttons and commands found elsewhere on the Macro menu. At the top of the dialog box, the name of the open macro file is listed. The file contents appear in a scrolling list, alphabetically by the first letter of their description.

The following paragraphs describe the purpose of each button in the Playback Macro File dialog box.

The Play Button

You can run a macro by selecting it and clicking Play. Before choosing the Playback And command, you should select the location where you want the macro to begin playing. When you click Play, the macro begins to run immediately, starting at the position of the insertion point, active cell, or field.

The Record Button

When you are prepared to record a new macro, you can begin by clicking the Record button. The Start Recording dialog box opens so that you can name your macro and assign a key code. You then click Record (in the Start Recording dialog box) to begin. However, choosing the Start Recording command from the Macro menu is often easier. This command opens the same dialog box without having to navigate deeper into the menu.

The Delete Button

The Delete button immediately removes the highlighted macro. Be sure you want to get rid of the macro because you cannot Undo your action. Note that the Delete button does not give you a dialog box to confirm the operation as do many other Delete commands in Works.

The Save Button

The principal purpose of the Save button is to quickly save an existing macro file that has been modified. If you click Save after creating a new file, the Save As dialog box described in the next section opens to enable you to choose a file name and location.

The Save As Button

To change the name or location of an existing macro file, choose the Save As button. The Save Macro File dialog box opens, with the file name displayed. You can click Save to use that name or enter another name or location in the Save Macro File As text box, and then click Save to rename the macro file.

The New Button

Choosing the New button immediately opens a new, empty macro file. The Playback Macro File dialog box disappears.

The Open Button

When you click the Open button, any changes in the open macro file are saved, and the Open Macro File dialog box appears. You can select macro files from the list. When you click Open in the Open Macro File dialog box, the file you selected is opened, enabling you to use the macros it contains or add a new macro.

Troubleshooting Macros

Many of the difficulties with macros can be traced to a few problems. The following list identifies common sources of difficulty.

- *The macro doesn't run when I press the correct key code.*
  Open the Window menu, choose Macro, and see whether a check mark appears beside the Macros On command. If not, choose the command to activate the macro feature.

- *The macro feature is turned on, but my macro still doesn't run.*
  Have you opened the macro file that contains the macro you want? If not, open the Window menu and choose Macro. On the Macro menu, choose Open Macro File and choose the file you want; then click Open.

- *Sometimes I can't start or stop my macro from the screen.*
  The Macro menu and recorder are disabled by the presence of a dialog box or message box on the screen. Cancel the dialog box or message to continue.

- *How can I interrupt a "runaway" macro that is not working correctly?*
  Hold down the ⌘ key, and then press the Period key. The macro stops, but any changes already made cannot be undone.

Practice: A Macro To Create Memos

This section presents an example of macro construction you can use to create a simple but useful macro. The macro creates a memorandum heading that includes your name and the current date.

Part VI

Using Advanced Features

Preparing To Record a Macro

To begin the lesson, start Works if necessary. Use the following steps to prepare for recording the macro:

1. Start Works by double-clicking the program icon.

2. When the Choose Type dialog box opens (see fig. 14.8), double-click the Word Processor icon to open a new word processor document.

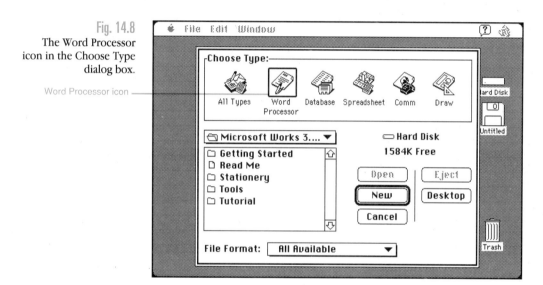

Fig. 14.8

The Word Processor icon in the Choose Type dialog box.

Word Processor icon —

3. Open the Window menu and choose the Macro command.

   Hold down the mouse button. A pop-up menu opens (see fig. 14.9).

4. Drag the pointer to choose the Macros On command.

The macro recording program is now ready to operate. In the steps that follow, you will go through the procedures to record your specific macro.

1. Open the Window menu and choose the Macro command.

   Hold down the mouse button. A cascade menu opens.

2. In the Macro cascade menu, choose the Start Recording command.

   The Start Recording dialog box opens (see fig. 14.10).

Chapter 14

Using Macros

Fig. 14.9
The Macro cascade menu.

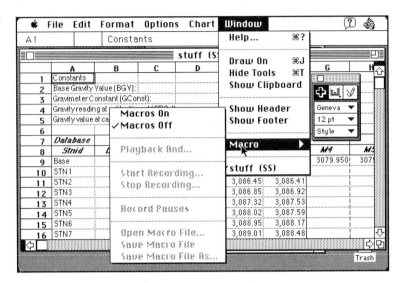

3. In the Key text box, type **m**.

This indicates that holding down the Option key and typing **m** will replay the macro.

4. Press Tab to move to the Description of New Macro box.

5. Type **Creates blank memo form**. Click the Record button.

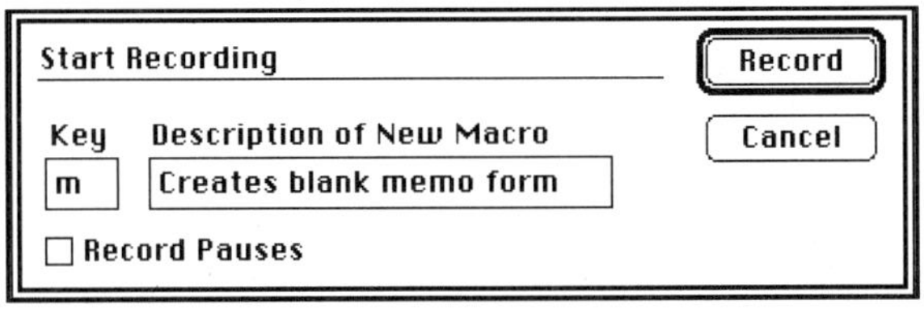

Fig. 14.10
The Start Recording
dialog box.

The recorder is now operating. Every action will be recorded. If you make a mistake, open the Macro cascade menu and choose Stop Recording. Your macro will stop at that point. Restart the process using the preceding steps. When asked if you want to record over the old macro, click Record and start your macro actions again.

Entering Macro Contents

Enter the macro contents using the steps that follow:

1. Type **Memorandum**.
2. Double-click the mouse to select the word Memorandum.
3. Open the Font menu and drag to select Times.

   If you don't have Times, select another font.

4. Open the Style menu and drag to select 18 (points).

   The word Memorandum will be formatted as 18-point Times.

5. Click at the right end of the word Memorandum.

   The selection is removed from the word, and you are positioned to press Return.

6. Press Return twice to insert two blank lines after Memorandum.
7. Open the Font menu and select Geneva.
8. Open the Style menu and select 12 (points).

   Your memo text is now formatted as 12-point Geneva.

When you prepare your own customized Memo form, you can add other enhancements, such as pictures, color, and borders, using the preceding principles.

Continue entering the Memo heading:

1. Click the Calendar icon on the ruler to place the date on your form.

   It looks like a page containing the number 3.

2. Press Return.
3. Type **From:** [Tab] [**Your Name**] [Return].
4. Type **To:** [Tab] [Return].
5. Type **Subj:** [Tab].
6. Open the Window menu and choose the Macro command.
7. Choose Stop Recording on the Macro cascade menu.
8. Click Stop in the Currently Recording dialog box.

Saving Your Macro

You have completed recording your memo macro, but it exists only in computer memory at the moment.

Works uses a default macro file called *Microsoft Works 3.0 (keys)* to store macros. You can use this file or create others for macros with different purposes. A macro file can contain as many macros as disk storage space will allow. To save the macro for future use, follow these steps:

1. Open the Window menu and choose the Macro command.

2. Choose Save Macro File As from the Macro cascade menu.

    The Save Macro File dialog box appears (see fig. 14.11).

Fig. 14.11
The Save Macro File
dialog box.

3. Click Save to store your macro.

Using Your Macro

When you turn on the macro feature, Works loads the default macro file, Microsoft Works 3.0 (keys) into memory. Any macros the file contains are available for immediate use. The quickest way to run a macro is to hold down the Option key and press the key associated with the macro.

You also can play a macro by opening the Macro cascade menu and choosing the Playback And command, which opens the dialog box shown in figure 14.12. There, you can select the macro and locate the key associated with it. Clicking the Play button in this dialog box will run the macro.

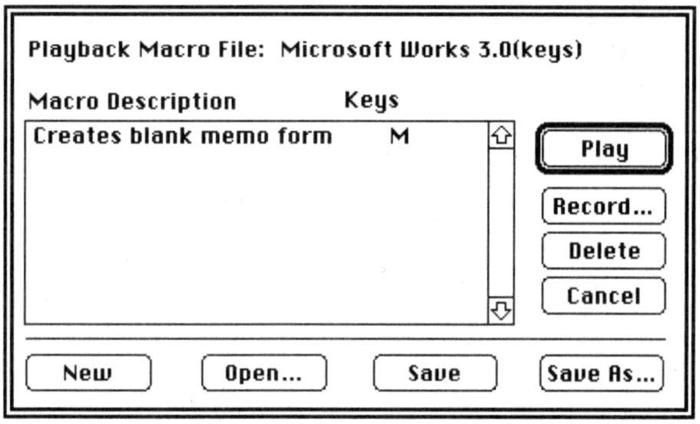

Fig. 14.12
The Playback Macro File
dialog box.

```
Playback Macro File:  Microsoft Works 3.0(keys)

Macro Description          Keys

Creates blank memo form      M          ⇧      [ Play ]

                                               [ Record... ]

                                               [ Delete ]

                                        ⇩      [ Cancel ]

  [ New ]      [ Open... ]     [ Save ]     [ Save As... ]
```

To conclude this short practice session, run your new macro using the steps that follow:

1. Select and delete the contents of the screen where you built your macro.

2. Click to place the insertion point in the upper left corner of the screen.

   The macro will begin running at the location of the insertion point.

3. Hold down the Option key and type **m**.

   Your memo form is created automatically.

Chapter Summary

Macros may seem complex, but when you are familiar with Works, you can use them easily to simplify and speed your work. This chapter explained the use of macros, which is the same in all Works modules. Techniques for creating, running, and managing macro files were described. Macro troubleshooting tips and a practice macro also were included.

Works Command Reference

This appendix first covers the menus common to all modules, and then describes the unique menus found in the individual modules. The commands are listed in alphabetical order under the following module names:

- Word processor
- Draw module
- Spreadsheet module
- Database module
- Communications

Once you understand the commands they represent, keyboard shortcuts are the way to fly. Quick two-key combinations that activate frequently used commands, shortcuts simplify your work. If you are using Works with System 7, you can access a handy pop-up listing of the shortcuts by clicking the Help balloon on the menu line and choosing Shortcuts from the menu that opens. In this appendix, the shortcuts are listed next to the command names.

Menus Common to All Modules

The Edit, File, and Window menus appear in all Works modules. Other menu names change depending on the module you are using.

Edit Menu

The Edit menu contains the commands you use to change your documents. You can move, remove, or revise material you select. Some of the Edit menu commands appear only in particular modules; this is noted appropriately in the text.

Absolute Reference (⌘-E)

In the spreadsheet module only, Absolute Reference converts a relative reference to an absolute reference.

Clear

The Clear command removes selected material from the document without storing the material on the Clipboard. The command is useful when you want to bypass the Clipboard to preserve something that is currently on it. In spreadsheets, the command is useful in emptying cells of their contents. You can recover cleared material by immediately choosing Undo from the Edit menu.

Clear Overflow Area

When the window in which you view and type information becomes full, information scrolls into an overflow area. Use the Clear Overflow Area command to empty the overflow area.

Copy (⌘-C)

Copy works like the Cut command, except the material selected to copy remains in the document. The copied material is placed on the Clipboard. You use the Paste command to place the material into another area of the document or into another document.

Cut (⌘-X)

The Cut command removes selected material from the document to the Clipboard. The material is kept on the Clipboard until you cut or copy something else. You use the Paste command to place the contents of the Clipboard into another location.

Duplicate (⌘-D)

Available only in the Draw module, the Duplicate command combines the features of Copy and Paste. When applied to a selected object, the command copies the selection and pastes it slightly offset from the original.

Duplicate Previous

In the database module only, the Duplicate Previous command is used in the list view. Highlight the entry below the one you want to duplicate and choose Duplicate Previous. The contents of the field above is copied into the highlighted field.

Fill Down (⌘-D)

In the spreadsheet module, the Fill Down command copies the cell contents of the starting cell (at the top) to every other selected cell below. In the database module, this command copies the cell contents of the starting field (at the top) to every other selected field below.

Fill Right (⌘-R)

In the spreadsheet module only, the Fill Right command copies the cell contents of the starting cell (at the left) to every other selected cell to its right.

Find (⌘-F)

The Find command is available in the word processor, the spreadsheet, and the database. The command opens a dialog box that lets you search for a character, word, or phrase.

In the word processor, you can search for words, numbers, and the special tab and paragraph characters. The search proceeds from the location of the cursor and continues until all occurrences of the search target are found or the search is canceled.

In the spreadsheet and database modules, you can locate text or cell references by entering them in the Find dialog box and clicking OK. Because the command matches exactly what you enter, be careful about capitalization and blank spaces. Find also looks at numbers as you entered them, which may be different than how they appear in a formatted cell (1000 as opposed to 1,000.00, for example).

Find Again (⌘-G)

If you want to edit a found item, you have to close the Find dialog box. To continue your search, choose the Find Again command (available only in the word processor). The command uses the contents of the Find dialog box to continue the search but does not display the dialog box.

Go To Page

The Go To Page command, available only in the word processor, opens a dialog box where you enter the number of the page to which you want to go. When working with footnotes, this command becomes Go To Footnote and lets you type in the number of the footnote to which you want to jump. A shortcut for this command is to double-click the status bar, and the Goto dialog box appears.

Insert (⌘-I)

In the spreadsheet module only, you can use this command to insert rows and columns in the spreadsheet. Select either a row or a column by clicking its row number or column letter. Choose Insert to add a new row above a selected row or new column to the left of a selected column.

Move

In the spreadsheet module only, choosing the Move command opens a dialog box where you can specify the destination of selected cells.

Paste (⌘-V)

The Paste command copies the contents of the Clipboard into the active document at the location of the insertion point. Because the data remains in the Clipboard, you can paste the same information repeatedly.

Appendix A
Works Command Reference

Paste Function

In the spreadsheet module only, the Paste Function enables you to place equations in the Formula box using a dialog box that lists Works functions, gives a short description of their purpose, and pastes the functions onto the entry bar. Chapter 8, "Applying Spreadsheet Functions," contains a full explanation and listing of all functions.

Paste Special

In the spreadsheet module only, you can use Paste Special to copy only the values generated by formulas or copy the values and formulas together. The capability to copy values only is a useful way to unlink data from formulas. This command is also used when transposing rows and columns.

Preferences

The Preferences command appears in each module. In every module, the command opens a dialog box where you specify the default font and font size for that module. In the word processor, you also can set footnote location and separator line. In Draw, you can set Snap to Grid and Snap to Vertex on or off for all documents. In the spreadsheet, you can set the default chart type. In the database, you can specify the default field type. In the communications module, you can use the Preferences command to set the overflow area size and turn Always Capture on or off. You also can toggle the Notify Before Closing Connections command on or off. Note that you can change the preferences of any module while in another module.

Replace

Available only in the word processor, the Replace command locates the word, phrase, or number you specify in its dialog box and replaces the item with a specified item. You can approve the replacements on an instance-by-instance basis or allow all items to be replaced at once.

Select

In the spreadsheet module only, the Select command opens a small cascade menu in which you can choose the All option to select all active cells or Last Cell to select only the last cell in the spreadsheet. Because empty formatted cells are considered part of the active spreadsheet, the

Last Cell selection will sometimes reveal why your spreadsheet is larger than expected.

Select All (⌘-A)

In all modules except the spreadsheet and communications, everything in the current document is selected when you choose Select All. The command is useful for changing an entire word processing document to a new line spacing, font, or other whole-document revision, or for selecting the entire contents of the active database. In the Draw module, Select All enables you to change text formats, line widths, and fill patterns globally. You also can grab the total drawing to move it.

Undo (⌘-Z)

The Undo command reverses your most recent formatting or editing change. Undo also reverses any changes made during a Find and Replace search and removes any changes made with the thesaurus. Remember that Undo changes only your most recent change.

File Menu

The File menu commands enable you to open, close, and save files; set document margins, numbering, and footnotes; print; and, if you use Microsoft Mail, receive and send electronic mail. You also quit Works from this menu. The File commands work the same in all modules.

Close (⌘-W)

The Close command removes the current document from the screen, while keeping the module open, after asking whether you want to save any unsaved changes. You also can click the close box in the upper left corner of the window to close a document.

Close All

Depending on how much memory your Macintosh has, you can have a number of documents open at once. Close All closes each open document, pausing to ask you to save if there are unsaved changes unless you have checked the Save All Files Without Further Prompting box. All documents are closed by this command, but Works itself is left running.

New (⌘-N)

The New command opens a new document from any module. Choosing the command opens a dialog box where you select the Works module you want. Clicking the module's icon opens a new, blank document with that module's filter. Choosing the Show Stationery box lets you base your new document on a stationery document.

Open (⌘-O)

The Open command is used to open an existing document. Choosing the command opens a dialog box where you can select the types of documents to open from a Document list box. You also can specify non-Works file formats that can be converted and opened by Works.

Open Mail and Send Mail

The Open Mail and Send Mail commands are available only to network users of Microsoft Mail. The commands enable you to access your mailbox from within Works so that you can use its word processor to compose and send mail or read received mail. If you have this program, you will also have instructions about how to use it.

Page Setup

The Page Setup command is part of the group of printer commands. The dialog box that appears depends on the printer you use, but generally, the dialog box lets you select paper type, size, orientation, and any special settings available from your printer. This dialog box contains a Document button that opens an important dialog box where you can set margins and page numbering.

Print (⌘-P)

The Print command opens the standard Macintosh Print dialog box appropriate for your printer. You can set number of copies, pages to print, and other printer-specific settings.

Print One

The Print One command immediately prints one copy of the document using the current settings in the Print dialog box. No dialog box opens on the screen. This is the command of choice when you know your printer settings are correct and you want only one copy.

Appendix A

Works Command Reference

Print Preview

The Print Preview command has saved many a tree from being turned into paper. Instead of printing endless draft copies, you can use Print Preview to view your document. Print Preview shows a small but accurate illustration of the way your document layout and page breaks will appear in print. Use the zoom out magnifying glass to view the full-page preview. Click the close button to return to the thumbnail preview screen.

Quit (⌘-Q)

This command shuts down Works completely. If any open files contain unsaved changes, dialog boxes will appear asking whether you want to save. You cannot lose work by choosing Quit. Many people use the Save command before Quit, but because Quit will prompt you to save any changed work, it is quite safe and more efficient to choose Quit.

Save (⌘-S)

The Save command saves the active document to the originally selected location of the file or to the place where it was last saved. No dialog box appears, so the process is quick. One of the most common problems encountered by new computer users is loss of work because a problem occurred and the files hadn't been saved.

Save As

The Save As command enables you to save a new document or rename a saved document. The command opens a dialog box where you can apply a file name and a destination to the document. This box appears the first time you save a file so you can replace the generic name (Untitled 1, for example) that Works gives to unsaved files. In the Save As dialog box, you also can save a file in formats other than normal Works format so they can be used with other programs.

Save Workspace

In Works, you can routinely have several documents open at once. If you want to save the entire group to reopen quickly later, use the Save Workspace command. When you choose the command, a dialog box opens where you can name the group of files. When you want to reopen the workspace, use the Open command and select the workspace name.

Appendix A
Works Command Reference

Note that the Save Workspace command does not include any unsaved files in the workspace, so make sure that you save document(s) before saving the workspace if you want it (them) included.

Window Menu

The Window menu is found in all Works modules although the commands it contains vary somewhat from one module to another. This menu lets you show or hide headers, footers, and footnotes; access tools such as the Draw program, the Clipboard, or the ruler; and get help with the program. The macro utility is started from this menu, and the list of open windows at the bottom lets you change the active window.

Draw On (⌘-J)

In the word processor, spreadsheet, and database modules, the Draw On command activates a drawing layer that overlays your document and provides drawing tools for limited drawing within the module. When you choose the command, the menu bar changes to include Draw commands, and icons for the drawing tools are added to the tool palette. To return to your document layer, click the pencil icon on the tool palette or select Draw Off from the Window menu. Working with Draw is discussed in Chapter 5, "Creating Drawings."

Help (⌘-?)

The Help command activates the Works Help program. The Help box is also available from the Help menu on the menu bar. Help on help is available when you select a module icon from the Help box.

Macro

The Macro command opens a cascade menu that contains commands to create and run macros. Use of macros is discussed in Chapter 14. The Macro command appears on the Window menu of every module. This section describes the commands that appear on the cascade menu that opens when you choose the Macro command.

Macros Off

Choosing Macros Off inactivates the macro feature. A check mark to the left of the command indicates it is chosen.

Macros On

Choosing Macros On activates the feature, allowing you to record and play macros. When the feature is active, a check mark appears to the left of the command on the menu.

Open Macro File

The Open Macro File command opens a dialog box that contains a listing of available macro files. You can double-click to open a selected file, or use the Desktop (or Disk) button or current folder pop-up menu to navigate to other folders that hold macro files.

Playback And

The all-purpose macro command, Playback And opens a dialog box where you can choose to record, play, delete, create, open, save, and rename macros. The principal use of the command is activating macros from the scrolling list it displays as well as managing the macros you create.

Record Pauses

With the Record Pauses command selected, your macro is recorded in "real time," placing pauses where you stop and continue.

Save Macro File

When a macro file is open, choosing Save Macro File immediately saves the file with any changes. No dialog box appears unless it is the first time a specific macro file has been saved, in which case the Save As dialog box opens.

Save Macro File As

The Save Macro File As command opens a standard Save As dialog box where you can change the file name if desired or save the file to a new folder or disk.

Start Recording

Choosing Start Recording opens a dialog box where you choose a key code, name your macro, and begin recording.

Appendix A
Works Command Reference

Stop Recording

Stop Recording can be used either to end or to pause macro recording. When chosen, a dialog box opens where you can record pauses, continue with your recording, or stop the process.

Show Clipboard

The Clipboard is a tool of the Macintosh system that is shared among all the Works modules as well as all other Macintosh applications. Choosing Show Clipboard opens a window that shows you the current contents of the Clipboard. You cannot directly edit Clipboard contents, but you can change or delete the contents of the Clipboard by copying other text, including blank spaces, from your document.

Show Footnotes

In the word processor only, the Show Footnotes command opens a window at the bottom of the screen where you can view and edit footnotes.

Show/Hide Ruler (⌘-R)

In the word processor and Draw modules, the Ruler provides a measurement scale for use in keeping track of text and objects in your document. Use the Show Ruler command in Draw to display its ruler. The word processing module shows its ruler (with tools for justification, tabs, and date and time stamping) as a default. If you want to see as much of your document as possible on the screen, you can turn off the ruler with the Hide Ruler command. When the ruler is hidden, the command changes to Show Ruler.

Show/Hide Tools (⌘-T)

Choosing Show Tools opens the tool palette on the screen. (The default in most modules is to automatically present the tool palette and offer the Hide Tools command if you want to put the palette away.) The palette contains icons and buttons that let you add a Draw layer and change font, point size, and style from pop-up menus. If you switch to the Draw layer, drawing tools are added to the bottom of the palette window.

In the database module, the displayed palette also lets you switch between the design and data views, and scroll through your records in the data view, as well as select font styles and formats in the design view. In the communications module, the palette contains icons to control communications.

Show Header and Show Footer

Show Header and Show Footer are related commands that open windows at the top and bottom of the screen. You can view and edit headers and footers in these windows.

Window Names

At the bottom of the Window menu is a list of open windows. A check mark appears next to the active window. Selecting a window from this list makes it active and brings it to the top of any overlapping windows. If more windows are open than fit in the menu space, an arrow appears at the bottom. Clicking it enables you to scroll through the remaining window names.

Word Processor

This section lists commands unique to the word processor module. Additional word processor commands are listed in the section "Menus Common to All Modules."

Document Menu

The Document menu contains commands used to add data to your document or to copy edit your document. The spelling checker and thesaurus are controlled from the Document menu. You also can control footnote insertion and choose to have menu equivalents of the icons on the ruler that insert date and time in headers and footers. You can select text and insert it as a footnote from this menu, and you also can run a word count utility.

Copy Ruler Settings (⌘-K)

The Copy Ruler Settings command lets you transfer tabs, paragraph spacing, indents, and line spacing from a selected paragraph to another paragraph or group of paragraphs. It copies the settings, and its companion command, Paste Ruler Settings, applies them in a new location.

Insert Current Date

The Insert Current Date command reads your computer's clock and pastes the current date at the location of the insertion point. The result is identical to choosing the Date button on the ruler.

Insert Current Time

The Insert Current Time command reads your computer's clock and pastes the current time at the location of the insertion point. The result is identical to choosing the Time button on the ruler.

Insert Document Title

In a header or footer window, the Document menu changes. Insert Page Break is replaced by Insert Document Title, which inserts document's title at the insertion point.

Insert Footnote (⌘-E)

The Insert Footnote command places a footnote number at the insertion point and opens the footnote window so that you can either type or paste a note next to the corresponding number. Click the close button or select Close from the File menu to close the footnote window and return to your document.

Insert Page Break (Shift-Return)

The Insert Page Break command places a manual page break just above the line containing the insertion point. Although automatic pagination cannot be changed, you can select a manual page break. The command then changes to Remove Page Break. Choosing the command removes the selected manual page break.

Merge Fields (⌘-M)

You use the Merge Fields command to create form letters using a mail merge document in your word processor and database. Merge fields correlates a place holder and its associated data to build the form letter. The Merge Fields command displays a dialog box, enabling you to select the database fields to merge.

Paste Ruler Settings (⌘-Y)

Paste Ruler Settings, the mirror twin of Copy Ruler Settings, pastes the copied settings into their new location. You can paste in a single paragraph or select an entire group of paragraphs to receive the settings.

Show Field Names

When the Show Field Names command is selected in a form letter, Works displays the field names rather than their contents from the database.

Spelling (⌘-L)

The Spelling command starts the spelling checker. The extensive dictionary can check for misspellings, improper hyphenation or capitalization, and repeated words.

Spelling Options

The Spelling Options command opens a dialog box where you specify whether the spelling checker ignores words in all caps, ignores words containing numbers, and whether it presents suggested corrections when it finds a misspelled word. More importantly, Spelling Options enables a user to create, use, and edit custom dictionaries.

Thesaurus (⌘-D)

The Thesaurus command opens the new 190,000-word thesaurus. You can locate synonyms and antonyms. You also can search for synonyms for common short phrases to add variety to your writing.

Word Count

Choosing Word Count activates a small utility program that counts the number of characters, words, lines, paragraphs, and pages in the current document or in a selection you made before choosing the command.

Font Menu

The Font menu contains no commands. It is a list of the fonts installed on your system. A small selection of fonts is provided with the system software, but you can obtain and install additional fonts. Please note that fonts are software and should be purchased, not illegally copied.

Style Menu

The Style menu controls font size and appearance. Paragraph alignment and spacing are also controlled from this menu.

Alignment

Choosing the Alignment command opens a small cascade menu that contains four selections for paragraph alignment. Choosing one of the alignments—left, right, centered, or justified—is identical in result to choosing the related alignment button on the ruler.

Font Sizes

The numbers toward the bottom of the Style menu represent standard point sizes for Macintosh bit-mapped fonts. Selecting characters and choosing a size will change the characters to that size. If the number is outlined, a font of that size is installed. If not, the size will be approximated and may not print smoothly. See the Format Character command for information on nonstandard font sizes.

Format Character

Choosing the Format Character command opens a dialog box where you can completely control font, size, style, and color of characters. If using TrueType fonts, you can specify virtually any point size, and smooth characters will be created. This dialog box is the only location where you can apply superscript or subscript formatting to characters.

Increase Size and Decrease Size

When bit-mapped fonts are in use, choosing Increase Size or Decrease Size changes the font to the next standard size higher or lower. Standard sizes are the ones listed on the menu. If you are using TrueType fonts, choosing the commands will increase or decrease size by one point.

Spacing

Choosing the Spacing command opens a small cascade menu that contains four selections for line spacing. Choosing single, double, or

1.5 spacing is identical in result to choosing the related spacing button on the ruler. The actual measurement between lines is based on the font size. The command 6 Lines Per Inch, available only from the menu, is used to force lines to fit standard forms, which commonly use that spacing.

Style Choices

Plain (⌘-spacebar), Bold (⌘-B), Italic (⌘-I), Underline (⌘-U), Outline, and Shadow specify font styles that can be applied to selected characters by choosing the desired style name. You can choose more than one style for a selection; for example, bold italic.

Draw Module

This section lists commands unique to the Draw module. Additional Draw commands are listed in the section "Menus Common to All Modules."

Arrange Menu

The principal use of the Arrange menu is to control the layering and alignment of Draw objects. Through rearranging stacked layers, grouping and ungrouping objects, and activating the grid and vertex snap features, you can exercise both overall and detailed control of objects. This menu also contains commands that control character formatting, alignment, and text spreading.

Alignment

The Alignment command provides the menu-based equivalent of the four paragraph alignment icons found on the ruler. You can choose left, right, centered, or justified alignment.

Bring To Front and Send To Back (⌘-F) /(⌘-B)

Bring To Front and Send To Back are complementary commands that reorder the stacking of Draw objects. Each object has its own layer, as though your drawing was a stack of transparent acetate sheets, each one containing only one object. By selecting an object and bringing it to the front or sending it to the back, you can restack objects that may obscure other objects.

Appendix A
Works Command Reference

Crop

The Crop command enables you to reorganize an imported graphic so that it can be made to fit in your design. Cropping removes excess white areas by moving the graphic's boundaries. A portion of an imported drawing can be selected by drawing a rectangle with the cropping tool. When you click outside the cropping rectangle, any parts of the illustration outside the cropping rectangle disappear. Cropping differs from resizing because you do not change the size of the drawing—you select a portion of it.

Format Character

Choosing the Format Character command opens a dialog box where you can completely control font, size, style and color of characters. If using TrueType fonts, you can specify any point size, and smooth characters will be created.

Grid Settings

The dimensions of the alignment grid are established using the dialog box opened by choosing the Grid Settings command.

Group and Ungroup (⌘-G) /(⌘-U)

The Group and Ungroup commands lock together or unlock a grouping of objects. A drawing often consists of many small objects that can be difficult to move together. By grouping objects, you merge them into a single object with one set of handles. The Ungroup command reverses the grouping process so you can edit individual components of a composite object.

Hide/Show Column Borders

If borders are hidden, the Hide Column Borders command becomes Show Column Borders. Its purpose is to turn on or off the dotted lines that can surround column borders. These nonprinting guides can be helpful in aligning columns, but you may want to turn them off to see the effect of the finished document.

Snap To Grid

The Snap To Grid command activates an invisible grid on the Draw screen. Draw objects, column boundaries, and text boxes will align to the grid as though it was magnetic. This feature is indispensable for organizing complex documents with multiple parts. If the command is active, a check mark appears next to it. Choose the command again to turn it off.

Spread Text

A line of text can be spread along a line or arc by creating the text and the line or arc, choosing both, and then choosing the Spread Text command. The text object is spread along the path of the line or arc as separate letters that can be manipulated individually.

Vertex Snap

A *vertex* is the intersection of two sides of a figure. In Draw, Vertex Snap is a feature that ensures that when you use the Polygon tool to draw an object, the final side will "snap" to the end of the first side without leaving a gap. Vertex Snap consists of a toggle (either on or off); a check mark indicates its status. Hold down the N key to temporarily turn on the Vertex Snap.

Draw Menu

Many of the commands on the Draw menu let you reshape or add effects to objects. You also can break an object into its component parts and lock objects in place. You can invoke the Draw menu in any module by selecting the Draw On command on the Window menu or by clicking the pencil in the tool palette.

3-D Effect

Applying the 3-D Effect command to an object automatically extends its depth to produce a three-dimensional appearance. A dialog box lets you specify the object's depth and rotation. You can move and edit a 3-D object by undoing the effect or by dragging apart the object's components.

Add Handles and Remove Handles

Handles enable you to manipulate the shape of your objects. This pair of commands doubles (Add) or halves (Remove) the number of handles applied to a selected object. The number of handles needed depend on the complexity of editing you intend. Freehand lines often have too many handles to be managed effectively.

Break Up and Join

This pair of commands applies to objects composed of line segments. Applying the Break Up command turns each segment into an independent line that can be moved and sized separately. Join reverses the process, fusing adjacent line segments into a single segmented line.

Lock Objects and Unlock All

The Lock Objects command sends an object to the lowest level of an object stack so you cannot select it. This prevents moving or reshaping the object. This technique is useful for complex objects where you may want to arrange objects on top of other objects while holding a background shape in place. You can lock objects one at a time, but you can only unlock all objects at once by using the Unlock All command.

Rotate

A selected object can be rotated clockwise any specified number of degrees by applying the Rotate command. The command does not apply to text objects or bit maps. You also can flip an object 180 degrees around its horizontal or vertical axis.

Shadow

The Shadow command duplicates an object and places the copy below and to the right of the original to produce the appearance of a shadow. The shadow is actually a second object that can be selected and edited independently, if needed.

Smooth

The Smooth command automatically turns straight lines in an object into smooth curves. It provides an easy way to add a rounded appearance to items without having to modify each line by hand.

Page Menu

You can add, remove, and turn to the pages of a multipage document using the Page menu. The multipage feature lets you create a document such as a newsletter as a single document rather than a series of separately created, saved, and printed pages.

Add Pages and Delete Pages

Add Pages and Delete Pages are complementary commands that work almost identically. Choosing one opens a simple dialog box that lets you choose how many pages to add or delete and specify which pages will be affected.

Go To Page (⌘-K)

Using the Go To Page command, you can type the page number you want in the command's dialog box and Works moves to that page. If your document is more than one page long, you can double-click the status bar (next to the page numbers), and the Go To Page dialog box opens.

Next Page and Previous Page (⌘-=) /(⌘--)

Next Page and Previous Page are simple commands that let you flip pages, forward or back, one at a time.

Spreadsheet Module

This section lists commands unique to the spreadsheet module. Additional spreadsheet commands are listed in the section "Menus Common to All Modules."

Chart Menu

The Chart menu contains the commands used to create and format charts.

Define Chart

Choosing the Define Chart command, with a chart on the screen will open the Define a Chart dialog box, showing the values of the existing chart and allowing you to change various aspects of the chart.

New Chart

Choosing New Chart, with cells highlighted on an open spreadsheet, causes Works to create a chart representing the selected material. If Works cannot successfully interpret the selected cells, the Define a Chart dialog box will open.

Touch Up

When a chart is open and the Draw layer is active, choosing Touch Up enables you to select, alter, and move text and graphic elements of the chart. You can use Draw tools to change fills, line widths, and font properties.

Format Menu

Using the Format menu, you can change the format of cells and characters, set and remove page breaks, and "freeze" split windows to show nonscrolling titles.

Column Width

The Column Width command displays a dialog box where you can set the width of a column.

Format Cells

The dialog box opened with the Format Cells command lets you change the type of cell format, numeric format, the alignment of cell contents, and add or remove cell borders. You also can double-click a cell to open the Format Cells dialog box.

Format Character

Format Character opens a dialog box that controls font, font size, style, and color for selected cells.

Freeze Titles Horizontal and Vertical

Freeze Titles Horizontal and Freeze Titles Vertical are commands that lock and remove scroll bars from upper or left panes on a screen with split windows. See Chapter 7's sections "Splitting the Display" and "Freezing Split Panes."

Appendix A

Works Command Reference

Protect Cell

Selecting a cell or a range of cells and applying the Protect Cell command prevents any alteration to cell contents. Selecting the cells and the command again removes protection.

Remove Page Break

The Remove Page Break command removes manual page breaks set by the Set Page Break command. Highlight the cells used to create the page break to guide Remove Page Break. See the Set Page Break command.

Set Page Break

With a single cell selected, Works sets vertical and horizontal page breaks with the selected cell as the upper left corner of the page. If an entire row is selected, choosing Set Page Break inserts a horizontal break above the row. If a column is selected, a vertical break is placed left of the column.

Options Menu

The Options menu commands control the appearance and behavior of the spreadsheet screen. Display of the cell grid, values, formulas, and cell notes is controlled here, as is spreadsheet calculation. The Sort command also is located on the Options menu.

Calculate Now

The Calculate Now command lets you recalculate the spreadsheet when Manual Calculation is selected.

Manual Calculation

The spreadsheet recalculates formulas every time you make a change or an entry. If you want to make all your spreadsheet entries and calculate when you finish, choose Manual Calculation. Then the spreadsheet will recalculate only when you choose Calculate Now.

Open Cell Note

The Open Cell Note command opens a small note window for the active cell. Enter your note and click the note close box to remove the window.

Appendix A
Works Command Reference

Pressing the ⌘ key and double-clicking a cell opens a note window.

Show Grid

When chosen, Show Grid displays a grid around each cell. Turning off the command removes the grid and produces a screen that looks more like a printed document.

Show Note Indicator

The note indicator, a small rectangle in the upper right corner of a cell containing a note, can be turned on or off by choosing the Show Note Indicator command. You may want to turn off the note indicators while printing and then restore them while working on the spreadsheet.

Show Values and Show Formulas

The Show Values command shows the values resulting from a formula. The Show Formulas command shows the actual formula underlying the result. Columns usually have to be widened to show the entire formula.

Sort

Sort displays a dialog box that lets you specify the sort order of high-lighted columns. You can designate sort keys and choose ascending or descending sort order.

Database Module

This section lists commands unique to the database module. Additional database commands are listed in the section "Menus Common to All Modules."

Data Menu

Commands on the Data menu control the selection and filtering of database records. Records also can be inserted and deleted and sorted using commands found here. A list at the bottom shows all filters associated with the current database.

Define Filter (⌘-K)

The Define Filter command lets you edit an existing filter to modify its criteria. Define filter displays a dialog box where you can change or add to the data contained in the three filters.

Delete Filter

Delete Filter removes the selected filter from the database. Works displays an alert box before deleting the filter.

Delete Record

The Delete Record command removes the selected record. If you change your mind, immediately use Undo.

Duplicate Filter

Duplicate Filter duplicates and renames a selected filter to simplify the creation of similar filters.

Insert Record (⌘-I)

Choosing Insert Record places a new record immediately before the current record.

Match Records

The Match Records command searches database fields for entries matching the information you enter in a dialog box.

New Filter

The New Filter command enables you to create new filters. A dialog box appears where you name the filter and set its three parameters: field, comparison type, and compare to.

Next Record (⌘-=)

When chosen, Next Record selects the next record in the database. The data view tool palette enables you to use arrows to scroll through your records.

Previous Record (⌘--)

Previous Record selects the previous record in the database. The data view tool palette enables you to use an arrow to scroll backwards through your document.

Show All

The Show All command removes the effect of a filter. When chosen, all records in the database are visible. When filters exist, they are listed below the Show All command. Choosing a filter name applies the filter. Choosing Show All removes the filter. A check mark appears next to Show All or the selected filter.

Sort

Database records can be sorted alphabetically or numerically in ascending or descending order using the Sort command.

Form Menu

Using the Form menu, you can change views, as well as create and edit forms and fields. A list at the bottom of the menu shows all forms associated with the current database.

Data View

Choosing the Data View command switches you to a form-based view of the database. Individual fields are arranged to show you the entire contents of a single record.

Delete Field

Delete Field immediately deletes the selected field. Use Undo immediately to reverse.

Delete Form

Delete Form deletes the currently selected form.

Design View

The design view enables you to create, move, and edit fields on forms as you create layouts that meet your data entry and reporting needs. The Design View command opens a blank form and enables you to edit fields. Use the tool palette to switch between the data and design view. A check mark appears to the left of the current view.

Duplicate Form

Duplicate Form creates a renamed duplicate of the selected form that you then can modify.

Field Name

Field Name names or renames selected fields.

Format Character

Format Character sets font, font style, and color for selected fields.

Format Field

The Format Field command designates the format of selected fields as text, number, date, or time. Formulas or default values also can be inserted.

Form Names

A list of existing forms appears at the bottom of the Form menu. Choosing a form name makes that form the current form.

List View

The List View command switches you to a grid-based view of rows of records arranged in columns that correspond to the fields of the database. A check mark appears next to the List View command in the Form menu, indicating that the command is selected.

New Form

New Form opens the New/Set Up Form dialog box for creation of new form.

Place Field

The Place Field command lets you add fields to both data and design views. In design view, a list box shows the names of any fields not contained on the form, enabling you to add them to the form.

Set Up Form

Set Up Form opens the New/Set Up Form dialog box for revision of the currently active form.

Show Field Border

When Show Field Border is chosen, a check mark appears and selected fields show a border. Select the command again to remove the check mark. Show Field Border applies only to data and design views.

Show Grid

The Show Grid command applies only to list view. This command displays the spreadsheet grid. A check mark appears next to the command name to indicate that the command is turned on.

Report Menu

The Report menu contains commands that let you organize, print, and analyze database information.

Delete Report

Choosing Delete Report opens a dialog box asking you to confirm deletion of the current report. Choosing OK removes the report. If you delete a report in error, immediately open the Edit menu and choose Undo to restore the report. The change does not occur until the database is saved.

Duplicate Report

The Duplicate Report command enables you to "clone" an existing report as the basis of a new report that has many of the same features. This procedure saves the time involved in creating a new report from scratch.

List of Reports

A list of existing reports appears at the bottom of the Report menu. Choosing a report name makes that report the current report and adds a check mark next to the report name in the list.

New Report

The New Report command opens a dialog box where you name the report and choose Create. You then use the report view screen to arrange and enhance report elements.

Report Name

The active report can be renamed for clarification or repositioning on an alphabetical list using the Report Name command.

Report View

The Report View command switches between report view and the previously selected view. When the report view is active, a ruler and four icons appear at the top of the database window. A check mark appears next to the Report View command when it is selected.

Totals Menu

The Totals menu appears only when you are in report view. The four commands it contains are the same as the commands chosen by using the four icons on the report view ruler. The currently chosen field name appears in gray at the top of the menu as a guide to which field is affected by the commands. Replicas of the icons appear next to the commands.

New Page after Subtotal

New Page After Subtotal is a "global" command that applies to an entire report that uses subtotals. When the command is selected, each time a subtotal is printed, a page break will be inserted.

Subtotal When Contents Change

The Subtotal When Contents Change command specifies the key field that triggers a subtotal in a second field when the key field contents change. For instance, if the Department field changes from "Sales" to "Manufacturing," a subtotal would be triggered in the "Salary" field. Note that the Salary field must also be tagged with the Sum This Field command.

Subtotal When 1st Char Changes

The Subtotal When 1st Char Changes command also specifies a key field that triggers a subtotal in a second field, but in this case, only the first character of the key field needs to change. This command applies to either text or numeric values, but it often works well with numeric values. For example, if a part number changes from 200 to 300, a subtotal could be placed in a "Quantity" or "Cost" column.

Sum This Field

The Sum This Field command inserts the sum of the selected field in the printed report. The sum does not show in the report view, but can be examined using the Print Preview command or the Copy Totals command on the Edit menu, which places the totals on the Clipboard.

Communications

This section lists commands unique to the communications module. Additional communications commands are listed in the section "Menus Common to All Modules."

Connection Menu

The Connection menu controls your communications session; connecting and disconnecting, transmitting and receiving files, and providing information about the cost and duration of your sessions.

Close Connection (⌘-K)

The Close Connection command ends your communication session and breaks the connection to the remote computer.

Listen For Connection

If the remote computer is originating communication, you can wait for the call by opening the proper communications document and choosing

Listen For Connection. When the call comes, you will automatically be connected.

Open Connection (⌘-D)

The Open Connection command directs Works to dial the specified number and open a connection. An icon on the tool palette also activates this command.

Receive File (⌘-L)

The Receive File command prepares your computer to receive a file originating from a remote computer using the file transfer protocol specified in the current communications document.

Reset Terminal

If you have temporarily changed terminal settings during a communications session, choosing Reset Terminal returns the settings to those last saved in the communications document.

Reset Timer

The Reset Timer command resets the status bar timer to zero.

Resume Capture

When capturing has been paused, the Resume Capture command restarts the capture process.

Send File (⌘-U)

The Send File command starts the process of transmitting a file using a file transfer protocol.

Show Info (⌘-I)

The Show Info command opens a dialog box showing current and cumulative time and dollar expenditures for communication. The cost per unit of time used for calculation is entered in this dialog box.

Appendix A
Works Command Reference

Start/Pause Capture

The Capture commands record text information on the screen in a designated file. This procedure is different from the one used to receive files using a protocol. Capture is a way of preserving the flow of on-screen activity during communication. Use Start Capture to begin the procedure. When capture is under way, the command becomes Pause Capture.

Status Bar

Choosing the Status Bar command opens a small cascade menu that lets you select time, date, and cost options to be displayed on the status bar in the lower left corner of the communications screen.

Stop/Start Timer (⌘-G)

Stop Timer stops the status bar timer. The command becomes Start Timer when the timer is stopped.

Settings Menu

The Settings menu is at the center of successful communications. Although many connections can be made with default settings, this menu contains the commands to correct problems or fine-tune successes.

Connection (⌘-1)

The Connection command opens a dialog box that gives access to the four methods of communication provided by Works. Each method has a number of settings that can be altered to establish or improve communications.

File Transfer (⌘-3)

Three file transfer protocols are available for transferring complex files. File Transfer opens a dialog box that gives access to the protocols and related commands.

Options

Choosing the Options command opens a dialog box where you can choose to open connections automatically, play a sign-on script automatically, and regulate the speed with which copied material is pasted to the screen.

Play Sign-On (⌘-E)

When a sequence of Sign-on commands has been recorded, the Play Sign-On command replays them when a connection is made.

Record Sign-On (⌘-R)

The Record Sign-On command starts a process that records your actions as you sign on. While recording is active, the command becomes End Record Sign-On.

Select Receive Folder (⌘-F)

Choosing the Select Receive Folder command opens a file and folder selection dialog box where you can designate a location for received files.

Terminal (⌘-2)

Works can emulate three types of terminals to meet the needs of the remote computer. The dialog box associated with the Terminal command enables you to select and modify emulation procedures.

New Features of Version 3.0

n the upgrade-driven world of Macintosh software, Works has not been revised in quite a while. In one way, the delay is a testimonial to the quality of the program. Works has been on the list of Macintosh best-sellers since its release. Works' strength is simply that it gets the job done. No fuss, no flash, just solid performance of the core activities for which most people buy a Macintosh.

The following sections detail the enhancements found in Version 3.0. The improvements are solid but not spectacular. The database and drawing modules are the most changed. Experienced users welcome this type of thoughtful upgrade as an enhancement of what they already know well. New users don't recognize the changes, but they benefit from a richer, more refined product.

USING
MICROSOFT
WORKS

Word Processor Enhancements

Works includes word processing features that can make your documents more accurate and professional. This section covers the spelling checker, thesaurus, footnotes, and mail merging.

Spell Checking

The spelling checker is faster than before and now includes the capability to add a word to a custom dictionary. You can create multiple custom dictionaries for specialized purposes. You also can edit the contents of customized dictionaries.

Thesaurus

Works has an entirely new 190,000-entry thesaurus.

Footnotes

You now can add footnotes either at the end of each page or the end of a document.

Mail Merge

The print merge process is streamlined to ease the job of creating form letters and other documents that merge database information into word processing documents.

Draw Module Enhancements

The Draw module includes features that enable you to enhance your graphics efficiently and effectively. This section describes Draw's stand-alone status; the use of color, rotation, smoothing, and cropping; and 3-D effects.

Stand-Alone Status

The Draw module is now an independent module, which allows enhanced features and better performance. Draw layers are still available in the word processing, database, and spreadsheet modules, enabling you to enhance documents easily with a full range of Draw tools.

Color

With a color monitor, you can work with a 256-color palette on-screen.

Rotation

You can rotate and flip graphics horizontally or vertically.

Smoothing

Works can smooth polygons automatically to produce rounded corners. This process greatly simplifies modification of straight-edged shapes.

Cropping

You easily can crop bit-mapped images imported from other applications to reduce their size.

3-D Effects

You can extrude graphic objects to produce three-dimensional effects. You can specify depth and degree of rotation. You also can place automatic drop shadows behind objects.

Spreadsheet Enhancements

You can use the special features in the spreadsheet module to enhance the presentation of data in your documents. This section describes quick charting, function pasting, chart touch-up, the new Hi-Lo-Close chart, and automatic date/time formatting.

Quick Charting

Selecting information and choosing Quick Chart automatically creates a bar chart of the data. You can use charting and drawing tools to modify and enhance the chart if necessary.

Function Pasting

You can filter function types and read a description of each function's purpose in the enhanced Paste Function dialog box.

Chart Touch-Up

You can enhance or modify linked charts directly in the spreadsheet.

Hi-Lo-Close Chart

Works has a new chart type, the Hi-Lo-Close chart, which is suitable for tracking stocks.

Automatic Date/Time Formatting

Works now recognizes standard date and time formats as they are entered in a cell and adjusts the cell format accordingly.

Database Enhancements

The database module includes features that enable you to present and view data in the most efficient way possible. This section includes descriptions of forms, data view, design view, multiple named filters, and improved mailing labels.

Forms

You can design up to 16 data-entry forms for each database. Forms enable you to specify the fields to be shown and their exact position. Forms can be printed.

Data View

The data view enables you to enter information one record at a time. Data view forms can mimic paper forms, easing the job of entering information.

Design View

Design view is a new view used for creating and enhancing forms. You can use draw tools to add graphics to forms.

Multiple Named Filters

Up to 16 filters can be associated with a database. Each can have up to six record-selection rules, allowing complex searches.

Improved Mailing Labels

You can create mailing labels entirely within the database using prepared forms.

Communications Enhancements

The communications module is a capable program that shares Works' easy-to-use features. The communications enhancements enable you to use the module efficiently and effectively. These enhancements include new terminal emulation, auto log-on, and the Communications Toolbox.

New Terminal Emulation

You can choose VT102, VT220, and VT320, as well as TTY terminal emulation.

Auto Log-On

Automatic log-on scripts can be recorded, enabling you to quickly reach frequently used remote computers.

Communications Toolbox

Works installs and uses an enhanced series of data transfer and emulation tools provided as part of the Apple Communications Toolbox.

General Program Enhancements

Works 3.0 provides you with many features that will improve your performance and productivity. These features include easy installation, tool palettes, the Preferences command, stationery documents, expanded file conversion, new Help and tutorial, and improved headers and footers.

Easy Installation

With the Macintosh Installer, program installation has been automated. Standard installation puts the program and all supporting material on your disk. Custom installation enables you to choose the features to install.

Tool Palettes

All modules now have a small floating window containing icons that activate tools that differ from module to module. Tool palette items provide a quick shortcut for reaching frequently used menu commands.

Preferences

The Preferences command enables you to customize aspects of each module and the entire program. You can specify default settings for features such as fonts and formats.

Stationery

Stationery documents are templates that can be reused to open a document containing specific information and settings. Several stationery documents are furnished with Works, or you can create your own.

Expanded File Conversion

Works is able to convert to and from a large number of Macintosh and PC file formats thanks to a new set of file translators.

New Help and Tutorial

Works has an entirely new Help system. The Help system and a new HyperCard-based tutorial give quick access to information from basic to advanced.

Improved Headers and Footers

You now can add automatic page, date, and time numbering. You can create multiline headers and footers and add graphics.

Works with System 6 and 7

Whether you use Macintosh System 6 or System 7, Works runs well on your computer. A decision to use Works does not require you to change systems. Depending on the system you choose and your hardware configuration, Works appears on your screen and performs certain activities differently. This appendix lists the differences in the way Works appears and behaves under the two systems.

Works with System 6

You need a recent version of System 6—Version 6.0.4 or later to be exact. Works Version 3.0 does not work properly with earlier versions. You can obtain system hardware upgrades from an authorized Apple dealer. As mentioned in the discussion of installation, you also need a minimum of one megabyte of random-access memory (RAM). More than a megabyte of memory enables you to open more documents and larger documents.

USING
MICROSOFT
WORKS

The following features are available only on a Macintosh using System 7. The features are described in the next section called "Works with System 7."

> Balloon Help
>
> Help menu icon
>
> Shortcuts command
>
> TrueType
>
> Finder-created stationery
>
> Desktop button

Works with System 7

System 7 brings additional features to Works. Some, like TrueType, are part of the system software; others, the Shortcuts command for instance, are built into Works but are available only when System 7 is running.

Balloon Help

Clicking the Help icon that System 7 places toward the right end of the menu bar opens a menu where you can activate Balloon Help. With the function active, pointing to a screen feature such as a command or a scroll bar causes a small dialog balloon, like those used in the comics, to open. The balloon contains a brief description of the item. Moving the mouse away or using a button causes the balloon to disappear. Choosing the command again disables it.

Help and Shortcuts Command

The menu that opens when you click the Balloon Help icon also contains two commands used to obtain additional help specific to Works. The Works Help menu duplicates the Help command found on the Window menu. You can choose either command; the result is identical. Choosing the Works Shortcuts command opens a window containing an electronic booklet of shortcuts you can page through to locate keyboard and command shortcuts.

Appendix C

Works with System 6 and 7

TrueType

System 7 brings TrueType fonts to the Macintosh. TrueType enables you to accurately scale screen and printer fonts to any size in one point (1/72") increments. Fonts at any size are drawn and printed without the ragged edges characteristic of non-TrueType fonts for which font files are not installed. TrueType fonts are managed within the system software. Consult your System 7 documentation for additional information.

Stationery

Stationery is available in Works regardless of the system you use. With System 7, you need to be aware that you can designate a document as stationery using either the Finder or Works. Unfortunately, Works cannot display a preview of Finder-created stationery as it can with its own stationery. To prepare a version containing a preview, open the Finder-created stationery in Works, and then save it as Works stationery. You can find instructions in the chapters describing each Works module that is capable of creating stationery.

The Desktop Button

In the Works dialog boxes used for Open and Save As, System 7 includes a button called Desktop that can be used to navigate through folders and disks. In earlier versions of the Macintosh system, this button was called the Drive button.

Appendix C

Works with System 6 and 7

Index

Index

Index

D

N

Index

X–Y–Z

Computer Books from Que Mean PC Performance!

Spreadsheets

1-2-3 Beyond the Basics	$24.95
1-2-3 for DOS Release 2.3 Quick Reference	$ 9.95
1-2-3 for DOS Release 2.3 QuickStart	$19.95
1-2-3 for DOS Release 3.1+ Quick Reference	$ 9.95
1-2-3 for DOS Release 3.1+ QuickStart	$19.95
1-2-3 for Windows Quick Reference	$ 9.95
1-2-3 for Windows QuickStart	$19.95
1-2-3 Personal Money Manager	$29.95
1-2-3 Power Macros	$39.95
1-2-3 Release 2.2 QueCards	$19.95
Easy 1-2-3	$19.95
Easy Excel	$19.95
Easy Quattro Pro	$19.95
Excel 3 for Windows QuickStart	$19.95
Excel for Windows Quick Reference	$ 9.95
Look Your Best with 1-2-3	$24.95
Quattro Pro 3 QuickStart	$19.95
Quattro Pro Quick Reference	$ 9.95
Using 1-2-3 for DOS Release 2.3, Special Edition	$29.95
Using 1-2-3 for Windows	$29.95
Using 1-2-3 for DOS Release 3.1+, Special Edition	$29.95
Using Excel 4 for Windows, Special Edition	$29.95
Using Quattro Pro 4, Special Edition	$27.95
Using Quattro Pro for Windows	$24.95
Using SuperCalc5, 2nd Edition	$29.95

Databases

dBASE III Plus Handbook, 2nd Edition	$24.95
dBASE IV 1.1 Quick Reference	$ 9.95
dBASE IV 1.1 QuickStart	$19.95
Introduction to Databases	$19.95
Paradox 3.5 Quick Reference	$ 9.95
Paradox Quick Reference, 2nd Edition	$ 9.95
Using AlphaFOUR	$24.95
Using Clipper, 3rd Edition	$29.95
Using DataEase	$24.95
Using dBASE IV	$29.95
Using FoxPro 2	$29.95
Using ORACLE	$29.95
Using Paradox 3.5, Special Edition	$29.95
Using Paradox for Windows	$26.95
Using Paradox, Special Edition	$29.95
Using PC-File	$24.95
Using R:BASE	$29.95

Business Applications

CheckFree Quick Reference	$ 9.95
Easy Quicken	$19.95
Microsoft Works Quick Reference	$ 9.95
Norton Utilities 6 Quick Reference	$ 9.95
PC Tools 7 Quick Reference	$ 9.95
Q&A 4 Database Techniques	$29.95
Q&A 4 Quick Reference	$ 9.95
Q&A 4 QuickStart	$19.95
Q&A 4 Que Cards	$19.95
Que's Computer User's Dictionary, 2nd Edition	$10.95
Que's Using Enable	$29.95
Quicken 5 Quick Reference	$ 9.95
SmartWare Tips, Tricks, and Traps, 2nd Edition	$26.95
Using DacEasy, 2nd Edition	$24.95
Using Microsoft Money	$19.95
Using Microsoft Works: IBM Version	$22.95
Using Microsoft Works for Windows, Special Edition	$24.95
Using MoneyCounts	$19.95
Using Pacioli 2000	$19.95
Using Norton Utilities 6	$24.95
Using PC Tools Deluxe 7	$24.95
Using PFS: First Choice	$22.95
Using PFS: WindowWorks	$24.95
Using Q&A 4	$27.95
Using Quicken 5	$19.95
Using Quicken for Windows	$19.95
Using Smart	$29.95
Using TimeLine	$24.95
Using TurboTax: 1992 Edition	$19.95

CAD

AutoCAD Quick Reference, 2nd Edition	$ 8.95
Using AutoCAD, 3rd Edition	$29.95

Word Processing

Easy WordPerfect	$19.95
Easy WordPerfect for Windows	$19.95
Look Your Best with WordPerfect 5.1	$24.95
Look Your Best with WordPerfect forWindows	$24.95
Microsoft Word Quick Reference	$ 9.95
Using Ami Pro	$24.95
Using LetterPerfect	$22.95
Using Microsoft Word 5.5: IBM Version, 2nd Edition	$24.95
Using MultiMate	$24.95
Using PC-Write	$22.95
Using Professional Write	$22.95
Using Professional Write Plus for Windows	$24.95
Using Word for Windows 2, Special Edition	$27.95
Using WordPerfect 5	$27.95
Using WordPerfect 5.1, Special Edition	$27.95
Using WordPerfect for Windows, Special Edition	$29.95
Using WordStar 7	$19.95
Using WordStar, 3rd Edition	$27.95
WordPerfect 5.1 Power Macros	$39.95
WordPerfect 5.1 QueCards	$19.95
WordPerfect 5.1 Quick Reference	$ 9.95
WordPerfect 5.1 QuickStart	$19.95
WordPerfect 5.1 Tips, Tricks, and Traps	$24.95
WordPerfect for Windows Power Pack	$39.95
WordPerfect for Windows Quick Reference	$ 9.95
WordPerfect for Windows Quick Start	$19.95
WordPerfect Power Pack	$39.95
WordPerfect Quick Reference	$ 9.95

Hardware/Systems

Batch File and Macros Quick Reference	$ 9.95
Computerizing Your Small Business	$19.95
DR DOS 6 Quick Reference	$ 9.95
Easy DOS	$19.95
Easy Windows	$19.95
Fastback Quick Reference	$ 8.95
Hard Disk Quick Reference	$ 8.95
Hard Disk Quick Reference, 1992 Edition	$ 9.95
Introduction to Hard Disk Management	$24.95
Introduction to Networking	$24.95
Introduction to PC Communications	$24.95
Introduction to Personal Computers, 2nd Edition	$19.95
Introduction to UNIX	$24.95
Laplink Quick Reference	$ 9.95
MS-DOS 5 Que Cards	$19.95
MS-DOS 5 Quick Reference	$ 9.95
MS-DOS 5 QuickStart	$19.95
MS-DOS Quick Reference	$ 8.95
MS-DOS QuickStart, 2nd Edition	$19.95
Networking Personal Computers, 3rd Edition	$24.95
Que's Computer Buyer's Guide, 1992 Edition	$14.95
Que's Guide to CompuServe	$12.95
Que's Guide to DataRecovery	$29.95
Que's Guide to XTree	$12.95
Que's MS-DOS User's Guide, Special Edition	$29.95
Que's PS/1 Book	$22.95
TurboCharging MS-DOS	$24.95
Upgrading and Repairing PCs	$29.95
Upgrading and Repairing PCs, 2nd Edition	$29.95
Upgrading to MS-DOS 5	$14.95
Using GeoWorks Pro	$24.95
Using Microsoft Windows 3, 2nd Edition	$24.95
Using MS-DOS 5	$24.95
Using Novell NetWare, 2nd Edition	$29.95
Using OS/2 2.0	$24.95
Using PC DOS, 3rd Edition	$27.95
Using Prodigy	$19.95
Using UNIX	$29.95
Using Windows 3.1	$26.95
Using Your Hard Disk	$29.95
Windows 3 Quick Reference	$ 8.95
Windows 3 QuickStart	$19.95
Windows 3.1 Quick Reference	$ 9.95
Windows 3.1 QuickStart	$19.95

Desktop Publishing/Graphics

CorelDRAW! Quick Reference	$ 8.95
Harvard Graphics 3 Quick Reference	$ 9.95
Harvard Graphics Quick Reference	$ 9.95
Que's Using Ventura Publisher	$29.95
Using DrawPerfect	$24.95
Using Freelance Plus	$24.95
Using Harvard Graphics 3	$29.95
Using Harvard Graphics for Windows	$24.95
Using Harvard Graphics, 2nd Edition	$24.95
Using Microsoft Publisher	$22.95
Using PageMaker 4 for Windows	$29.95
Using PFS: First Publisher, 2nd Edition	$24.95
Using PowerPoint	$24.95
Using Publish It!	$24.95

Macintosh/Apple II

Easy Macintosh	$19.95
HyperCard 2 QuickStart	$19.95
PageMaker 4 for the Mac Quick Reference	$ 9.95
The Big Mac Book, 2nd Edition	$29.95
The Little Mac Book	$12.95
QuarkXPress 3.1 Quick Reference	$ 9.95
Que's Big Mac Book, 3rd Edition	$29.95
Que's Little Mac Book, 2nd Edition	$12.95
Que's Mac Classic Book	$24.95
Que's Macintosh Multimedia Handbook	$24.95
System 7 Quick Reference	$ 9.95
Using 1-2-3 for the Mac	$24.95
Using AppleWorks, 3rd Edition	$24.95
Using Excel 3 for the Macintosh	$24.95
Using FileMaker Pro	$24.95
Using MacDraw Pro	$24.95
Using MacroMind Director	$29.95
Using MacWrite Pro	$24.95
Using Microsoft Word 5 for the Mac	$27.95
Using Microsoft Works: Macintosh Version, 2nd Edition	$24.95
Using Microsoft Works for the Mac	$24.95
Using PageMaker 4 for the Macintosh	$24.95
Using Quicken 3 for the Mac	$19.95
Using the Macintosh with System 7	$24.95
Using Word for the Mac, Special Edition	$24.95
Using WordPerfect 2 for the Mac	$24.95
Word for the Mac Quick Reference	$ 9.95

Programming/Technical

Borland C++ 3 By Example	$21.95
Borland C++ Programmer's Reference	$29.95
C By Example	$21.95
C Programmer's Toolkit, 2nd Edition	$39.95
Clipper Programmer's Reference	$29.95
DOS Programmer's Reference, 3rd Edition	$29.95
FoxPro Programmer's Reference	$29.95
Network Programming in C	$49.95
Paradox Programmer's Reference	$29.95
Programming in Windows 3.1	$39.95
QBasic By Example	$21.95
Turbo Pascal 6 By Example	$21.95
Turbo Pascal 6 Programmer's Reference	$29.95
UNIX Programmer's Reference	$29.95
UNIX Shell Commands Quick Reference	$ 8.95
Using Assembly Language, 2nd Edition	$29.95
Using Assembly Language, 3rd Edition	$29.95
Using BASIC	$24.95
Using Borland C++	$29.95
Using Borland C++ 3, 2nd Edition	$29.95
Using C	$29.95
Using Microsoft C	$29.95
Using QBasic	$24.95
Using QuickBASIC 4	$24.95
Using QuickC for Windows	$29.95
Using Turbo Pascal 6, 2nd Edition	$29.95
Using Turbo Pascal for Windows	$29.95
Using Visual Basic	$29.95
Visual Basic by Example	$21.95
Visual Basic Programmer's Reference	$29.95
Windows 3.1 Programmer's Reference	$39.95

For More Information,
Call Toll Free!
1-800-428-5331

*All prices and titles subject to change without notice.
Non-U.S. prices may be higher. Printed in the U.S.A.*

Que Gives You the Latest Macintosh Information

Que's Big Mac Book, 3rd Edition
Neil J. Salkind
Macintosh Hardware & Software
$29.95 USA
0-88022-903-9, 1,020 pp., 7³/₈ x 9¹/₄

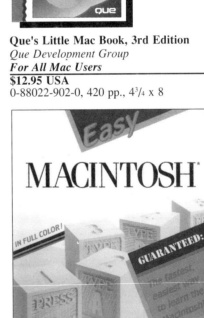

Que's Little Mac Book, 3rd Edition
Que Development Group
For All Mac Users
$12.95 USA
0-88022-902-0, 420 pp., 4³/₄ x 8

**Que's Computer User's Dictionary,
2nd Edition**
Bryan Pfaffenberger
Macintosh, Apple II, IBM, & Programming
$10.95 USA
0-88022-697-8, 550 pp., 4³/₄ x 8

Easy Macintosh
Que Development Group
All Macintosh Computers
$19.95 USA
0-88022-819-9, 200 pp., 8 x10

 To Order, Call: (800) 428-5331 OR (317) 573-2500

Free Catalog!

Mail us this registration form today, and we'll send you a free catalog featuring Que's complete line of best-selling books.

Name of Book _____

Name _____

Title _____

Phone ( ) _____

Company _____

Address _____

City _____

State _____ ZIP _____

Please check the appropriate answers:

1. Where did you buy your Que book?
   - ☐ Bookstore (name: _____)
   - ☐ Computer store (name: _____)
   - ☐ Catalog (name: _____)
   - ☐ Direct from Que
   - ☐ Other: _____

2. How many computer books do you buy a year?
   - ☐ 1 or less
   - ☐ 2-5
   - ☐ 6-10
   - ☐ More than 10

3. How many Que books do you own?
   - ☐ 1
   - ☐ 2-5
   - ☐ 6-10
   - ☐ More than 10

4. How long have you been using this software?
   - ☐ Less than 6 months
   - ☐ 6 months to 1 year
   - ☐ 1-3 years
   - ☐ More than 3 years

5. What influenced your purchase of this Que book?
   - ☐ Personal recommendation
   - ☐ Advertisement
   - ☐ In-store display
   - ☐ Price
   - ☐ Que catalog
   - ☐ Que mailing
   - ☐ Que's reputation
   - ☐ Other: _____

6. How would you rate the overall content of the book?
   - ☐ Very good
   - ☐ Good
   - ☐ Satisfactory
   - ☐ Poor

7. What do you like *best* about this Que book?
   _____
   _____

8. What do you like *least* about this Que book?
   _____
   _____

9. Did you buy this book with your personal funds?
   - ☐ Yes   ☐ No

10. Please feel free to list any other comments you may have about this Que book.
   _____
   _____
   _____

— Que —

Order Your Que Books Today!

Name _____

Title _____

Company _____

City _____

State _____ ZIP _____

Phone No. ( ) _____

Method of Payment:

Check ☐ (Please enclose in envelope.)

Charge My: VISA ☐   MasterCard ☐

American Express ☐

Charge # _____

Expiration Date _____

Order No.	Title	Qty.	Price	Total

You can **FAX** your order to **1-317-573-2583**. Or call **1-800-428-5331**, ext. **ORDR** to order direct.
Please add $2.50 per title for shipping and handling.

Subtotal	
Shipping & Handling	
Total	

— Que —

BUSINESS REPLY MAIL

First Class Permit No. 9918   Indianapolis, IN

Postage will be paid by addressee

que®

11711 N. College
Carmel, IN 46032

NO POSTAGE
NECESSARY
IF MAILED
IN THE
UNITED STATES

BUSINESS REPLY MAIL

First Class Permit No. 9918   Indianapolis, IN

Postage will be paid by addressee

que®

11711 N. College
Carmel, IN 46032